D1103869

THE ART OF THE GOOD AND EQUITABLE

A *Festschrift* in Honor of Lawrence G. Wrenn

Frederick C. Easton, Editor

Commissioned by the Canon Law Society of America

At the 61st Annual Convention in Minneapolis, Minnesota

October 1999

ISBN 0-943616-97-2
SAN 237-6296

Printed in the United States of America

Canon Law Society of America
The Catholic University of America
Washington, DC 20064

ARCHDIOCESE OF DETROIT
1234 WASHINGTON BLVD.
DETROIT, MICHIGAN 48226

OFFICE OF THE CARDINAL

PREFACE

When I heard that the Canon Law Society of America had commissioned a *Festschrift* in Honor of Father Lawrence G. Wrenn, I wanted to make a contribution, and so, I am happy to be able to offer these prefatory remarks.

Larry and I have been friends for many years, dating back to our time as graduate students in Rome forty-some years ago. We have traveled together and have come to know one another's families. Over and above these more personal connections, I have also known him as an outstanding scholar in canon law as well as an eminent practitioner of the law. It would be hard to imagine anyone involved in tribunal work in the dioceses of the United States not being familiar with his written words, especially the several editions of *Annulments* and, most recently, *The Invalid Marriage*.

Larry Wrenn's work in the revision process which led up to the 1983 Code of Canon Law and his work on the Pontifical Council for the Interpretation of Legislative Texts, as well as his presentations at meetings of canonists outside the United States, have also made him known and revered throughout the canonical world. Closer to home, he has been serving our episcopal conference as a consultor to the Canonical Affairs Committee.

This book in his honor is not the first recognition of Lawrence Wrenn by the Canon Law Society of America. He received the "Role of Law Award" in 1976 and was made an honorary member of the Society in 1994. The commission of this work offers canonists another occasion to thank him for his continuing contributions to the field. I commend this *Festscrift* to all canonists as a work which will be of assistance to them in their ministry. I want to offer my appreciation once again to Larry and extend my best wishes. AD MULTOS ANNOS!

Sincerely yours in the Lord,

+ Adam Cardinal Maida

Adam Cardinal Maida
Archbishop of Detroit

Iuri operam daturum prius nosse oportet, unde nomen iuris descendat. Est autem a iustitia appellatum: nam, ut eleganter Celsus definit, ius est ars boni et aequi, cuius merito quis nos sacerdotes appellet: iustitiam namque colimus et boni et aequi notitiam profitemur, aequum ab iniquo separantes, dicitum ab illicito discernentes, bonos non solum metu poenarum, verum etiam praemiorum quoque exortatione efficere cupientes, veram nisi fallor philosophiam, non simulatam affectantes.

Ulpianus, Liber Primus Institutionum, D. 1, 1, 1.

TABLE OF CONTENTS

Acknowledgements

The editors of this festschrift are proud to offer their contribution in honor of Lawrence G. Wrenn.

The editors wish to acknowledge the assistance of Marianne Burchard, OSB in translating the original Italian text of the chapter provided by Professor Emeritus Luigi de Luca, "Nullity of Marriage by Error of Quality." They likewise acknowledge the work of Arthur J. Espelage, OFM, CLSA Executive Coordinator, in formatting the text and seeing to the printing and publishing this book. The assistance of Jennifer H. Miller, administrative assistant in the office of the Canon Law Society of America, is also gratefully acknowledged.

Frederick Easton, General Editor
Patrick Cogan, SA, Editor

PUBLICATIONS OF LAWRENCE G. WRENN

Common Sources of Marriage Nullity, Washington, DC: Canon Law Society of America, 1966.

"Marriage and Cohabitation," *The Jurist*, 1967, 85-89.

"Updating the Law on Marriage," *The Jurist* 1967, 267-282.

"Metropolitan (Canon Law)," *The New Catholic Encyclopedia*, Volume 9, 1967, 758-759.

"Simple Error and the Indissolubility of Marriage," *The Jurist*, 1968, 84-88.

"An Outline of a Jurisprudence on Sociopathy," *The Jurist*, 1968, 470-485.

"Notes on Canonical Jurisprudence," *The Jurist*, 1969, 57-69.

"Integration or Segregation of Grounds," *The Jurist*, 1969, 183-188.

Annulments – 1st Edition, Washington, DC: Canon Law Society of America, 1970.

"Notes but mostly Footnotes on Presumptions" *The Jurist*, 1970, 206-215.

"It's Unbelievable, yet I believe it," *National Catholic Reporter*, June 1, 1971, 5A.

"The American Procedural Norms," *The American Ecclesiastical Review,* November 1971, 74-186.

"Invalid Convalidation," *The Jurist* 1972, 253-265.

Annulments, 2nd Edition, Hartford, CT: Canon Law Society of America, 1972.

"Epilepsy and Marriage," *The Jurist* 1972, 91-101.

Divorce and Remarriage in the Catholic Church, editor and contributor, New York, Newman Press, 1973.

"A New Condition Limiting Marriage," *The Jurist* 1974, 292-315.

Remarks on Receiving Role of Law Award, *Proceedings of the Canon Law Society of America*, 1976, 219-221.

Annulments, 3rd Edition, Toledo, Ohio: Canon Law Society of America, 1978.

"Law and the Brothers Grimm," *Studia Canonica*, 1979, 429-454.

"The Canon Law of Marriage, a Summary of Developments from 1966 to 1978," *The New Catholic Encyclopedia*, Volume 17, 1979, 384-388.

John Witherspoon and Church Law, An Exploration into Comparative Church Law, Rome: Lateran University, 1979.

Decisions, Toledo: Washington, DC: Canon Law Society of America, 1980.

"A Sneak Preview of the New Code," *National Catholic Reporter,* February 6, 1981, 917.

"Giustiniani and Quirini, A Reflection on Church Reform," *Studia Canonica,* 1981, 481-496.

"Law and the Local Church: The Contribution of a Presbyterian Debate," *The Jurist,* 1982, 422-448.

Decisions, 2nd edition, Washington, DC: Canon Law Society of America, 1983

Annulments, 4th edition, Washington, DC: Canon Law Society of America, 1983.

"Some Notes on the Petrine Privilege," *The Jurist* 1983, 394-405.

"Canon 1095: A Bird's Eye View," *The Jurist*, 1984, 220-242.

"Processes," *The Code of Canon Law, A Text and Commentary,* New York, Paulist, 1985, 943-1022.

"Charles Augustine, OSB: Excerpts from a Journal," *The Jurist* 1985, 297-320.

"The New Law of Marriage," translation from the Italian of an article by Luigi de Luca, *The Catholic Lawyer,* Winter, 1985, 70-93.

"The Scope of the Church's Judicial Competence," *The Jurist*, 1985, 639-652.

"Refining the Essence of Marriage," *The Jurist* 1986, 532-551, and *Proceedings of the Canon Law Society of America*, 1986, 12-28.

"In Search of a Balanced Procedural Law for Marriage Nullity Cases," *The Jurist*, 1986, 602-623. See also *Il Diritto Ecclesiastico*, 1987, 1191-1218.

Procedures, Washington, DC: Canon Law Society of America, 1987.

Annulments, 5th Edition, Washington, DC: Canon Law Society of America, 1988.

"Urban Navarrete, S.J. and the Response of the Code Commission on Force and Fear," *The Jurist* 1991, 119-137.

Authentic Interpretations on the 1983 Code, Washington, DC: Canon Law Society of America, 1993.

Law Sections, Washington, DC: Canon Law Society of America, 1994.

Annulments, 6th edition, Washington, DC: Canon Law Society of America, 1996.

"When Is an Invalid Marriage Null?" *Proceedings of the Canon Law Society of America* 1998, 31-43.

The Invalid Marriage, Washington, DC: Canon Law Society of America, 1998.

"The Joyful Vocation of the Canonist," *The Jurist,* 1998, 515-525.

"Requesting and Receiving Marital Consent: A Chronology," *The Jurist,* 1999, 39-59.

"A Commentary on Canons 1400-1500," in *The New Commentary on the Code of Canon Law,* New York, Paulist, 2000, 1609-1654.

"The Place of Law in the Church," *The Jurist,* forthcoming.

"Sacramentality and the Invalidity of Marriage," *The Jurist,* forthcoming.

"*In Diebus Illis*: Some Canonical Giants in Days of Yore," *Studia Canonica* 35 (2001) 485-514.

Judging Invalidity, Washington, DC: Canon Law Society of America, forthcoming

CURRICULUM VITAE
LAWRENCE G. WRENN

June 26, 1928	Born in New Haven, Connecticut
May 14, 1953	Ordained a priest for the Archdiocese of Hartford
1953-1956	Assistant Pastor, St. Paul Parish, West Haven, Connecticut
1956-1958	Assistant Pastor, St. Patrick Parish, Hartford, Connecticut and Notary, Metropolitan Tribunal, Archdiocese of Hartford
1960	JCL, Lateran University
1960-1965	Secretary, Metropolitan Tribunal, Archdiocese of Hartford
1965-1983	Officialis, Archdiocese of Hartford
1968-1972	Lecturer, The Tribunal Institute, The Catholic University of America
1976	JCD, Lateran University
1976	Received Role of Law Award, Canon Law Society of America
1978-1981	Consultant, NCCB Committee on Canonical Affairs
1983-1995	Judicial Vicar, Provincial Court of Appeals, Province of Hartford Consultor, the Pontifical Commission for the Authentic
1984	Interpretation of the Code of Canon Law (renamed in 1989 as the Pontifical Council for the Interpretation of Legislative Texts). Presently serving third five-year term.
1994	Named Honorary Member, Canon Law Society of America
1995-Present	Judge, Metropolitan Tribunal, Archdiocese of Hartford
1999-Present	Consultant, NCCB (USCCB) Committee on Canonical Affairs
2000	Awarded Johannes Quasten Medal by School of Religious Studies, The Catholic University of America

INTRODUCTION

Like hundreds of others, when I began working in the tribunal, even before I had the opportunity for further canonical studies, my essential guidebook was Lawrence Wrenn's *Annulments.* That would have been the first edition of a publication which has since been through five more editions and has culminated (for the time being at least) in *The Invalid Marriage* in 1998. Its prolific author, as virtually every canonist in the United States of America knows, has contributed so extensively and so unselfishly to the development of canonical doctrine and practice that it came as no surprise that the Canon Law Society of America should have resolved at its 1999 annual convention to commission a *festschrift* in honor of Lawrence Wrenn as "an expression of its appreciation, gratitude, and esteem for his contributions to its publications."

For those of us who have had the good fortune to encounter Lawrence Wrenn, not only through his writings but personally as well, we easily recognize that along with his keen intellect and sure knowledge he possesses a civility, modesty, and wit that are both remarkable and attractive. And although he himself would be loath to agree, he has served as a model for many of us who have spent or still spend our lives in daily canonical tasks. 'Doing canon law' is for Lawrence Wrenn not just an office or an assignment, but a vocation. When in 1976 he received the Role of Law Award of the Canon Law Society of America, one of his many honors and achievements, the citation read in part "his scholarship and practical experience is that of a deeply feeling man, committed to the pastoral and practical service of people." How true! It is indeed fitting that the same Society, which awarded Lawrence Wrenn one of its highest honors twenty-five years ago, would now commission a *festschrift* in honor of his continuing contributions to canon law.

The contributors to this volume give us a rich and varied fare. John Beal explores the possible usefulness of the acts of a previous matrimonial case in three instances: a case between the same parties, previously given a negative decision, but now introduced on new grounds; a case involving a marriage which failed subsequent to a declaration of nullity of the previous marriage of one of the parties; and a case involving a non-cooperative respondent whose immediate family member received a declaration of nullity. The author also conducts a thorough review of the law in order to establish canonical justification for such use of the acts of a previous case, particularly in view of the confidentiality of those acts.

Through a historical overview of the Church's judicial involvement – and in some cases non-involvement – in matrimonial issues, including marriage nullity, James Coriden attempts to "illustrate the complexity and variety of the Church's encounter with unsuccessful marriages" over the centuries. Richard Cunningham provides an informative sketch of the work, method, and significance of the eleventh-century predecessor of Gratian, Ivo of Chartres.

In his contribution Luigi de Luca sets out to interpret the meaning of canon 1097, § 2, whereby marriage is stated to be invalid by virtue of error concerning the quality of a person only when the quality is "directly and principally" intended, and also addresses whether this is a matter of ecclesiastical or natural law. He cites rotal jurisprudence, scholarly studies, and papal teaching, while considering likewise canons 1098 on fraud and 1099 on error that "determines the will." The key to interpreting the law on error of quality of a person, the author concludes, is to be found in the "unification of the different faculties of the human person," i.e., intellect and will.

Noting concerns expressed in various quarters about the extensive use of grounds of psychological incapacity in matrimonial cases today, Frederick

Easton urges re-visiting and developing the so-called traditional grounds of marriage nullity, particularly partial and total simulation. In presenting his case, the author makes use of rotal jurisprudence, canonical studies, and psychological categories as found in the DSM-IV. Thomas Green gives what he calls "a general overview of some significant similarities but especially procedural differences" between the *Code of Canon Law* and the *Code of Canons of the Eastern Churches*. He also summarizes the process of the drafting of the *Code of Canons of the Eastern Churches* and discusses briefly a few of the principles that guided the drafting process.

In his article on prenuptial agreements, John Johnson offers some thoughtful considerations of what constitutes an invalidating exclusion of matrimonial indissolubility as well as the probative value of documentary evidence. Aidan McGrath treats, clearly and concisely, the role and conduct of the judge in marriage nullity cases, especially with respect to the nature of proofs and their evaluation. Drawing mainly on statements of Pope Paul VI and Pope John Paul II, Kevin McKenna highlights the theological and pastoral dimension of ecclesiastical law.

Augustine Mendonça summarizes and explains decisions rendered by Roman tribunals in three matters. In a case involving the transfer of three pastors, the Signatura decrees that an improper procedure has been followed. Secondly, in a case, involving a suspension from priestly ministry, the Signatura initially upholds the priest's recourse; later, however, *restitutio in integrum* is granted, and a new panel of the Signatura upholds the action of the bishop. Finally, a rotal sentence mitigates the penalty of dismissal from the clerical state which had been imposed by a first-instance tribunal.

Despite the fact that in the 1983 *Code of Canon Law* the norm that marriage enjoys the favor of the law is found essentially unchanged from its formulation in the 1917 code, Elissa Rinere traces what she considers to be a "subtle evolution" of the interpretation of that norm. She cites evidence of a "shift to a better balance between the rights of the bond of marriage and the rights of individuals."

In the final contribution, through the use of questionnaires Myriam Wijlens arrives at a statistical profile of petitioners and respondents in matrimonial cases for the tribunal of the Diocese of Münster, Germany, in the years 1998-2000. The information obtained includes the number of people affected by the tribunal procedure, the gender and age of the petitioners, the religion of petitioners and respondents, the age of the parties at the time of the wedding, and whether there was a pregnancy at the time of the nuptials. The author suggests that the use of such profiles may assist the Church in a number of ways, including the discovery of additional methods for informing persons of the availability of the tribunal process.

The contributions to this *festchrift* do just honor to Lawrence Wrenn. They are examples of the spirit of scholarship and helpfulness with which he has always approached his craft. As he states in a recent article, "The Joyful Vocation of a Canonist" (*The Jurist* 58:2 [1998] 515-525), to enjoy their work, canonists should be students, shepherds, and ministers. Within the parameters he sets out, Lawrence Wrenn has surely been all three; and he has earned the gratitude and respect of countless of us canon lawyers.

Most Rev. David E. Fellhauer
Bishop of Victoria, Texas

ACTS FROM PREVIOUS CASES AS A NEGLECTED SOURCE OF EVIDENCE

JOHN P. BEAL

Introduction

Lawrence G. Wrenn has contributed enormously, arguably more than any single individual, to the transformation of ecclesiastical marriage tribunals in the English speaking world from moribund bureaucracies whose primary role seemed to be an affirmation to divorced and remarried members of the faithful that there was no hope for them to have anything more than a marginal role in the life of the Church. Thanks in large part to Lawrence Wrenn's books in their multiple editions[1] and his ministry in the tribunal of the Archdiocese of Hartford, North American tribunals have become effective agents of pastoral care for the divorced. As a result, during the seventeen years since the promulgation of the revised Latin code, tribunals in the United States, applying lessons learned from Lawrence Wrenn, have concluded over three quarters of a

[1] See Lawrence Wrenn, *Annulments*, 1st edition (Toledo, OH: CLSA, 1970); id., *Annulments*, 2nd edition (Toledo, OH: CLSA, 1972); id., *Annulments*, 3rd edition revised (Toledo, OH: CLSA, 1978); id., *Annulments*, 4th edition revised (Washington, DC: CLSA, 1983); id., *Annulments*, 5th edition revised (Washington, DC: CLSA, 1988); id., *Annulments*, 6th edition (Washington, DC: CLSA, 1996); id., *The Invalid Marriage* (Washington, DC: CLSA, 1998); id., *Decisions* (Toledo, OH: CLSA, 1980); id., *Decisions*, 2nd edition revised (Washington, DC: CLSA, 1983); id., *Procedures* (Washington, DC: CLSA, 1987); id., *Law Sections* (Washington, DC: CLSA, 1994); id., "Processes," in *The Code of Canon Law: Text and Commentary*, ed. J. Coriden, et al. (Mahwah, NJ: Paulist Press, 1985) 945-1028; id., "Trials in General," in *A New Commentary on the Code of Canon Law*, ed. J. P. Beal, et al. (Mahwah, NJ: Paulist Press, 2000) 1609-1654.

million marriage cases and thereby allowed thousands of people to remarry in the Catholic Church and to return to the sacraments.[2]

Requirement that Tribunal Acts be Preserved

When these cases were concluded, the acts of the case and of the process[3] were filed away in the archives of the tribunals where the cases originated. In principle, the acts of these cases are to be preserved in perpetuity. However, the Apostolic Signatura has allowed tribunals to microfilm or microfiche these acts and destroy the originals after ten years have elapsed since the conclusion of the cases as long as hard copies of the definitive sentences are preserved.[4] Nevertheless, the principle remains that all of the documentation related to individual cases must be preserved in some readily retrievable form.

One obvious reason for the requirement that the acts of marriage cases be preserved is the fact that marriage cases, like other cases concerning the status of persons, never become *res iudicatae* or definitively judged matters (c. 1643). Consequently, these cases are always subject to reconsideration as the result of a complaint of nullity against the sentence (cc. 1619-1627), a legitimate appeal (cc. 1628-1640) or a petition for the favor of a new hearing of the case (c. 1644). Since these marriage cases are always susceptible to further review, it is important to insure the availability of the acts that served as the basis for the original decisions.

---

[2] Between the promulgation of the revised code in 1983 and the end of 1999, the last year for which statistics are available, tribunals in the United States have concluded 758,169 formal marriage cases in first instance: 66,668 in 1983, 43,464 in 1984, 44,170 in 1985, 40,117 in 1986, 47,949 in 1987, 48,287 in 1988, 40,685 in 1989, 48,741 in 1990, 49,542 in 1991, 48,678 in 1992, 38,280 in 1993, 42,603 in 1994, 39,419 in 1995, 42,230 in 1996, 40,165 in 1997, 38,504 in 1998, and 36,667 in 1999. See Secretariat of State, *Annuarium statisticum Ecclesiae* (Vatican City: Libreria Editrice Vaticana, 1983-1999).

[3] The acts of the case (*acta causae*) consist of the various forms of evidence (declarations of parties, documents, depositions of witnesses, reports of experts) collected during the instruction of the case; the acts of the process (*acta processus*) are the many procedural decrees issued in the course of the process. See c. 1472, §1 and Wrenn, "Trials in General," 1643.

[4] Apostolic Signatura, "Microfilming the acts of tribunal cases," in *Roman Replies and CLSA Advisory Opinions 1990*, ed. William Schumacher and Lynn Jarrell (Washington, DC: CLSA, 1990) 22.

In addition, tribunal records have served as an important source of information for historians. Documents from tribunal archives have greatly enriched our understanding of marriage and family life in the middle ages and in early modern Europe.[5] Unless these records had been carefully preserved for centuries, our knowledge of the past would be seriously impoverished. Future historians may find in tribunal archives a treasure trove of valuable glimpses into married life, as well as ecclesial life, in the late twentieth and early twenty-first centuries.

In fact, however, few cases are actually reopened for reconsideration after they have been concluded. Moreover, while historians have shown a keen interest in tribunal records from ages when there is little other extant evidence about married life and customs, they have not shown the same interest in tribunal records from the more recent past. In the modern era, there are ample written records and sociological data about marriage and family life in the public domain. Thus, it is not clear that retaining records of marriage cases will be a great boon to historians of the future. The apparently minimal usefulness of records stowed away in tribunal archives suggests that the requirement that tribunals preserve these records in perpetuity is something of an anachronism, an anachronism that requires tribunals and their supporting dioceses to dedicate immense amounts of precious, scarce space to house bundles of paper of no apparent value.

---

[5] See John T. Noonan, Jr., *Power to Dissolve: Lawyers and Marriages in the Courts of the Roman Curia* (Cambridge, MA: Belknap Press, 1972), which is based on documents from the archives of the Roman Rota and Congregations. However, the archives of local tribunals have also been a rich source of information. See Richard Helmholz, *Marriage Litigation in Medieval England* (Cambridge, MA: Cambridge University Press, 1978); Richard Wunderli, *London Church Courts and Society on the Eve of the Reformation* (Cambridge, MA: Medieval Academy of America, 1981); Nicholas Adams and Charles Donahue, ed., *Select Cases from the Ecclesiastical Courts of the Province of Canterbury, c. 1200-1301* (London: Selden Society Publications, 1981); James Brundage, "The Treatment of Marriage in *Questiones Londinenses* (MS Royal 9.E.VII)," in James Brundage, *Sex, Law and Marriage in the Middle Ages* (Brookfield, VT: Ashgate, 1993) 86-97.

The Value of Tribunal Records for New Cases

On the other hand, the 1983 *Code of Canon Law* suggests that the records of concluded cases, when properly preserved, may have a more immediately practical purpose. An instance of a marriage case can be concluded not only by a definitive sentence but also by peremption or abatement, i.e., when an unimpeded party fails to posit a required procedural act within six months (c. 1520), or by renunciation or abandonment by the petitioner (c. 1524, §1). Both peremption and renunciation extinguish the acts of the process, but not the acts of the case (cc. 1522 and 1525). Thus, if a new instance or trial is initiated by one of the parties after the original instance has been concluded by abatement or renunciation, all of the procedural acts need to be repeated during the new instance, but evidence collected during the original case can be incorporated into the acts of the new instance and has the same probative force that it would have had in the original instance, "provided that the case (*causa*) involves the same persons and the same issue" (cc. 1522 and 1525). However, in cases involving persons other than the original parties, the acts of the case have only the probative force of documents (c. 1522).

The code explicitly mentions the use of the acts of the case in a new instance when the previous instance had been concluded by abatement or renunciation, but its mention that these acts have only the weight of documents in cases involving others suggests that the acts of concluded cases, now slowly yellowing in tribunal archives, can also be used as evidence in new cases. Three scenarios suggest themselves immediately:

- when a case has been concluded by two conforming definitive negative sentences, but one of the parties now seeks to have the matter examined again on a different ground;
- when a party sought and received a declaration of nullity of a first marriage in order to be able to enter a new marriage in the Church, but the second marriage has now broken up and the petitioner in the earlier case is now an uncooperative respondent in a new marriage case; and
- when the respondent has refused to cooperate, but a member of his or her immediate family recently received a declaration of nullity.

In all three scenarios, the evidence collected during the instruction of a previous case could be of critical importance to the resolution of a new pending case.

A New Case Between the Same Parties

Usefulness of Acts of Previous Cases

When a party seeks a declaration of nullity of his or her marriage on a new ground after a previous petition had received a negative decision, he or she is, strictly speaking, initiating a new case (*causa*) and not a new instance (*instantia*) of the previous case. Nevertheless, even though the new ground of nullity was not the focus of the instruction of the original case, its acts may be one of the few sources of evidence for new cases, especially if a considerable period of time has elapsed between the decision in the original case and the introduction of the new one. A party who participated in the original process may have disappeared or become uncooperative; witnesses who testified in the original case may have died or disappeared; memories of both parties and witnesses may have dimmed. In short, the just resolution of the new case may be impossible without the use of the evidence collected in connection with the original, unsuccessful case.

An Example

George and Mildred met in 1945 while singing in the choir of their Methodist Church. They began dating and were married in the Methodist church in 1947. They lived together happily, or so George thought, for twenty years until Mildred deserted George for another man. After their divorce, George met and fell in love with Joan, a Catholic widow. When George and Joan decided to marry, they approached the local tribunal to see if it was possible to secure a declaration of nullity or dissolution of George's marriage to Mildred. After a preliminary investigation of George's petition, the tribunal concluded that there was no basis for an annulment or dissolution and rejected the petition. George and Joan married civilly. In 1985, George once again approached the tribunal to inquire whether changes in Church practice had opened the way for a declaration of nullity so that he could convalidate his marriage to Joan and be received into full communion with the Catholic Church.

After taking an extensive declaration from George, the tribunal could still find no apparent basis for nullity. However, since George mentioned his previous attempt at an annulment, the tribunal unearthed the record of the case from its archives. The file indicated that the absence of a baptismal record for Mildred at the Methodist church had prompted the tribunal to explore the possibility of seeking a favor of the faith dissolution of George's marriage to Mildred. This approach was abandoned when the tribunal received a letter from Mildred's mother attesting that she herself had baptized Mildred in the bathtub when she was an infant and had done so "as the good sisters in Ireland had taught me." She also attested that she had always considered this baptism to be "Catholic" and that she had taught Mildred the *Baltimore Catechism* and Catholic prayers, including the rosary when she was a girl.

On the basis of this letter from Mildred's now deceased mother, the tribunal contacted Mildred, who was willing to confirm that her mother had told her about baptizing her in the bathtub and that she had learned the Catholic catechism and prayers from her mother and even wore a Miraculous Medal. On the basis of the letter and Mildred's testimony, the tribunal concluded that Mildred had been baptized and raised in the Catholic Church[6] and declared her marriage to George invalid on the ground of lack of form in a formal process. If the tribunal had not preserved the records of George's earlier petition for a declaration of nullity, a favorable resolution of his case would have been impossible.

[6] Canon 1099, §2 of the 1917 code exempted from the obligation of observing the canonical form of marriage those who, although baptized in the Catholic Church, were born to non-Catholics (*ab acatholicis nati*) and raised in heresy, schism or without any religion from infancy. This provision of the 1917 code was interpreted to include those, like Mildred, born to mixed marriages. This clause of the 1917 code was abrogated by Pope Pius XII in 1949. See Pius XII, *motu proprio*, 1 August 1948, *AAS* 40 (1948) 305.

The Uncooperative Respondent Formerly A Petitioner

The Usefulness of Acts of Previous Cases

The evidence from a previous case may also be particularly important when the respondent in a newly submitted case was a petitioner in an earlier case decided affirmatively by a tribunal, but now is uncooperative. Although the acts of the previous case may provide little usable information about the marriage whose validity is now being challenged, they may provide invaluable testimony about the family history of the now uncooperative respondent and his or her developmental history, reports of psychological experts identifying psychic causes for grave lack of due discretion or inability to assume the obligations of marriage or raw material from which an expert could reach such a diagnosis, characterological bases for an intention to simulate matrimonial consent, or evidence of deeply rooted error about the substance of marriage. Indeed, unless the acts of the previously decided case are entered into evidence in the new trial, the just resolution of the new case involving the former petitioner who is now an uncooperative respondent may be impossible.

An Example

Henry and Patricia, both non-Catholics, entered marriage in 1975 and divorced in 1980. Henry then met Cynthia, a Catholic. Out of deference to Cynthia's desire to be married in the Catholic Church, Henry petitioned for a declaration of nullity of his marriage to Patricia in the local tribunal. The declaration of nullity on the ground of Henry's lack of due discretion was granted in 1982 and Henry and Cynthia promptly married in the Catholic Church. This marriage ended in divorce in 1987 and Cynthia petitioned for a declaration of nullity.

In her own declaration, Cynthia was unable to identify the reason for the break-up of her marriage to Henry. She said that one day he suddenly announced that he was unhappy and was leaving her. He promptly moved out. She described Henry as emotionally distant and apparently depressed. However, this general description was rather vague and insufficient to pinpoint a basis for lack of due discretion. Cynthia's witnesses were no more helpful, and Henry failed to respond to all requests of the tribunal for assistance.

When the tribunal retrieved the records of Henry's own annulment case, however, it found a wealth of relevant information. Prior to his marriage to Patricia, Henry had served two tours of duty in Vietnam and the combat experience had left him emotionally shattered. With the help of Henry's own testimony and that of his witnesses, the psychological expert in the previous case had diagnosed Henry as suffering from post-traumatic stress disorder. This information gave substance to the rather vague description of Henry by Cynthia and her witnesses and enabled the tribunal to reach an affirmative decision on the ground of Henry's lack of due discretion, a decision that would have been difficult if not impossible without the records from the previous case.

Cases Involving Relatives of an Uncooperative Respondent

The Usefulness of Acts of Previous Cases

Acts of previously decided cases may also be useful in resolving new cases when a respondent is uncooperative, but a member of his or her immediate family has recently been granted a declaration of nullity. Although the information in the acts of the family member's case may not bear directly on the marriage whose validity is now being challenged, it may be helpful in sketching the dynamics of the respondent's family of origin and corroborating testimony from the petitioner and his or her witnesses. This data about the culture and dynamics of the respondent's family can be especially helpful in identifying pathologies that may have led to lack of due discretion or inability to assume the essential obligations of marriage or the familial atmosphere that may have provided a remote motive for simulating or been a breeding ground for error about the substance of marriage.

An Example

Charlene, a Catholic, and Alexander, a baptized but non-practicing Catholic, married in the Catholic Church in 1987. The marriage, like the courtship before it, was troubled. Charlene and Alexander argued frequently about religion, starting a family, work, and various other issues. In 1990, the day after a particularly bitter shouting match, Charlene returned home from work to discover that Alexander had moved out and filed for divorce. When the divorce was final, Charlene petitioned the local tribunal for a declaration of nullity.

When cited by the tribunal, Alexander made clear his intention not to cooperate in the case and threatened the tribunal with a lawsuit for invasion of privacy if it contacted him again. Charlene acknowledged the frequent arguments during the marriage, but could not identify any problems in Alexander's family of origin, except for the fact that both his parents had been divorced twice before marrying, or any symptoms of a psychological disorder. The witnesses she offered were equally unhelpful. As a result, the tribunal was leaning toward a negative decision until one of the tribunal judges recalled a recent case involving Alexander's half-sister Sheila.

When the tribunal retrieved the acts of Sheila's case, it found considerable testimony about Alexander's family's attitude toward divorce. His parents had testified that, although they had had their children baptized, they had done so out of "residual Catholic guilt" and had done nothing to see to their religious education. They admitted that they had been estranged from the Catholic Church since their own first divorces and considered the Church's position on the indissolubility of marriage "quaint." Alexander himself had testified: "Sheila believed that, if two people don't get along, they should go their separate ways instead of making each other miserable. Every idiot knows that." With the help of this and other testimony in the acts of Sheila's case, the tribunal was able to issue an affirmative decision on the ground of Alexander's hypothetical intention *contra bonum sacramenti*. Without these records, the tribunal's decision would almost certainly have been a negative one.

The Law Governing Use of Tribunal Archives

While the acts of cases previously decided may be valuable resources for deciding new cases, does the Church's law allow tribunals to rummage in their own archives as part of the instruction of marriage cases or to request documentation from the archives of other tribunals? Although canons 1522 and 1525 explicitly address only the value of the acts of the case when an instance has been concluded by abatement or renunciation, they also suggest a wider possible usage for this documentation. If the acts of cases were not available as evidence in cases other than those concluded by abatement or renunciation, the reference to cases involving "those not party to the [original] case" (*ad extraneos quod attinet*) in canon 1522 would make no sense.

Suppletory Law

The code is silent about the use of the acts of previously concluded cases when a new marriage case is initiated between the same parties about the same marriage but under the rubric of a new *caput nullitatis*, when a petitioner in a previously decided marriage case has become an uncooperative respondent in a new case, and when an uncooperative respondent has immediate family members who were parties to marriage cases recently decided by an ecclesiastical tribunal. However, this silence does not imply that the code has no guidance to offer about the use of the acts of cases previously concluded in such cases. Canon 19 stipulates:

> If a custom or an express prescription of universal or particular law is lacking in a certain matter, a case, unless it is penal, must be resolved in light of laws issued in similar matters, general principles of law applied with canonical equity, the jurisprudence and practice of the Roman Curia, and the common and constant opinion of learned persons.

Canons 1522 and 1525 are clearly laws enacted to deal with circumstances similar to those envisaged in the three scenarios sketched above. Thus, canon 19 would seem to authorize the use of the acts of previously concluded cases to supplement the acts of new cases, either with the same probative weight as they would have had in the original case when a case has been proposed between the same parties about the same marriage but on a new ground of nullity or merely with the weight of documents in cases involving a different marriage.

The Nature of Documents in Tribunal Archives

The same conclusion can be reached by considering the nature of the acts of previously concluded cases now filed away in the tribunal archives. The acts of cases seem to be public ecclesiastical documents. The 1983 code is content to define public ecclesiastical documents as "those which a public person has drawn up in the exercise of that person's function in the Church, after the solemnities prescribed by law have been observed" (c. 1540, §1) without giving specific examples of these documents.

Nevertheless, in ecclesiastical trials, "a notary is to take part in any process, so much so that the acts are null unless the notary has signed them" (c. 1437, §1). Both the acts of the process and the acts of the case are to be put in writing, numbered, and authenticated (c. 1472, §§1-2). The signature of notary establishes the presumption that judicial acts are authentic (c. 483, §1), i.e., that they have "authoritativeness as having been executed by the proper public officer."[7] Although tribunals are sometimes remiss in authenticating acts of marriage cases submitted to them for resolution while the cases are active, "the absence of the proper signature does not invalidate the entry as a credible public record," provided that, after the cases were concluded, the acts were retrieved from a legitimate ecclesiastical archive and authenticated by a notary.[8] Thus, it is clear that the acts of concluded marriage cases are public ecclesiastical documents that can, in principle, serve as evidence in future cases.

---

[7] Francis Wanenmacher, *Canonical Evidence in Marriage Cases* (Philadelphia: Dolphin Press, 1935) 207.

[8] Ibid., 211.

This conclusion is confirmed by a comparison of the present norm with the parallel provisions of the 1917 code. The 1917 code was not as reticent as the present code in identifying documents that are to be considered "public ecclesiastical documents." Canon 1813, §1, 3° of the 1917 code listed among the principal public ecclesiastical documents "ecclesiastical judicial acts" (*acta iudicialia ecclesiastica*). This designation of ecclesiastical judicial acts as public ecclesiastical documents was repeated in the instruction *Provida Mater.*[9] These "ecclesiastical judicial acts" include "[j]udicial decisions and acts of procedure (*acta processus*) or of proof (*acta causae*) (see c. 1738), such as sworn reports of designated experts."[10]

Although the 1983 code does not attempt to list the various documents that are to be considered public ecclesiastical documents, there is no indication that the drafters of the revised code intended to alter the, admittedly non-taxative, listing of these documents in canon 1813 of the 1917 code. Instead, the drafters of the revised code chose to use a conceptual criterion for identifying public ecclesiastical documents rather than the enumerative criterion used by the 1917 code and the instruction *Provida Mater.*[11] While the 1917 code was content to list the "principal" (*praecipua*) public ecclesiastical documents without offering criteria for identifying others, the 1983 code provides criteria for identifying public ecclesiastical documents by defining them as "those which a public person has drawn up in the exercise of that person's function in the Church, after the solemnities prescribed have been observed" (c. 1540, §1) without providing examples. Commentators on the 1983 code who address the issue simply presume that the documents listed in canon 1813 of the 1917 code continue to be classified as public ecclesiastical documents.[12]

---

[9] Sacred Congregation of the Sacraments, instruction *Provida Mater*, August 15, 1936, §156: *AAS* 28 (1936) 344.
[10] Wanenmacher, 211.
[11] Juan José García Faílde, *Nuevo Derecho Procesal Canonico* (Salamanca: Publicaciones Universidad Pontificia de Salamanca, 1992) 135.
[12] See, for example, Donata Horak, "La prova documentale," in *I mezzi di prova nelle cause matrimoniali secondo la giurisprudenza rotale*, Studi Giuridici 38 (Vatican City: Libreria Editrice Vaticana, 1995) 34.

Parallel to Public Civil Documents

In the United States, the records of pleadings, transcripts of testimony, and decisions in criminal and civil cases, including divorce cases, are public records, authentic copies of which can, except in unusual circumstances, be acquired by interested parties by paying for the costs of duplication. Canon law recognizes these transcripts of court records as public civil documents and a legitimate source of proof in canonical trials (c. 1540, §2). Indeed, article 168 of the 1936 instruction *Provida Mater* required that:

> If the civil bond is dissolved by divorce, or declared null, the auditor should take care that the parties produce both the petition submitted to the civil court and the decision issued by the civil magistrate and even the record of the civil suit if the case suggests this.[13]

Doheny commented, "Sometimes all the acts of the divorce suit may be necessary. At least, the petition and the decree of divorce are required."[14]

Although article 168 and the other provisions of *Provida Mater*, an instruction given to clarify the prescriptions of the procedural law of the 1917 code, are no longer binding since the promulgation of the 1983 code (c. 34, §3), article 168 does constitute canonical recognition that the records of civil trials are admissible evidence in canonical trials about related matters. American tribunals still generally require petitioners in marriage nullity cases to submit authentic copies of the civil divorce decree for their marriages. However, with the advent of the regime of "no fault" divorce in the United States, the other documents of the civil divorce proceeding no longer contain a great deal of information relevant to an ecclesiastical annulment process.[15] As a result,

---

[13] Instruction *Provida Mater*, §168, 345.
[14] William J. Doheny, *Canonical Procedure in Matrimonial Cases* (Milwaukee, WI: Bruce, 1948) 1: 411.
[15] Mary Ann Glendon, *Abortion and Divorce in Western Law* (Cambridge, MA: Harvard University Press, 1987) 79: "The legal categories of adultery, cruelty, and desertion were represented as too crude and superficial to deal with the infinite variety of ways in which people in a close relationship can do harm to each other. Some critics of fault divorce opposed it also because they thought the adversarial litigation process was ill suited to ascertaining or sorting out the relative degree of fault of the spouses in a troubled marriage. The system had degenerated into a formal recitation of perjured testimony, leaving acrimony in its wake, and supposedly engendering disrespect for the

tribunals no longer routinely seek the complete transcripts of divorce proceedings in secular courts. Nevertheless, psychological evaluations conducted in connection with child custody hearings, if available, can still be of significant value to the marriage tribunal process. If, even under the regime of the 1917 code and the instruction *Provida Mater*, both of which were relatively hostile to the involvement of secular courts in marriage cases involving the baptized, tribunals were sometimes encouraged and sometimes required to admit into evidence public civil documents related to divorce proceedings, *a fortiori* tribunals can and should seek the acts of cases already decided by themselves or other ecclesiastical tribunals when these acts are relevant to the instruction of new cases.

Concern about the Confidentiality of Tribunal Records

The most frequently cited objection to incorporation of the acts of previously decided cases into the acts of new cases is that such incorporation would violate the confidentiality due to tribunal records and promises made to parties, witnesses, and experts that the content of their testimony would not be revealed. The acts of marriage cases often contain information about the most intimate details of married life, which, if divulged, could result in considerable embarrassment to parties and witnesses. Tribunals' failure to protect the appropriate confidentiality of acts of cases could easily result in loss of public confidence in the tribunal process. Since tribunals in the United States have no power to compel witnesses to testify in marriage cases, such loss of confidence could lead to the refusal of potential witnesses to participate in the annulment process and the reluctance of potential parties to approach the tribunal. However, tribunals sometimes promise greater confidentiality to parties and witnesses than either canon or civil law[16] authorizes them to grant.

---

legal system."

[16] It is fairly clear that, in most jurisdictions, the contents of records in ecclesiastical archives, including the tribunal archives and even the secret archives of dioceses, have quite limited immunity from discovery by secular courts when they are clearly relevant to a pending criminal or civil

Limits on the Publicity of Canonical Trials

Of course, canonical trials do not have the same publicity as trials in our secular courts where trials are generally open to the public and any interested party can usually acquire a transcript of a trial simply by paying the costs of duplication. Canonical trials are not open to the public. Instead, only those whose presence is necessary to expedite the process are permitted to be in attendance (c. 1470, §1). In particular, parties to marriage cases are not permitted to be present for the interrogation of witnesses (c. 1678, §2). Moreover, only the parties and their advocates have the right to examine the evidence at the time of the publication of the acts (c. 1598, §1) and to receive a copy of the definitive sentence (c. 1615).

The judge in a canonical trial also has considerable discretion to withhold the petition from the respondent until after he or she has offered a declaration during the trial (c. 1508, §2) and to withhold the names of witnesses from the parties until shortly before the publication of the acts (c. 1554). The evidence collected during the instruction of the case is normally not made available for review by the parties until the publication of the acts at the end of the probatory phase of the process (c. 1598, §1). Nevertheless, the parties' advocates have the right to be present at the interrogation of witnesses and to examine evidence collected prior to the publication of the acts (c. 1678, §1). Despite these limitations on the publicity of the marriage nullity process, canonical trials are still public processes which, in the case of marriage nullity cases, determine the parties' public status in the Church.[17]

The code attempts to assure the appropriate confidentiality of the trial itself. Judges and other tribunal personnel are bound by the secret of office in marriage

---

proceeding. See Hutchison v. Luddy, 606 A. 2d 905 (Pa. Super. Ct. 1992) and Patrick Shea, "Clergy Records: Part I – Civil Law Considerations," *CLSA Proceedings* 58 (Washington, DC: CLSA, 1996) 330-338. Outside Louisiana, where state law specifically privileges tribunal records, "the protection of tribunal documents is not so clear." Donna Krier Ioppolo, "Civil Law and Confidentiality," in *Confidentiality in the United States: A Legal and Canonical Study* (Washington, DC: CLSA, 1988) 26. See also Patrick Geary, "Civil Discovery and Confidentiality of Church Documents," *CLSA Proceedings* 35 (Washington, DC: CLSA, 1977) 82-86.

nullity cases "if the revelation of some procedural act could bring disadvantage to the parties" (c. 1455, §1). Moreover, the judge can require parties, their advocates or procurators, witnesses and experts to take an oath to maintain secrecy about evidence in a case that is known to them if disclosure "will endanger the reputations of others, provide opportunity for discord, or give rise to scandal or some other disadvantage" (c. 1455, §3). However, both the secrecy of office which binds judges and other tribunal personnel and the secrecy imposed on others by oath are primarily intended to protect the integrity of the process by avoiding the impression that tribunal officials are biased and by preventing collusion among parties and witnesses.[18] Thus, these requirement of secrecy generally cease when the case has been concluded or, in the case of parties and witnesses, after the publication of the acts. However, they can be extended indefinitely if the circumstances warrant.[19] Despite these provisions to insure the confidentiality, in canonical trials "the principle is openness, the exception is secrecy."[20]

Protection of Witnesses

Witnesses can refuse to testify if they fear that, as a result of their testimony, "ill repute, dangerous hardships, or other grave evils will befall them, their spouses, or persons related to them by consanguinity of affinity" (c. 1548, §2, 2°). However, once they have testified during a trial, witnesses (and parties) cannot dictate what will be done with their testimony by the tribunal. The transcript of their testimony is part of the public record, i.e., the acts of the case. While the judge can order the production of documents common to both parties

---

[17] See Manuel J. Arroba Conde, *Diritto processuale canonico* (Rome: EDIURCLA, 1994) 250-254.
[18] Francis Xavier Wernz and Peter Vidal, *Ius Canonicum,* Tome V, *Ius Matrimoniale* (Rome: Gregorian, 1946) §155; Arroba Conde, 252; Klaus Lüdicke, *Der kirchliche Ehenichtigkeitprozeß nach dem Codex Iuris Canonici von 1983* (Essen: Ludgerus Verlag, 1994) 58-59; Francisco Ramos, *I tribunali ecclesiastici* (Rome: Millenium Romae, 1998) 202; Pio Pinto, *I Processi nel Codici di Diritto Canonico* (Vatican City: Libreria Editrice Vaticana, 1993) 164; André Cardinal Jullien, *Juges et avocats des tribunaux de l'Église* (Rome: *Officium Libri Catholici,1970*) 326-327.
[19] Arroba Conde, 250; Lüdicke, 59; Jullien, 326.
[20] Edward Dillon, "Confidentiality in Tribunals," *CLSA Proceedings* 45 (Washington, DC: CLSA, 1983) 174.

to a marriage case (c. 1545), parties who believe that these documents cannot be submitted without causing grave harm to themselves or their families can legitimately refuse to submit these documents (c. 1546, §1). Nonetheless, "if at least some small part of a document can be transcribed and presented in copy without the above mentioned disadvantages, the judge can decree that it be produced" (c. 1546, §2). Once documents are submitted to a tribunal, however, they become part of the acts of the case and a matter of public record.

Required Publicity of Acts of Cases

Publication of the Acts

When the instruction of the case has been completed, the judge is to issue a decree publishing the acts of the case, i.e., making them available for review in the chancery of the tribunal by the parties and their advocates (c. 1598, §1). Although the judge has limited discretion in cases affecting the public good like marriage cases to withhold some act (*aliquod actum*) from the parties to avoid most grave dangers (*ad gravissima pericula evitanda*) when the acts are published, he or she must still insure that the parties right of defense is not denied as a result of the decision to restrict the evidence made available for review by the parties.[21] Publication of the acts is required "under pain of nullity" (c. 1598, §1), and failure to do so will almost certainly result in a declaration of nullity of the sentence for denial of the right of defense, if the sentence is challenged (c. 1620, 7°). In principle, therefore, the acts of a marriage case are not strictly confidential but must be made available for review by the parties and their advocates. Indeed, advocates can request and receive copies of the acts (c. 1598, §1).[22]

---

[21] John Johnson, "Publish and Be Damned: The Dilemma of Implementing the Canons on Publishing the Acts and the Sentence," *The Jurist* 49 (1989) 221-222.

[22] Cappello and other commentators on the 1917 code had argued that parties and their advocates had a strict right to receive copies of the acts of the case at the time of the publication of the acts, unless, in the judgment of the judge, the party could not be trusted to honor the terms of an oath not to disseminate the contents of the acts. Felix Cappello, "*Quaestio canonica,*" *Periodica* 19 (1930) 71-73. See also Dillon, 174-175.

Publication of the Sentence

Moreover, the sentence in a marriage case, which usually contains an ample recapitulation of the evidence adduced during the process lacks effect until it is published to the parties (c. 1614). A sentence can be published either by mailing a copy of it to the parties or their procurators or by allowing them to come to the tribunal office to receive a copy (c. 1615). In either case, the publication of the sentence places both the sentence and the reasons in law and fact on which it is based in the hands of the parties or their procurators, who are free to give them as much publicity as they wish. The practice of the Roman Rota, whose decisions are to provide assistance to lower tribunals,[23] is to publish its most significant decisions and decrees in annual volumes of *Romanae Rotae Decisiones seu Sententiae* and more recently *Romanae Rotae Decreta* with minimal attempts to conceal the identities of the parties and witnesses in the case.

Transmission of the Acts to the Appellate Tribunal

When an appeal against a sentence is lodged either by one of the parties or by the defender of the bond and when an affirmative sentence is transmitted *ex officio* to the appellate court, a copy of the acts of the case authenticated by a notary is to be transmitted to the appellate court as well (cc. 1634, §3; 1682, §1; 1474, §1). Thus, concern for confidentiality of the acts of cases does not prevent their being transmitted to other tribunals; in some cases at least, the law actually requires such transmittal.

Furnishing Acts To Those Who Legitimately Ask

When a case has been concluded in one of the methods recognized by law, documents belonging to private persons are to be returned after authentic copies have been made and retained in the acts of the case (c. 1475, §1). Canon 1475, §2 stipulates: "Without a mandate of the judge, notaries and the chancellor are

---

[23] John Paul, Apostolic Constitution *Pastor bonus*, June 28, 1988, art. 126: *AAS* 80 (1988) 892.

forbidden to furnish a copy of the judicial acts and documents acquired in the process." Although this canon frames the issue of furnishing copies of archived tribunal records negatively, it can also be expressed positively. With the mandate of the judge, notaries may provide judicial acts and documents to those who seek them. Indeed, one of the duties of notaries is to furnish acts or instruments to one who legitimately requests them from the records and to declare copies of them to be in conformity with the originals" (c. 484, 3°). It is hard to imagine a more legitimate reason for requesting copies of tribunal records than to admit them into evidence in a new marriage case.

Probative Weights of the Acts of the Case

If acts of previously decided cases are admitted into evidence in new marriage cases, it is important to assess their probative weight. Public documents are fully probative of "everything which they directly and principally affirm" (c. 1541). However, what the declarations of parties, documents, affidavits, transcripts of witness testimony, and expert reports, which comprise the bulk of the acts of the typical marriage case, directly and principally affirm is that a party or witness appeared before a judge or auditor and offered the testimony transcribed in the acts of the case or that a party or affiant appeared before an ecclesiastical or civil notary with a written document and attested that its contents were true. These documents do not direct and principally affirm that what was said or written is, in fact, true and accurate. The truth of the information contained in the documents must, therefore, be assessed independently.

Documents from tribunal archives are formally public documents but materially private documents. Depositions or affidavits signed by the parties themselves have the same probative weight as an extrajudicial confession (c. 1542), i.e., the judge is to decide how much probative weight to attribute to such a document after having considered all the circumstances of the case (c. 1537). Documents signed by third parties have the same force as declarations of the parties that are not confessions (c. 1542). The judge must evaluate such declarations in light of all the circumstances of the case, but cannot attribute the weight of full proof to them, "unless other elements are present which thoroughly corroborate them" (c. 1536, §2).

Inter-Tribunal Cooperation and Sharing

Canon 1545 stipulates: "The judge can order a document common to both parties to be presented in the process." Documents can be common to both parties in several ways: 1) by reason of common ownership of the document; 2) by reason of the fact that the document deals with a matter common to both parties; and 3) by reason of the fact that the matter with which the document deals, although it is not common to both parties, concerns both of them.[24] The acts of a marriage case involving a previous case of the same parties are clearly common to both of them. Since documents from previously decided cases involving only one of the parties or the immediate family of one the parties can still shed considerable light on a marriage whose validity is now being challenged, these documents too can be considered common to both parties.

When documents common to the parties are in the possession of some public office, whether civil or ecclesiastical, the judge may order their production for use in a pending trial.[25] Doheny commented:

> The tribunal is to search diligently on its own authority for documents of both kinds [i.e., both public and private], unless they submit them voluntarily, and should interrogate the parties and witnesses about them in the examination. . . . Hence, the plain duty of the tribunal is to make a thorough search of ecclesiastical and civil records, whether of a public or private nature, in an effort to ascertain the entire truth in a case.[26]

---

[24] Wernz and Vidal, 5: §512; Fernando Della Roca, *Canonical Procedure* (Milwaukee, WI: Bruce, 1961) 237.
[25] Arroba Conde, 375. See also Wernz and Vidal, 5: §512 and Felix Cappello, *Summa Iuris Canonici* (Rome: Gregorian University Press, 1955) 3: §295.
[26] Doheny, 1: 402-403.

Thus, a judge has the right to order his or her own tribunal to make available the acts of cases decided there and to ask other tribunals to provide authentic copies of cases previously decided for use in cases currently pending.

Does a tribunal have the obligation to make the acts of cases they have decided available to other tribunals that have cases pending before them for which their archival material seems to be relevant? Canon 1418 makes it clear that ecclesiastical tribunals have "the right (*ius*) to call upon the assistance of another tribunal to instruct a case or to communicate acts." To this right of one tribunal corresponds a strict duty of the other tribunal to provide the assistance requested.[27] Although the assistance sought from other tribunals usually consists in communicating citations and other procedural acts and interviewing parties and witnesses who cannot come to the tribunal where the case is pending without grave inconvenience, it can also involve transmitting from one tribunal acts of cases concluded in one tribunal that are relevant to a distinct case pending in another tribunal. Indeed, a tribunal would be remiss if it did not seek such documents from another tribunal to assist in the instruction of a pending case, and the other tribunal would fail in its duty to assist other tribunals if it refused to honor such a request.

Conclusion

Although American tribunals have been rightly concerned about preserving the confidentiality of tribunal records, in doing so they have sometimes turned basic principles of canonical procedure on their heads. The code does make provisions for secrecy during canonical trials, especially those involving marriage cases and by barring access to the acts of tribunal cases to those who do not have a legitimate interest in reviewing them. However, this confidentiality of the canonical process is not absolute. It yields to the openness and transparency that is necessary for the tribunal process to be just and, perhaps as importantly, to be perceived as just.

Thus, the parties and their advocates must be given the opportunity to review and refute the evidence gathered in the process, the parties at the time of the publication of the acts and their advocates at any point in the process. The parties have a right to a copy of the decision with its arguments in law and in fact. Appellate courts have the right to have the whole acts of the case and of the process transmitted to them so that they can decide whether to confirm the previous decision. Without the openness and transparency assured by these procedural requirements, the tribunal process will be, in the words of one participant in it, "Catholic gobbledygook."[28] When the process is lacking in transparency, an annulment can easily be characterized as "a fiction obtained as an adjunct of a hoax," "the magical product of an incomprehensible process in which legal reasons play no part and curial discretion is absolute."[29]

Fairness is also not served by withholding from the tribunal process documentary evidence in tribunal archives, which may be crucial for the resolution of a case. Care must be taken with this evidence, of course, lest it be misused to embarrass or damage the reputations of persons. Nevertheless, claims that these archived documents are entitled to absolute confidentiality are exaggerations. In 1973, the Supreme Court of the United States compelled President Nixon to hand over to the courts tapes of confidential conversations in the Oval Office for use in pending criminal cases. The Court held:

> [When] the ground for asserting privilege as to the subpoenaed materials sought for use in a criminal trial is based only on the generalized interest in confidentiality, it cannot prevail over the fundamental demands of due process of law in the fair administration of criminal justice. The generalized

---

[27] Arrobe Conde, 128; Lüdicke, 13.

[28] Sheila Rausch Kennedy, *Shattered Faith* (New York: Pantheon Books, 1997) 10-11.

[29] Noonan, xiii. Rausch Kennedy, 54, somewhat inaccurately cites Noonan, but ignores the fact that this is not Noonan's own view of the actual annulment process, but his description of Chaucer's portrayal of the fraudulent annulment obtained by Walter for his marriage to Griselda in *Canterbury Tales*, "The Clerks Tale," lines 737-749. As is evident from the six careful studies in *Power to Dissolve*, Noonan's own view is that the annulment process is one in which legal reasons are paramount and curial discretion is relatively marginal.

> assertion of privilege must yield to the demonstrated, specific need for evidence in a pending criminal trial.[30]

If the confidentiality of private conversations of the President of the United States with his closest advisors must yield to the need for evidence in pending criminal cases, the confidentiality of acts of marriage cases in tribunal archives should also yield to the need for just resolutions of pressing pastoral problems.

The current law of the Church, like the law of the 1917 code and the instruction *Provida mater*, allows the use of evidence gathered for one case to be used to resolve another, as long as care is taken to ascertain the authenticity and reliability of these documents. The acts of the three quarters of a million marriage cases concluded by American tribunals during the past seventeen years is a resource too valuable to be ignored.

---

[30] United States v. Nixon, 418 U.S. 683 (1973).

Historical Perspectives on Marriage Nullity Cases

James A. Coriden

Introduction

The argument of this historical essay is that the Church has dealt with the divorced and remarried, not only in a judicial mode, but in a variety of ways. This is an examination of the procedures employed in dioceses to discern the validity or nullity of marriages. It is not a study of the doctrine of indissolubility, nor of the Church's jurisdiction over the marriages of Christians, two related but larger issues.

Historical summaries tend to stress continuity and sometimes portray past trends as smooth trajectories in a single direction. Some historical overviews of the Church's treatment of marriage nullity cases fall into this pattern. Beginning with the Apostle Paul, they trace a continuous development from his admonitions to the church at Corinth to the tribunal of the 21st century as though it was a straight line, a smooth and uninterrupted path. They infer that the bishop of the local church, through all periods of the Church's history, as one of his functions, acted as a judge in matrimonial matters. The impression is given that the bishop always adjudicated the validity of disputed marriages in much the same way that diocesan judges do today. Take these summary statements by two distinguished authors as examples.

Colin Morris wrote about the bishop's consistory court in 12th century England:

> Among the functions of the bishop were his judicial duties, which may, even in the earliest days of the Church, be divided into two groups. He had to correct and bring to repentance those who offended against the moral law (1 Cor 5, 3, Paul passed sentence on the incestuous man in Corinth); this was later called correction, ex officio or 'office' jurisdiction. There was also the quite separate duty to restore to amity those who were in dispute, preferably by persuading them to come to agreement, but, failing that, by determining which of them was in the right (1 Cor 6, 5: "Can it be that there is no one among you wise enough to settle a case between one member of the Church and another?"). This was later known as 'instance' jurisdiction as it was provoked by the parties themselves, *ad instantium partium*. This distinction was, therefore, similar to the separation, more familiar to us, of criminal and civil actions.[1]

Morris' text leaves the reader with the impression that the leader of the local church consistently exercised this twofold judicial office from the first century straight through to the twelfth.

Another example is that of Francis Xavier Wernz, SJ, who, in a section entitled "*De Iudicio Canonico in Causis Matrimonialibus*," offered two pages of historical notes. He began: "Since the earliest Christians would not contract marriage without the *sententia* of the bishop, so much the less would they be able to dissolve a contracted marriage without consulting their ecclesiastical Superiors."[2]

Wernz went on to say that although we do not know of any matrimonial cases which were brought before *an ecclesiastical judge* (his italics) in those first centuries on the grounds of a diriment impediment, silence is not a

[1] C. Morris, "A Consistory Court in the Middle Ages," *Journal of Ecclesiastical History* 14:2 (1963) 150-151.

[2] F. X. Wernz, *Ius Decretalium,* Tome IV, *Ius Matrimonii Ecclesiae Catholicae* (Prati: Giachetti, 1911) n. 715. The same text was reproduced verbatim in Wernz-Vidal, *Ius Canonicum,* Tome V, *Ius Matrimoniale* (Rome: Gregorian, 1946) n. 686. Wernz cited in support of his view the same two texts of Paul to the Corinthians and St. Ignatius of Antioch in his letter to Polycarp: "It is proper for men and women who wish to marry to be united with the consent (*sententia*) of the bishop, so that their marriage will be acceptable to the Lord, and not entered upon for the sake of lust."

conclusive argument. He wrote that the infrequency of cases in those first centuries is partly explained by the fact that there were only a few diriment impediments at that time. When the number of diriment impediments increased in the 8th and 9th centuries, then the disputes about the nullity of marriages in the ecclesiastical forum became more frequent.

Wernz skipped ahead in his historical narrative to Gratian and the decretists (12th century) on the scope of the Church's matrimonial jurisdiction, to Clement V's (1311) permission to use a summary process in marriage cases, and then to the Council of Trent's restoration of exclusive matrimonial jurisdiction to the bishop's court (excluding the courts of lesser prelates). Wernz concluded his historical notes with the procedures issued by Benedict XIV in 1741 (in the constitution *Dei miseratione*), and some procedural concessions made in the late 19th century.

Recognizing the limitations of a very brief historical synopsis, even when it was the work of a brilliant canonist, still the impression given is that our judicial process is *the* way that the Church has addressed matrimonial nullity controversies from the very beginning.

History struggles against the all-too-human presumption that the way things are is the way that they always have been. Some suppose, for instance, that the papal office was always a centralized monarchy, that presbyters were always required to be celibate, that practicing Catholics always received Holy Communion frequently.

History responds to the questions asked of it. When asked about the origins and evolution of marriage tribunals, it serves up answers like those above.[3]

[3] Another example is the article of Charles Lefebvre, "Origines et l'Évolution de l'action en déclaration de nullité de Mariage," *Revue de droit canonique* 26 (1976) 23-42. His study is well worth consulting, but it gives the same impression, namely, that the Church dealt with the nullity of marriage in a judicial mode (*une preuve administrée à autorité judiciaire*) right from the beginning. In coming to this conclusion Lefebvre seems to attach special significance to the use of the word *probatio* in c. 2 of the Council of Vannes (461-491): one had to give *proof* in the bishop's court of his wife's adultery in order to dismiss her and marry another. The canon makes no reference to any court and the term *probatio adulterii* does not necessarily indicate a formal judicial hearing; in fact, two manuscripts have the expression *provocatio adulterii* instead (*Corpus Christianorum*, vol. 148, *Concilia Galliae*, 152).

However, if asked for the historical evidence of the ways that the Church has dealt with its divorced and remarried members, then different answers emerge.

This study, by means of a series of historical observations from the first to the fifteenth centuries, will attempt to illustrate the complexity and variety in the Church's encounter with unsuccessful marriages.

Clarifications and Limitations

Two preliminary clarifications are in order before proceeding to the individual observations. First, there is a difference between making a judgment and utilizing a judicial procedure. Human judgments are of all sorts, most of them not made by judges. Confessors make judgments about absolution and suitable penances. Pastors make judgments about readiness for admission to sacraments. Parents make judgments about the wisdom of their children's marriages. To observe that someone with authority in the Church made a judgment about a matrimonial matter does not necessarily mean that the person acted as a judge in a judicial proceeding.

Second, a judicial process usually implies at least these elements: a petition, a judge with jurisdiction, a framing of the issue, notice to the parties, the gathering of evidence, a decision based on the evidence, and a pronouncement of that judgment. These elements generally characterize the judicial process.

This study has four limitations. These explorations are very tentative; much more investigation would be needed to confirm them. While the influence of Jewish law and practices on the early Church was considerable, this study is limited to the impacts of Roman law. The developments described here did not take place simultaneously everywhere in the Church, and observations about what happened in a particular period must admit regional differences, e.g., between Syria and Spain, England and Italy. The practices and experiences of

---

Lefebvre's article appears to have been written in response to J. Gaudemet, "*Le lien matrimonial: les incertitudes de haut Moyen Age,*" *Revue de Droit Canonique* 21(1971) 81-105. Gaudemet's interpretation of the historical evidence reveals much greater diversity in the Church's practice.

our sister churches of the East and of the Reformation traditions are not considered here and must be a part of any larger assessment.

Language of Paul

The words used by the Apostle Paul in the two passages of First Corinthians are often cited as the biblical grounds for judicial action (in general) within the Church and with regard to the nullity of marriage (in particular). Do his words imply a judicial process? Is it legal language which implies the action of a judge parallel to that of a Jewish or Roman law court?

Paul established the Christian community in the port city of Corinth about 50 A.D. A few years later word reached him of troubles there. Among the difficulties was the issue that they were tolerating a man living in an incestuous liaison with his own stepmother. Paul wrote to them in about 56 A.D. and reprimanded the community: "As for me, though absent in body I am present in spirit, and have already passed sentence in the name of our Lord Jesus Christ on the man who did this deed" (1 Cor 5, 3). The main verb, "I have passed sentence, I have judged," is a form of the Greek verb, *krino,* which has as broad a range of meanings as the English word, "to judge." Here it does mean "to try, to sit in judgment on," but the critical point is not that Paul acted like a secular judge (or wanted the Corinthian community to act like one), but that he acted "in the name of our Lord Jesus Christ." Paul, with the authority of Christ, made a spiritual judgment so that the guilty man's "spirit may be saved on the day of the Lord."[4]

In the very next chapter Paul remonstrated with the Corinthian Christians for suing one another in the secular courts:

> How can anyone with a case against another dare bring it for judgment to the wicked and not to God's holy people? . . . Can it be that there is no one among you wise enough to settle a case between one member of the Church and another? (1 Cor 6, 1 and 5)

---

[4] W. Orr & J. Walther, *I Corinthians*, Anchor Bible (Garden City, NY: Doubleday, 1976) 185.

Paul did not urge the Corinthians to set up their own system of courts, parallel to the Roman magistrates, nor did he recommend that the leader of the local church should judge disputes among the members. Paul wanted the Christians to resolve their disputes among themselves. Their unity and fellowship demanded that they settle their differences "within the family." Justice and reconciliation should be sought and found within the community of faith.[5]

Paul's language about judging in these two passages reaches our ears through the echo chamber of our Church's long tribunal tradition. But these church courts began in the 12th century, not in the 1st. And although Paul's words have resonance to our juridical ears, they do not give a mandate for deciding the status of freedom to marry or declaring the nullity of marriages exclusively in a judicial setting.[6]

The Second and Third Centuries: A Matter of Roman Law

The post-apostolic period, that is, from the last of the New Testament writings to the Emperor Constantine, roughly the 2nd and 3rd centuries, did not witness "judicial activity" on the part of bishops in matrimonial matters. In other words, it would not be accurate to speak of church "courts" in that period, much less courts which weighed the validity of marriages.

It is not that church leaders were indifferent to the marriages of church members or indecisive about them. They taught about marriage and family relationships and gave pastoral guidance to their people.[7] The bishops also imposed penances and granted reconciliation within the context of sacramental public penance. The bishop, gathered in synod with his presbyters and deacons,

---

[5] Ibid., 193-197. The verbs "bring for judgment" and "settle a case" are forms of the same Greek verb, *krino*.

[6] For a thorough discussion of marriage and of justice in the Christian communities of the first century, see J. Dauvillier, *Les Temps Apostoliques: Ier Siècle,* Tome II of G. LeBras, *Histoire du Droit et des Institutions de l'Église en Occident.* (Paris: Sirey, 1970) 363-415, 571-597.

[7] St. Ignatius' remark to Polycarp (about 110 A.D., cited by Wernz; see note 2 above) has that moral tone, much like the paternalistic advice sometimes given in marriage matters within modern charismatic communities. The word *sententia* (*gnomaes* in the Greek text) conveys a general sense of approval or consent, not the technical sense of a judge's decision. Confer W. Schoedel, *Ignatius of Antioch: A Commentary* (Phildelphia, PA: Fortress, 1985) 272-273.

set policies for the diocesan church and sometimes made disciplinary decisions regarding individuals, according to Charles Lefebvre.[8] Lefebvre refers to these conciliar proceedings as 'tribunals,' but he admits that they could not be distinguished from arbitration or conciliation proceedings. In summary, Lefebvre says that those early processes were essentially pastoral, founded in charity and in truth.[9]

There is no evidence that the bishops declared the nullity of marriages in those early years. The principal reason for this is that marriage was not within the jurisdiction of the Church. Marriage and divorce were matters of Roman law. At that time marriage was entered into by mutual consent, and it could be dissolved the same way. If there were disputes about married status or coerced divorce or collateral matters of dowry or inheritance, then a magistrate intervened. But the magistrate was an imperial officer, not an official of the Church. Marriage was secular matter, not an ecclesial one.[10]

The Audientia Episcopalis

The Emperor Constantine extended judicial authority to Christian bishops, probably as early as 318.[11] It was called the *audientia episcopalis* or bishop's

---

[8] C. Lefebvre, *"De Iudicio Reddendo in Ecclesia (Lineamenta Historica)" Monitor Ecclesiasticus* 101 (1976) 222-223. He bases his evaluation of these synodal events on a letter of St. Cyprian (North Africa, around 250-258 A.D.) and passages in the *Didascalia Apostolorum* (Syria, probably in the first half of the 3rd century). The passages refer to synod-like gatherings of bishop and clergy for the purpose of investigating and discerning matters, like accusations against presbyters. Most of the texts (e.g., chaps. v-vii, x-xi of the *Didascalia*) sound more like judgments in the context of public penance (the language is of sin, repentance, and prayer) than in a court of law. The *Didascalia* states in one place that the bishop with his presbyters and deacons should hear arguments on Monday so that there would be time to negotiate a reconciliation in time for the eucharist on the following Sunday. R. Connolly, *Didascalia Apostolorum* (Oxford: Clarendon Press, 1969) chap. XI, p. 111.

[9] *Lefebvre, "De Iudiciò Reddendo,"* 223.

[10] The Roman law regarding marriage and divorce has been well studied. See A. Watson, *The Spirit of Roman Law* (Athen, GA: University of Georgia Press, 1995) 9-11, 46-47, 173; S. Treggiari, *Roman Marriage:* Iusti Coniuges *from the Time of Cicero to the Time of Ulpian* (Oxford: Clarendon Press, 1991) 446-482; P.E. Corbett, *The Roman Law of Marriage* (Oxford: Clarendon Press, 1930) 211-251.

[11] The authorization was never rescinded by subsequent emperors, though it was modified considerably. A nominal vestige of the term *audientia episcopalis* is still found in medieval England. It should be noted that Jews were also given their own courts by the Roman imperial authority, and in some respects the two "systems" were treated analogously. See J. Gaudemet, *L'Église dans*

court, but it operated explicitly according to Roman law, not by the canons of the Church. Some contemporary authors assume that this episcopal duty was one of the early stages of the evolution of the Church's action to declare the nullity of marriage by means of a judicial process.[12]

The *audientia episcopalis* was a kind of judicial function, but mainly one that we today might characterize as "alternative dispute resolution." The bishops acted most often as arbitrators, seekers of compromise, negotiators of reconciliation, rather than as judges.[13] Originally these alternative courts had general competence, but during the course of the 4th century their scope was narrowed, first by excluding criminal matters from them, then by limiting them to arbitration, and only in matters of religion. By the time of the Theodosian Code (438) the *audientia episcopalis* was arbitration *inter volentes,* that is, a negotiation of settlements between disputants who willingly submitted their cases to the bishop.[14]

Marriage and divorce remained secular affairs, regulated by imperial law, not religious matters over which the Church claimed or exercised any jurisdiction. They were also private matters, not governed by public law. Divorce, like marriage, could be accomplished by mutual consent; no judicial authority had to intervene. When proper notice of one partner's withdrawal of *affectio maritalis* was not given, or when there was a collateral dispute, for example, over the return of a dowry or division of property, then the case could be brought before a civil magistrate. These marital disputes could have been brought before the bishop in his *audientia episcopalis,*[15] but there is no evidence

---

l'Empire Romain (IVe-Ve siécles), Histoire du Droit et des Institutions de l'Église en Occident, G. Le Bras, ed., Tome III (Paris: Sirey, 1958) 231.

[12] E.g., Lefebvre, "*Origins et Évolution,*" 25.

[13] H. Chadwick, *The Role of the Christian Bishop in Ancient Society* (Berkeley, CA: Center for Hermeneutical Studies in Hellenistic and Modern Culture, 1980) 6.

[14] Gaudemet, L'Église dans l'Empire Romain (IVe-Ve siécles) 230-240.

[15] The Theodosian Code seems to indicate that the bishop's court had competence, L. 16 and L. 28; confer especially *Novel* 35 (452) of Valentinian III, "De Episcopali Judicio," in the Mommsen-Meyer edition of 1854, vol. II, 144-145.

that they actually were, with the notable exception of Pope Innocent I's decision (about 415) in Ursa's case.[16]

Augustine of Hippo (354-430) functioned as a judge in this context every day:

> As a bishop, Augustine sat all morning arbitrating in law-suits. He would have to deal mainly with intricate and rancorous cases of divided inheritances. It was a rare thing for brothers to agree about their property; and Augustine would listen for hours while families of farmers argued passionately about every detail of their father's will.[17]

J. Lamoreaux, in a recent article, presents many examples of the kinds of cases and the burdens they caused to Augustine, Ambrose, and several other contemporary bishops. None of the cases were about marriage or divorce.[18] It is especially ironic that Augustine, the early Church's foremost theologian of marriage, left no evidence of having dealt with marriages as a judge.

Confessors' Absolutions and Bishops' Visitations

In the second half of the first millennium, ecclesiastical courts as we know them did not yet exist, but church authorities did make decisions about marriage and divorce. The laws of the northern peoples (Germanic peoples, Franks, Anglo-Saxons, Visigoths, etc.), like those of the Romans, permitted divorce for several reasons, and the Church's explicit teaching on the indissolubility of marriage was not yet fully in place.

The Frankish kings retained the judicial as well as the legislative authority over marriage. Under Charlemagne and his immediate successors the

[16] The case involved a wife, Ursa, held in captivity by invaders and later freed. While she was captive her husband remarried. Innocent declared that, under Roman law, Ursa was still his lawful wife. The case is well discussed by P. Reynolds, *Marriage in the Western Church: The Christianization of Marriage during the Patristic and Early Medieval Periods* (Leiden: Brill, 1994) 132-134; J. Noonan, in Ursa's Case, *Divorce and Remarriage in the Catholic Church,* ed. L. Wrenn, (New York, NY: Paulist, 1973) 36-38; G. Joyce, *Christian Marriage: An Historical and Doctrinal Study,* second edition (London: Sheed & Ward, 1948) 320.

[17] P. Brown, *Augustine of Hippo* (Berkeley: University of California Press, 1970) 226. Neither Brown nor Augustine's other major modern biographer, F. Van Der Meer, *Augustine The Bishop* (London: Sheed & Ward, 1961) make any mention of his treating issues of marriage in his work as a judge. (Van Der Meer in pp. 258-263 describes that work vividly.)

competence of the secular courts in regard of marriage cases was unquestioned.[19]

Prior to the tenth century, the Church lacked jurisdiction over marriage in any technical sense. Ecclesiastical authorities could and did make judgments about marriages, of course, but the Church had not yet developed a juristic routine for dealing with matrimonial disputes. . . . Only during the tenth and eleventh centuries did church officials seriously begin to assert exclusive jurisdiction over marriage. Prior to that time, the western church limited its intervention in marriage cases essentially to reviewing the legitimacy of particular unions, especially those of prominent persons, whose irregular marriages could create public scandal. Churchmen employed various kinds of pressure to persuade couples to separate and imposed sanctions in order to insure conformity with the Church's marriage rules.[20]

In this context two procedures operated to review the legitimacy of particular unions: private penance and episcopal visitations.

The penitential books, written to guide confessors in dealing with penitents, exercised great influence on Christian thinking and practice from the end of the 6th century to the beginning of the 11th. They were, in effect, new sources of law, and about two-fifths of their canons were concerned with sexual misconduct.[21] Many of these manuals condemned divorce and remarriage and assigned long penances (often seven years) for those who confessed it. Some of the books tolerated divorce and a second marriage when the grounds seemed adequate, e.g., desertion, captivity, enslavement, or a wife's adultery.[22] The point here is not the laxity or diversity of the recommended practices, but that the matrimonial situations were decided by the confessor.

---

[18] J. Lamoreaux, "Episcopal Courts in Late Antiquity," *Journal of Early Christian Studies* 3:2 (1995) 143-167.
[19] Joyce, *Christian Marriage*, 219.
[20] J. Brundage, *Law, Sex, and Christian Society in Medieval Europe* (Chicago, IL: University of Chicago Press, 1987) 137.
[21] J. Brundage, *Medieval Canon Law* (London: Longman, 1995) 25-26.
[22] Brundage, *Law, Sex, and Christian Society*, 164.

The other "forum" for dealing with matrimonial irregularities was the bishop's visitation of his diocese. This sometimes found expression in an informal, movable synod which investigated and took action against abusers of discipline. Abbot Regino of Prüm compiled a collection of canonical rules (in about 906) to aid Archbishop Radbod of Treves (883-919) in this pastoral task of visitation.[23] The visiting bishop, the abbot wrote, was to summon seven men of position and character in each district, put them under oath, and question them about faults in the neighborhood: Has any married man committed adultery with the wife of another? Has any married couple effected a divorce? Has any man separated from his wife, even if she was guilty, without the judgment of the bishop?[24] Such is the process the good abbot recommended; how it was actually carried out and how often it occurred we have little record. If and when it did take place, this form of inquiry followed by disciplinary action was probably as close as diocesan churches got to judicial procedures in marriage cases before the 12th or 13th centuries.

From Synod to Consistory:[25] Eleventh to Thirteenth Centuries

In the 9th century Hincmar of Rhiems (845-882) was settling marriage cases by letters of consultation, and referring some to secular courts. By the 13th century the Church had achieved exclusive jurisdiction over marriage and had developed a sophisticated system of courts for their adjudication.[26] The jurisdictional transfer from secular to religious courts took place in the 11th and

---

[23] *Libri duo de synodalibus causis et disciplinis ecclesiasticis, Patrologiae Latinae* 132: 185-370.

[24] Joyce, *Christian Marriage,* 223; Brundage, *Law, Sex, and Christian Society,* 172-173. Regino gave special attention to the reconciliation of separated couples, and finding a way to help restore their marital harmony. He restricted the grounds for divorce to adultery and impotence.

[25] The heading is taken from C. Morris, "From Synod to Consistory: the Bishops' Courts in England, 1150-1250," *Journal of Ecclesiastical History* 22:2 (1971) 115-123.

[26] P. Daudet, *L'Établissment de la Compétence de L'Église en Matière de Divorce & de Consanguinité (France – 10th-12th Siècles* (Paris: Sirey, 1941) 5, 122ff. Daudet's earlier work, *Études sur L'Histoire de la Jurisdiction Matrimoniale: Les Origines Carolingiennes de la Compétence Exclusive de L'Église (France et Germanie)* (Paris: Sirey, 1933), sets the scene for the jurisdictional shift from secular to ecclesial. Hincmar's treatment of six marriage cases is the centerpiece of his study (pp. 89-134).

12th centuries, and the establishment of a new court system in the 12th and 13th. At least, these are the rough parameters accepted by respected authors.[27]

It was in this period that the Church's judicial system was fully developed. The validity of marriages was one of the issues to which it was applied. It should be noted that marriage cases were not the largest part of the docket of the courts in these years,[28] and that suits for the *enforcement* of marriage contracts far outnumbered those which sought the nullity of marriages.[29]

It is also important to notice that the Church achieved and exercised jurisdiction over marriage well before it affirmed the doctrine that marriage is one of the seven sacraments.[30]

This development of the Church's judicial system in regard to matrimony was shaped by a confluence of factors which were distinctive characteristics of this period:

- Social and judicial anarchy reigned in the 10th and 11th centuries. The institutions of the Carolingian period had decayed. Feudalization allowed the Church to assume legal powers, while secular judges were under the influence of local political forces.[31]

---

[27] Daudet, *L'Établissment de la Compétence,* 127ff; Joyce, *Christian Marriage,* 223-233; Brundage, *Medieval Canon Law,* 120ff; idem, *Law, Sex, and Christian Society,* 223ff. M. Brett, *The English Church under Henry I* (London: Oxford University Press, 1975) 152ff, gives a picture of the relatively incoherent state of episcopal decisional structures in England at the outset of the 11th century. "It is impossible to determine the precise date at which the Church began to exercise proper judicial competence in questions of the marriage bond." A. Diacetis, *The Judgment of Formal Matrimonial Cases: Historical Reflections,* Canon Law Studies 492 (Washington, DC: The Catholic University of America, 1977) 48.

[28] Apparently it was not until the 19th century that marriage cases became the principal concern of the Church's judicial process. Lefebvre, "*De Iudicio Reddendo,*" 235.

[29] The causes brought to enforce marriage contracts predominated over divorce suits by preponderant ratios in English diocesan courts in the 14th and 15th centuries because of the problem of clandestine marriages. R. Helmholz, *Marriage Litigation in Medieval England* (Cambridge, MA: Cambridge University Press, 1974) 25ff.

[30] The system of seven sacraments was first articulated by Peter Lombard (about 1150), refined by Thomas Aquinas and others in the 13th century, but only authoritatively affirmed in the Council of Florence (1438-1445). Marriage was referred to as sacramental in the Council of Verona (1184), by Innocent III (1199), and in the Second Council of Lyon (1274), but the Church's juridical claims were prior to these and not specifically based on the sacramentality of marriage.

[31] Daudet, *Études sur Histoire,* 171; idem, *L'Établissment de la Compétence,* 127ff; G. Duby, *The Knight, The Lady and The Priest: The Making of Modern Marriage in Medieval France* (New York, NY: Pantheon, 1983) 119.

- The Gregorian Reform (beginning with Leo IX in 1049) provided motivation and energy to power the development of autonomous church courts, and to bring marriage under their jurisdiction.[32]
- Roman law, with the rediscovery of Justinian's *Corpus Iuris Civilis* and its systematic study (alongside canon law) at the University of Bologna in the late 11th century, greatly influenced all legal thinking and practice, especially the canonical.
- Canon law itself was stimulated by three great collections (those of Burchard of Worms, 1012, Ivo of Chartres, 1094-96, and Johannes Gratian, 1140) and the pressing needs of the Gregorian Reform. Canon law was studied intensely and achieved a whole new status as an organized and effective system of governance.
- Theology developed dramatically, under the impetus of philosophical systems and the ferment of scholastic debate. It also repositioned the relationship between theology and canon law which, in turn, refined convictions about the nature of marriage.

The convergence of these disparate factors provided the unique context within which the Church created its judicial system and began to use it for the determination of the validity of marriages. It was under these pressures that marriage became "the Church's thing," a religious matter rather than a secular one.[33]

It was in these singular circumstances that the synod gave way to the court. The annual (or semi-annual) gathering of bishop and clergy was replaced for judicial purposes by the consistory court with a judge-delegate, the bishop's *officialis,* hearing cases monthly (or more often).

---

[32] Brundage, *Law, Sex, and Christian Society,* 179ff. Brundage cites George Duby's compilation of seven fundamental principles upon which rested the model of marriage championed by the reformers: First, marriage must be monogamous; second, marriage should be indissoluble; third, marital unions should be contracted freely by the parties themselves, not by their parents or families; fourth, marriage represents the only legally protected type of sexual relationship, and therefore concubinage should be eliminated, even among the laity; fifth, all sexual activity outside of marriage must be punished by legal sanctions; sixth, all sexual activity, marital and non-marital, falls solely under ecclesiastical jurisdiction; and seventh, marriage must become exogamous, and intermarriage with related groups of families should therefore be eliminated.

Brundage, 183; G. Duby, *Medieval Marriage: Two Models from Twelfth-Century France* (Baltimore, MD: Johns Hopkins University Press, 1978) 3.

[33] Ivo of Chartres called marriage "the Church's business" (*negotium ecclesiasticum*). Rufinus (1156) used the expression, *causa spiritualis.* Bernard of Pavia taught that *divortium fieri non potest absque ecclesiastico judicio et sine causae cognitione. Solus ergo ecclesiasticus judex divortium facere potest.* (*Summa Decretalium,* c. 1198).

Colin Morris describes the change as "a managerial revolution" in which professional lawyers replaced ordinary churchmen, written pleadings replaced oral arguments, and the new rules were drawn from Roman civil law.[34] What remained constant was the principle that the jurisdiction belonged to the bishop.[35]

In the mid-twelfth century, then, although the bishop could hear causes in a variety of ways, the most formal and dignified tribunal in which he might settle a dispute or give sentence was the diocesan synod. A century later, the bishop had lost none of his independence of action, in the sense that he could still delegate causes specially to nominated judges, but the central tribunal had now been entirely transformed into a court devised for legal purposes, with a lawyer as president, meeting regularly for the hearing of cases. Although the synod continued for more pastoral purposes, in its legal activity it had been replaced by the consistory.[36]

The procedures for introducing a marriage case seem to have bridged this radical change in institutional forms. From the time of Gratian and the decretists there were three forms of canonical actions for the nullity of marriage. They were developments of the Church's disciplinary authority, and the procedures were modifications of criminal processes. The three ways to obtain the declaration of nullity of marriage were: *accusatio, denunciatio, and inquisitio.*

- *Accusation* of the nullity of a marriage could be brought by only one of the spouses, except in the case of the existence of a diriment impediment that was public. It had both criminal and civil effects in that it punished the person who had flouted the law, but it also resulted in the separation of the spouses.
- *Denunciation* (from *denunciatio evangelica,* Mt. 18, 17, "refer it to the Church") could also be made by anyone who knew of an invalidating impediment or some other source of nullity; it was a recognized part of the synodal process. Even though its purpose was the reform of the offender, still it could bring about separation.

---

[34] Morris, "From Synod to Consistory," 117.
[35] Ibid., 115.
[36] Ibid., 123.

- *Inquisition* was the investigation which a judge could undertake *ex officio* without any preceding accusation or denunciation, acting on persistent, widespread belief that a marriage had been contracted illegitimately. [37]

Full Deployment: Ordines Iudiciarii *and Case Loads*

"By the late twelfth century, church courts had secured jurisdiction over marriage and related matters, both in England and on the Continent."[38] This exclusive jurisdiction, combined with population growth in Europe and the moral vitality of the Reform movement, increased the need for effective courts and burdened them with larger case loads.

"A reasonably successful system of ecclesiastical courts only began to emerge in the second half of the thirteenth century."[39] Before that procedures were still *ad hoc* and unsystematic; bishops issued judgments as individuals or the multi-purpose assemblies called synods served as courts at the diocesan level.[40] The new courts were more professional and attended to higher standards of procedure and evidence. As a result a whole new literature developed: the *ordines judiciarii*.[41]

These procedural treatises, some theoretical studies, some practical manuals, some for use in secular courts, some for ecclesiastical courts, proliferated in the 12th and 13th centuries. They were all strongly influenced by the newly rediscovered Roman law. The church courts gradually modified and adapted their processes in accord with the Christian spirit (one book was entitled

---

[37] Lefebvre, "Origines et Évolution," 27-33, following A. Esmein-R. Genestal, *Le Mariage en Droit Canonique* (Paris: Sirey, 1929) 449-474. Brundage comments on these three forms as matters of criminal procedure, *Medieval Canon Law,* 89-96, 120-153. The first title of Book V of the *Decretales Gregorii IX* (1234) is entitled *De Accusationibus, Inquisitionibus, et Denunciationibus.*
[38] Brundage, *Law, Sex, and Christian Society,* 319.
[39] Brundage, *Medieval Canon Law,* 41; Morris, "A Consistory Court," 151.
[40] Ibid., 120ff.
[41] F. Claeys Bouuaert, *Dictionnaire de Droit Canonique,* vol. 6 (Paris: Letouzey & Ané, 1957) cols. 1132-1143. The authoritative *ordo iudiciarius* was that outlined in the twenty-nine titles of Book II of the *Decretales Gregorii IX* (1234).

Ordo "Invocato Christi nomine"), but the two systems, although independent, continued to exert influence on one another.

There were many *ordines* published during this time of establishment and consolidation of the Church's judicial system, but the two most influential and frequently cited were the *Ordo judiciarius* (1214-1216) by Tancred of Bologna and the *Speculum iudiciale* (versions in 1272 and 1287) by William Durand, called "The Speculator." Durand's work was said to sum up all that went before him and to be the source for all that followed. Dino Mugellanus, who collected the *Regulae Juris* for Boniface VIII, even wrote an *Ordo brevis* (1298) in verse form! Clearly the Church's new courts were well instructed on how to proceed.

Some recent studies provide glimpses of the kind and number of cases which these courts actually heard:

- During the years 1373 and 1374, thirty-nine and thirty-one matrimonial suits respectively were introduced into the Consistory Court of Canterbury, constituting approximately a third of the total number of suits heard in those years. Forty-seven suits were introduced during 1397, but between 1415 and 1507 the number of matrimonial suits for which a complete record survives never exceeded twenty, and was frequently less than ten."[42]
- The tribunal of Paris treated ten cases of the nullity of marriage in the three years, 1384-1387, two for impotence, eight for bigamy.[43]
- The roll of proceedings of the Diocese of Lincoln for the year 1430-1 listed ninety cases in which thirteen dealt with matrimony and divorce.[44]
- Robert Brentano narrates well over twenty cases in diocesan courts up and down the Italian peninsula in the course of the 13th century. They include disputes over land, privileges, olive oil, shop sites, and elections, but no marriage cases.[45]
- The fourteenth century books of acts from York show that marriage cases accounted for 38% of the case load.[46]

---

[42] B. Woodcock, *Medieval Ecclesiastical Courts in the Diocese of Canterbury* (London: Oxford University Press, 1952) 85.
[43] Lefebvre, "Origines et Évolution," 34.
[44] Morris, "A Consistory Court," 157.
[45] R. Brentano, *Two Churches: England and Italy in the Thirteenth Century* (Princeton, NJ: Princeton University Press, 1968) 140-172.
[46] C. Donahue, cited in Brundage, "The Treatment of Marriage in the *Quaestiones Londinenses* (MS Royal 9.E.VIII)" *Sex, Law and Marriage in the Middle Ages* (Brookfield, VT: Variorum, 1993) 97.

- "Of twenty-three marriage cases heard from April 1437 through April 1440 in the Rochester Consistory Court, only five were for divorce. . . . There are eighty-eight cases involving marriage in the York Cause papers of the fifteenth century, only twelve of them are divorce suits."[47]

Conclusions and Prospects

This series of observations leads to the conclusion that the Church has dealt with those who have divorced and have remarried (or who desire to remarry) in a variety of ways over the course of its history. Even when it was a question of the validity of the union, the leaders of diocesan churches have used several different approaches: pastoral admonition, moral guidance, penitential reconciliation, criminal punishment, synodal discernment, inquisitional inquiry, decretal response, advisory letter, administrative decision, and judicial procedure[48].

The judicial process of a contentious trial to declare the validity or nullity of a marriage was developed in the 12th and 13th centuries, after the rediscovery of Roman law and before the rise of nation-states. Secular juridical systems were in disarray. The Church acquired jurisdiction over marriage, before its convictions about the sacramentality of marriage were clear, and it employed its own developing judicial procedures to deal with matrimonial controversies.

But why raise the question? Why examine the assumptions about the Church's *judicial* determination of the validity marriages? Why bother to claim that for the first thousand years of the Church's historical journey it did not deal with marriage and divorce in what we would today identify as a judicial procedure?

---

[47] R. Helmholz, *Marriage Litigation in Medieval England,* 74. "Suits for divorce were not numerous; they were far outnumbered by cases involving the enforcement of marriage contracts. . . . Why were there so few divorce cases?

. . . Men and women invalidly married simply divorced themselves" (p. 75).

[48] Even within the judicial process the approaches have varied widely: criminal accusations, interpretations of contract law, and the determination of the status of persons (from the Roman law, *ius quod ad personas pertinet: status libertatis, status civitatis, status familiae.* P. Thomas, *Introduction to Roman Law* [Deventer, Netherlands: Kluwer, 1986] 135)

The answer is that it is time to reassess the bold American experiment with the annulment process.[49] The amazing explosion of annulments since 1970 needs to be soberly evaluated. It may be time for the churches to fashion a broader response to the culture of divorce. A new and more flexible pastoral strategy seems to be called for in order to meet this massive pastoral challenge.[50] The awareness of historical diversity should free us to fashion a more comprehensive and targeted pastoral plan for present-day Catholics who experience marriage failure.[51]

[49] This American experiment was the "American Procedural Norms," implemented in tribunals in the United States of America in July 1970. We were joined in this experiment by the able canonical forces of the Canadian, British, Irish, Scottish, and Australian churches. Lawrence G. Wrenn was and continues to be the outstanding guide and mentor for the thousands who have labored lovingly in this movement for Catholic families. The churches remain indebted to him for his brilliant, generous, and genial leadership.

[50] Confer James Coriden, "The Tribunal As Last Resort," *The Jurist* 59 (1999) 60-77.

[51] We are well aware that the present forms of canonical procedures are radically diverse: formal trials, documentary process, declaration of freedom to marry in the pre-nuptial investigation process, and the pastoral acknowledgment of de facto and civil unions.

Ivo of Chartres
An Earlier Master
of the Art of Interpretation

Richard G. Cunningham

Introduction

It was in the summer of 1969 when I first attended the Catholic University of America to participate as a student in its Summer Institute on Tribunals. My first professor there was Rev. Lawrence G. Wrenn who opened for me a whole new understanding of the Church's law and its application in practical matters (canon 19, 1917 *CIC*). From that day, Lawrence Wrenn in his teachings, writings and addresses has introduced a considerable portion of the canonical world to the prevailing present-day jurisprudence and we have learned much from his wisdom and words.

When I was honored with the request to make a contribution to this *festschrift* I immediately thought of an earlier master of the art of interpretation, the legendary bishop, Ivo of Chartres. We are indebted to him for the contributions he made to the science of interpreting the law as we are to Lawrence Wrenn, to whom I address this work with deep admiration, appreciation and affection.

"(A) French canonist of massive learning," observed Professor Brian Tierney of Cornell University in describing him.[1] "A major canon lawyer . . . an important forerunner of Gratian," wrote Dr. Lynn Barker of Mississippi State University.[2] Columbia University's Robert Somerville and West Texas A&M University's Bruce Brasington added ". . .(O)ne of the finest legal scholars of the reform era and one of the most significant figures in the history of medieval canon law. ."[3] High praise for this much admired canonist!

Born about 1040, Ivo was believed to be the son of land owning lesser nobility living north of Paris in the region of Beauvais, France. He was educated in a local church school and then was sent to St. Martin des Champs in Paris for the study of philosophy and the liberal arts. His intellectual and moral formation were most likely nourished in Normandy at a school well known throughout Europe, the Benedictine Abbey of Bec, where he was a student of its prior, the theologian, Lanfranc, who later became the Archbishop of Canterbury.[4]

Priest and Bishop

Following his ordination Ivo served as a priest at the church of Nesle in Picardy and later become prior of the canons regular of Saint Augustine at the monastery of Saint-Quentin at Beauvais. After serving in that office for a dozen

---

[1] Brian Tierney, *The Crisis of Church and State*. (Toronto: University of Toronto Press, 1988) 75.

[2] Lynn Barker, *History, Reform, and Law in the Works of Ivo of Chartres* (Ph.D. diss. University of North Carolina, 1989) 16.

[3] Robert Somerville and Bruce Brasington, *Prefaces to Canon Law Books in Latin Christianity. Selected Translations, 500-1245.* (New Haven: Yale University Press, 1998) 111. Contained in this work (132-158) is a complete English translation of Ivo's *Prologue*. My references in this paper to the English translation of the *Prologue* are taken from this work. It is based on another translation of the *Prologue* by Dr. Brasington in his doctoral dissertation, "The Prologue to the Decretum and Panormia of Ivo of Chartres: An Eleventh Century Treatise on Ecclesiastical Jurisprudence" (Ph.D. diss. University of California at Los Angeles, 1990) 295-321.

[4] Another future archbishop of Canterbury, St. Anselm Aosta, and possibly Anselm I of Lucca, the future Pope Alexander II, were also alumni of Bec around the time of Ivo's education in the eleventh century. Uta-Renate Blumenthal, *The Investiture Controversy: Church and Monarchy from the Ninth to the Twelfth Century.* (Philadelphia: University of Pennsylvania Press, 1988) 150, does not believe Anselm I of Lucca was among the young men who flocked to Bec. Nevertheless, an interesting study on the association of these persons with Lanfranc at Bec may be found in an article by Sally Vaughn, "Lanfranc at Bec: A Reinterpretation," *Albion* (17) 135-148. I am indebted to Ann Collins, Ph.D.

years, both the clergy and the people elected him, and Pope Urban II named him bishop of Chartres in 1090, having deposed the then reigning bishop Geoffrey who, after offering much resistance to the pope, had been fired for simony and other infractions of church rules.[5] Ivo served the See of Chartres until his death on December 23, probably in 1115.[6]

Although Ivo was never formally canonized, both in Chartres and northern France he is considered a saint.[7] In 1570 a constitution from Pope St. Pius V ratified the people's recognition of Ivo as saint and permitted the Canons of the Lateran Congregation to celebrate Ivo's memory on May 20th.[8]

Described as a man of charity, mercy, friendship and humanity,[9] Ivo was a gifted writer who was influenced by the aim of the eleventh century reform period at renewal of the old law in order to bring about reform of both the Church and Christian society.[10] This was to be accomplished by renewing the

---

cand. University of Pennsylvania of Wellesley, MA for calling this work to my attention.

[5] *Encyclopedia Britannica.* Chicago: 1958, 12, 834.

[6] Pope Urban II favored Ivo because he represented the ideals of the reform movement. In a letter to the clergy and people of Chartres, Pope Urban emphasized Ivo's erudition, a prized quality in a bishop of any era and his knowledge of the canons. Brasington, *Prologue to the Decretum*, 401.

[7] Stephan Kuttner, "*On Sources*" (Unpublished mimeographed class notes, Catholic University, 1941) 48.

[8] Amleto Cicognani, *Canon Law* (Westminister, MD: The Newman Press, 1949) 254. The *Columbia Encyclopedia* (NY: Columbia University Press, 1993), 1380 reports his feast day as May 24th and the *Encyclopedia Britannica,* Chicago, 1974, *Micropaedia* V, 478 reports it as May 23rd.

[9] Professor Colin Morris, in *The Papal Monarchy. The Western Church from 1050 to 1250* (Oxford, Clarendon Press, 1989) 317, wrote,

> Ivo found that human society had value in the eyes of God (and promoting a new spirit of humanism) Ivo wrote of "the dignity of the human condition," – an idea which is difficult to find in Gregory VII or his close associates. He held that need might overrule religious edicts so that the prohibition of swearing in MT 5:34-37 did not apply to 'human contracts', (see also, Barker, 335) and it was permissable to have dealings with excommunicates for the sake of humanity. He strove to secure peace between the *regnum* and the *sacerdotium*, "without whose concord affairs cannot be secure." The word, 'humanity', after 500 years in which it had mainly referred to the impotence of man in the face of the majesty of God, reappeared in Ivo's works in a good sense, shaped by its old classical meaning of 'philanthropy'. This was, of course, a Christian, not a secular humanism, shaped by the conviction that "honour or maltreatment of the poor refer to Christ." With widened sympathies and improved techniques of study, the church sought to instill the principles of Christian conduct in a broad range of human affairs.

Later on page 367 Morris mentioned that Ivo was first to call attention to the respect to be given to humanity "which was not confined to redeemed mankind, whose dignity had never been in doubt, but was directed also to man in the natural order."

[10] Barker, *History, Reform and Law*, 132.

individual in the image of God so as to restore harmony between the conflicting parties, especially the *regnum* and the *sacerdotium.*[11]

Canonist and Theologian

The most gifted canonical jurist[12] of his age, Ivo shared in the city of Chartres' eleventh century reputation as an intellectual center and he himself became well informed of the wider scientific renaissance then in progress.[13]

It appears that "Ivo had no university education" and that "he took no law degree."[14] Nevertheless, with a keen sense of history, an appeal to the past and emphasis on interpretation of 'time and place', Ivo's ideas and writings on the law were formed and influenced others. While we can discover only a little about the person of this talented man of learning, his writings point to a zealous bishop of faith and apparent holiness of life.[15] A shepherd deeply concerned with pastoral care, he was as well an industrious and thorough researcher, prudent and critical in his labors, respectful of tradition and able to make important and significant canonical distinctions, e.g., among illicit things that

---

[11] A common expression in Christian thought at Ivo's time used to describe the 'two-power' theory of cooperation between the state and the Church. It can be traced back to Pope Gelasius I (492-496). J.N.D. Kelly, *The Oxford Dictionary of Popes* (Oxford: Oxford University Press, 1986) 48.

The emperor Justinian (+565) wrote: "The greatest gifts given by God to man from his heavenly clemency are priesthood and empire (*sacerdotium et imperium)"* in his "Novella VI (535)" found in R. Schoell, ed., *Corpus Iuris Civilis,* vol. III *(Novellae),* (Berlin, 1895) cited by Tierney, 15. See also Robert McNally, "Middle Ages," *New Catholic Encyclopedia,* vol. IX (NY: McGraw Hill, 1967) 814-817 and Morris, 1-2 and 17.

[12] Brasington in *The Prologue,* 399, notes that while there are no traces of formal instruction in canon law at Lanfranc's Bec, it is likely that Ivo received there an initial, informal exposure to the subject, possibly some informal tutorial. He continues,

> We can only speculate on what Ivo studied while provost at the Augustinian house at Beauvais, however, it must have been here he made the leap from the *artes* to the canons and became a canonist, at least as defined by the standards of the late eleventh century. (401)

[13] Greek medical practices were being introduced to the West and increased writings on medicine began to appear out of the University of Salerno. From the East astronomic instruments for the study of stars were introduced into Europe and out of China came the mechanical water clock, the floating compass and the first moveable type.

[14] Barker, *History, Reform and Law,* 266-267.

[15] Brasington, *The Prologue,* 367, points out that Ivo himself provided a "distinctive portrait of the bishop . . . pastor, judge and jurisprudent."

are prohibited, necessary things that must be ordered, the highest things that are to be exhorted and milder things that can be permitted.[16] From this thinking came his corresponding categories in which he treats: prohibitions (prohibiting illicit things), precepts (commanding necessary things), admonitions (directing things most desirable) and remissions or indulgences (concerning things that are venial).[17]

Ivo was a man at home with the writings of Augustine and frequently drew on the psalms, gospels, Pauline letters, certain of the Fathers and many papal decretals. Mercy and truth appear as a priority to Ivo in seeking out the law as do faith and honesty. "Charity," above all, he wrote, "should be the mistress of every good thing."[18]

His Writings

In Ivo's writings, there was little distinction between the subjects of theology and law. His contemporary, the lay jurist, Irnerius, founder of the School of Roman Law at the University of Bologna early in the twelfth century, was one of the first to understand law as a separate discipline, to be cultivated for its own sake.[19]

As a theologian/canonist Ivo's writings had an influence on theologian Peter Lombard's *Book of Sentences* contributing to the fixing of the number of sacraments at seven. Ivo argued the pope could be tried only for heresy. He had serious reservations about the Crusades and his use of exclusively religious sanctions manifested his totally spiritual conception of the Church.

---

[16] Somerville and Brasington, *Prefaces to Canon Law Books*, 135.

[17] Yves de Chartres, *Le Prologue, Texte Latin. Introduction, Traduction et Notes* par Jean Werckmeister, vol. 6 (Paris: Les Editions du Cerf, 1997) 69-70. The Latin version of Ivo's *Prologue* used in this translation is based on a twelfth century manuscript, no. 14315, of the National Library of Paris, together with the manuscript published in J.P.Migne, *Patrologia Latina,* vol. 161 (Paris, 1889) 47B-60A. For an English translation, see Somerville and Brasington, 135.

[18] Yves de Chartres, 3, 67 and Somerville and Brasington, *Prefaces to Canon Law Books,* 134.

[19] Henri Daniel-Rops, *Cathedral and Crusade. Studies of the Medieval Church 1050-1350* (NY: E.P. Dutton & Co., Inc., 1957) 338.

He worked to promote the aims of the Gregorian Reform, '*libertas et puritas,*' [20] especially in monasteries and in the canonical life of the clergy. He was one of the principals involved in the controversy with Lanfranc's teacher, Berengarius, whose condemnation for his teachings on the Eucharist led to the adoption of the word "transubstantiation" at the IV Lateran Council in 1215.[21]

Acknowledged for his theological acumen, Ivo, above all, was the most accomplished canonical jurist of his age and one of the irreplacable artisans who enabled the further elaboration of classical canon law.[22]

Ivo wrote some three hundred letters containing his expert opinions on contemporary political, religious and liturgical questions. Along with his sermons and legal writings they are a valuable source for understanding his life and the culture of his times.

His Collections

In all likelihood, with the encouragement of Pope Urban II,[23] Ivo may have personally directed a group of copyists in composing the three collections of canonical materials attributed to him from 1093 to 1095. They were done in the cathedral school of Chartres, one of the most famous of the cathedral schools in the eleventh century, renowned for its classical studies and the center where Ivo promoted studies in canon law.

These collections were:

- *Tripartita* (a collection in three parts that possibly was Ivo's own work;)[24]

---

[20] "*Libertas,*" freedom for the Church plagued by lay investiture and "*puritas*", chastity among the clergy.

[21] Norman Tanner, *Decrees of the Ecumenical Councils,* vol. 1 (London & Washington, DC: Sheed & Ward, 1990) 230.

[22] L. Chevailler, "Yves de Chartres" *Dictionnaire de droit canonique* (hereafter *DDC)* 7, 1645.

[23] See footnote n. 54.

[24] For a discussion of this work see Kaaren Sorensen, *The Preface as a Hermeneutical Vehicle in Canon Law Collections, 1075-1175* (Ph.D. diss. Columbia University, 2000) 114-120.

- *Decretum* (an influential collection of some 3,760 decrees or canons; Paul Fournier, a leading authority of the past century in the history of canonical collections, in his study of this *Decretum*, referred to it as a great *"magasin des texts"*;[25] although there is much debate on who wrote this work, the *Decretum* did help to reconcile the strict Gregorian Reform with the Franco-German tradition and helped to introduce Roman law into the canonical tradition;)[26]
- *Panormia,* the more popular work, (collection of 'all the laws' almost universally recognized as Ivo's own work.)[27]

As mentioned above there are doubts about some of the sources, dates and circumstances of the editing of these collections, even doubts among some about the authorship.[28] These collections were extensive and the *Panormia,* a summary of canon law, gained popular success and remained in wide use in the ecclesiastical courts until supplanted by the even greater work of Gratian.[29]

His Sources

A general study of the numerous citations made by Ivo in his correspondence and other writings points to a man who was well educated in biblical, theological and canonical matters. He often referred to the Scriptures, the canons of the ecumenical councils, papal decretals, and a particular favorite source of his, the Fathers of the Church. Even the holy rule of St. Benedict along with Virgil, Horace, Cicero, Pliny the Elder and other Latin writers are often quoted as well. L. Chevailler in the *Dictionnaire de droit canonique* notes that

[25] Paul Fournier, Les Collections canoniques attribuees a Yves de Chartres, *Bibliotheque de l'École des Chartres*, vol. 57, 1896, 645-698; vol. 58 (1897) 26-77, 293-326, 410-444, 624-676.
[26] J. Joseph Ryan, "Ivo of Chartres, St.," *Dictionary of the Middle Ages*, vol. 7 (NY: Charles Scribner's Sons, 1982) 21-22.
[27] A version of the *Panormia* may be found in Migne, *Patrologia Latina*, 161, 1041-1344, but Stephen Kuttner and other scholars question the accuracy of this version.
[28] James Brundage, *Medieval Canon Law. The Medieval World* (London and NY: Longman, 1995) 38. See also Sorensen, 78-80.
[29] For a discussion of Ivo's work, see Somerville and Brasington, 112-117 and Paul Fournier and Gabriel LeBras, *Histoire des collections canoniques en Occident*, vol. II (Paris: Recueil Sirey, 1932) 55-114. For a rather thorough analysis of Ivo's works, see Paul Fournier, *Mélanges de droit canonique*, vol. I (Aalen: Scientia Verlag, 1983) 451-748.

Ivo's only passion was the good of the Church and he spoke of "zeal for the house of God,"[30] a phrase often used in his writings and sermons to describe himself, the reformers and others and always calling on them to maintain their zeal within the bounds of moderation.

The Gregorian Reform and Papal Supremacy

The Gregorian Reform had been instrumental in introducing a new kind of canon law, one that came out of Rome. It interested Ivo and his contemporaries but their enthusiasm was muted by the fear that it could take over the place of their own law.[31]

Ivo recognized the preeminent authority of the papacy and accepted and was influenced by the Gregorian reform in principle and substance but insisted as well on preserving among the ancient disciplinary norms taken into his compilation those of his own Frankish tradition. He favored tradition and progress simultaneously and tried to fuse the strict juridical principles of Roman-Gregorian law and the particular legislation of the Frankish-German tradition.[32]

Ivo wrote that it is the intention of Church Law

> either to tear down every structure that raises itself up against the knowledge of Christ, or to build up the enduring house of God in truth of faith and honesty of character, or if that house of God be defiled, to cleanse it with the remedies of penance.

Again he mentions:

> The mistress of this house is charity, which sees to the welfare of our neighbors, commanding that it be done for others what one wishes to be done for himself.[33]

---

[30] *DDC*, 7, 1645.
[31] S. Kuttner, "On Sources," 48.
[32] Theodore Mackin, *The Marital Sacrament* (NY: Paulist Press, 1989) 265 and idem, *Divorce and Remarriage* (NY: Paulist Press, 1984) 260-261.
[33] Yves de Chartres 3, 66; Somerville and Brasington, 134.

This period of change proved to be a challenge to ecclesiastics, especially those whose narrow view of the Church was by and large what they were already familiar with in their own country and culture. Burchard's early eleventh century *Decretum,* although by now a bit antiquated, would be a good example of a collection of law with which they could be comfortable. Following the cumulative practice that characterized the earlier collections of canon law,[34] Ivo incorporated into his *Decretum* virtually all of Burchard's work.[35] Both canonists stressed papal supremacy but called for some compromise and for some limits. They believed in the power of the pope but not his legates whose powers needed to be checked.[36]

For sources Ivo also drew from the Britannica collection,[37] the papal decretals, councils, church fathers and historians, together with the *Breviarium* of the Visigothic king Alaric, the capitularies of Charlemagne and some of Justinian's works.

The Panormia

Of the three collections attributed to Ivo or his associates the *Panormia* (what Fournier-Lebras refer to as a "compendious encyclopedia of Canon Law at the end of the 11th century").[38] was far and away the most successful and the most widely distributed because it constituted a systematic summary that was convenient to consult in seeking the essential canonical texts. Gratian later drew extensively from this *Panormia.*

---

[34] For observations on this "cumulative characteristic" of the early Church orders (manuals,) see J. Court, "The Didache and St. Matthew's Gospel," *Scottish Journal of Theology*, 34 (1981) April, 109-120.
[35] S. Kuttner, "On Sources," 49.
[36] A number of the papal legates were lay cardinals, not bishops or priests.
[37] The Britannica collection is so named because it survives only in a British Library manuscript, B.L. Addit, MS 8873. It is an important eleventh century collection compiled around 1089 in Italy.
[38] Fournier and LeBras, 2, 99.

Evidence of the *Panormia's* contribution to the development of canonical science may be found especially in the carefully worded summaries that precede each text, enhancing the general usefulness of the work and accounting for its attested popularity. Ivo's work in the *Panormia* offers an excellent example of the state of art of the science of canon law at the close of the eleventh century.[39] His *Panormia* even provided the philosopher and theologian Abelard with some material for his famous *Sic et non* which in turn was to serve as an influence on the development of Gratian's method of interpretation.[40]

In the *Panormia's* summaries there is evident legal scholarship along with the care taken in distinguishing the exact nature of juridical rules (precepts, counsels, unchangeable and contingent laws), the space given to exemption and the rules provided for reconciling conflicting texts (inspired partly by the works of the eleventh century chronicler, Bernold of Constance.) All these fine details reveal the talented guiding hand of the great canonist Ivo himself.

The Prologue

Ivo's major contribution to the art of interpretation was his work known as the *Prologue.*[41] "(T)he greatest part of the *Prologue* consists, not of abstract rules of interpretation, but of examples Ivo drew from history in order to justify his doctrine of dispensation."[42]

Brasington painted a picture of the structure of the *Prologue* which is outlined below:

- *Caritas* is introduced as the unifying, guiding principle in law that mediates between rigor and mercy.

---

[39] James Biechler, "Ivo of Chartres, Collecton of," *Encyclopedic Dictionary of Religion* (Washington, DC: Corpus Publications, 1979) F-N, 1854-1855.
[40] *The Westminster Dictionary of Church History*, Jerald C. Brauer, ed., s.v. "Ivo of Chartres," 446.
[41] The Latin version may be found in *PL*, 161, 47-60 and another Latin version, together with a French translation, in Yves de Chartres, *Le Prologue, Texte Latin. Introduction, Traduction et Notes,* par Jean Werckmeister (Paris, Les Editions du Cerf, 1997). An English translation is available in Somerville and Brasington, 132-158 (there are additional references to Ivo in their index on p. 244) and in Brasington, *The Prologue*, 295-321.
[42] Barker, 349.

- Ivo selects the subject, 'vow', analyzing it through a series of increasingly precise legal categories in order to extend and define the conflicting demands between rigor and mercy.
- From these categories there emerges his analysis of 'dispensation', (the core of his study which he understands to be a healing remedy) shaped by dialectical technique that made the *Prologue* one of the building blocks of the scholastic method. Ivo presents a sequence of scriptural, patristic and historical texts on the nature and limits of dispensation which, implicitly guided by *caritas*, resolves the conflict between rigor and mercy.
- Ivo offers a summary section returning to *caritas.*[43]

In this work Ivo articulated the dialectical hermeneutic of the scholastic method.[44] Not all agree on where the *Prologue* was meant to be placed, at the head of the *Decretum* or the *Panormia.* In whatever place, this work is "a milestone in the search for rules to harmonize discordant authorities and guide the application of church law with justice and mercy."[45]

It is Ivo's most personal contribution. He explained in his opening paragraph:

> I have gathered into one body – and not without labor – so that anyone who might not be able to have at hand the works from which these have been drawn may simply take here what he judges advantageous for his case.[46]

Interpreting Conflicting Canonical Texts

He thus provided a method by which church officials could address conflicting texts, viz., ". . . (One) should diligently consider what pertains to rigor, to moderation, to judgment, or to mercy."[47] They are to be treated with *justitia* (justice) or *misericordia* (mercy.)[48]

---

[43] Brasington, *The Prologue,* 470. The author states that "Ivo's pastoral concern as a bishop shaped his vision of law and ecclesiology in the *Prologue*" 472.
[44] Sorensen, 3.
[45] Ryan, *22.*
[46] Somerville and Brasington, 133.
[47] Idem, 133. Barker comments on the originality of Ivo's thinking as seen in his toleration, restraint and moderation:

> Drawing from Scripture, Fathers, Saints, Apostles, Popes and the supreme example for

In 1091 a few years before Ivo, the German priest chronicler, Bernold of Constance (+1100) penned several criteria for reconciling conflicting texts, viz: authenticity of the text; identity of the author; difference between law, counsel and dispensation, between universal and local law, between time and place and the different meanings of a word.[49]

Bernold of Constance further provided similar rules regarding some controversial matters at issue during the investiture controversy. Bernold's work entitled *De Excommunicatis Vitandis* edited in *Monumenta Germaniae,*[50] contained doctrine on interpretation of contradictory canon law sources and to what extent one must avoid the society of excommunicated persons, which was a very important concern at that time.

We do not know if Ivo knew of Bernold's writings. Both appear around the same time. Bernold has a more general approach than Ivo but they have the same spirit and their rules are of the utmost value for theologians and canonists. They helped the process of reflection and reasoning about the sources.[51]

Another contemporary of Ivo, the theologian and canon lawyer Alger of Liege, applied Ivo's criteria to the problem of the effects of the sacraments administered by heretics and simoniacs.

Professor James Brundage of the University of Kansas notes that in Ivo's *Prologue* ". . . (H)e sketched out a much more sophisticated canonical methodology than appears in the work of any of his predecessors."[52] In it Ivo

---

> every Christian, Christ himself, the Good Shepherd, merciful and tolerant. On this example he constructed his own teaching of relaxation of the law when the need of the Church warranted it and it did not prejudice doctrine or morals. (83 & 84)

Barker, 85, continues, ". . . If we say that we see in Ivo's Christ the foundation of dispensation, we may be sure that we have penetrated to the heart of Ivo's beliefs."

For more on Ivo's thoughts on this matter as it related to lay investiture see his letter to Pope Paschal II, *PL,* 162, 256-257.

[48] Kuttner, 50.

[49] *Encyclopedia Brittanica,* vol. 3, 776.

[50] "De excommunicatis vitandis, de reconciliatione lapsorum et de fontibus iuris ecclesiastici," *MGH. Libelli de lite imperatorum et pontificum saeculis XI. et XII. conscripti.* Tomus II: 112-142. *Hannoveriae: Impensis bibliopoli Hahniani,* 1892.

[51] Kuttner, 50. See also Petrus Huizing, "Canon Law," *Encyclopedia Britannica, Micropaedia* 16, (Chicago: Encyclopedia Britannica Inc. 1985) 321.

[52] Brundage, 38.

reveals his ideas, tendencies and spirit of compromise. He offers a number of general principles relating to the sources of canon law, e.g., in first place, among those mentioned above, are the Gospel texts and then the papal decretals, conciliar canons, rules laid down by the orthodox fathers, legal edicts of Catholic princes and custom.

The multitude of decisions over a long period of time can confuse and even sometimes contradict one another by quoting diverse sources and unequal authorities. It is this problem Ivo addressed with a remarkable system of interpretation.[53]

Caritas*: The Golden Rule*

Caritas is the cornerstone of Ivo's vision of the canonist. The mistress of the house of God is charity "which sees to the welfare of our neighbors, commanding that it be done for others what one wishes to be done for himself." This familiar "Golden Rule" cited by Ivo is found also at the start of the ancient *Didache* as well as at the start of Gratian's twelfth century *Decretum*, which Gratian called the *Concordia Discordantium Canonum.*[54]

On the subject of interpretation, near the start of Ivo's *Prologue* one finds his familiar declaration to canonists:

Every ecclesiastical doctor should thus interpret or moderate ecclesiastical rules so that he may refer to the kingdom of charity those matters that he

---

[53] Walter Ullman, *The Growth of Papal Government in the Middle Ages* (London: Methuen & Co. Ltd. 1962) 371, notes that a letter from Pope Urban II to the bishop of Pistoia first pointed to the need to distinguish between immutable norms and those that are changeable. The letter concerned the validity of holy orders conferred by a heretic and reordination. Thus Pope Urban II provided the start of a hermeneutic principle that "contradictions are merely apparent, not real." Pope Urban's letter which became a crucial canonical text in Ivo's work is discussed in Fournier and Lebras, 110 and 358.
See also Stephen Kuttner, "Urban II and the Doctrine of Interpretation: a Turning Point?" in *The History of Ideas and Doctrines of Canon Law in the MIddle Ages,* vol. IV (London: Variorum Reprints, 1980) 57-58 in which Kuttner challenges Fournier-Lebras' reading of Pope Urban's letter; and Sorensen, 75-77.

[54] Somerville and Brasington, 134; James Kleist, *The Didache*, in Johannes Quasten and Joseph Plumpe, eds., *Ancient Christian Writers* 6 (Westminster, MD: The Newman Press, 1948) 3-25, 151-166; Gratian, *Decretum* from *Corpus Iuris Canonici*, 2 vols. Ed. Aemilius Friedberg (Leipzig: B. Tauchnitz, 1879; repr. Graz: Akademische Druck-U-Verlagsanstalt, 1959).

teaches; nor does he err or sin here, because, concerned for the welfare of his neighbors, he endeavors to achieve the required goal in the holy institutes.[55]

As mentioned above, Ivo drew liberally from what he lists as

> (T)he letters of the Roman pontiffs, partly from the deeds of the councils of Catholic bishops, partly from the treatises of the orthodox Fathers, partly from the institutes of Catholic kings[56]

A perfectionist when it came to methodology Ivo gathered into his work

> (W)hat pertains to the ecclesiastical sacraments, to the institution or correction of morals, to the investigation and resolution of every matter, so that it should not be necessary for the investigator to turn through the whole volume but simply to note the general title appropriate to his question, and then to run through the canons under it without pause.[57]

He distinguished between immutable and invariable precepts (such as the Ten Commandments) and those that are not (oaths are an example, not that they are always forbidden but abuses must be prevented);[58] also between sanctions of eternal law and those which are contingent. Then there are ecclesiastical precepts which do not present a character of absolute necessity, and disciplinary rules to assist the faithful in their salvation.

---

[55] Yves de Chartres, 4, 66. A related thought is found at the conclusion of the 1983 *Code of Canon Law:* ". . . (T)he salvation of souls, which must always be the supreme law in the Church, is to be kept before one's eyes." (canon 1752)

Barker notes that in the *Prologue* Ivo observes that some laws derive from judgment and others from mercy. They are united in God's nature and dealings with his people. It is from this basic distinction that other principles of interpretation arise as Ivo points out in this famous opening passage of his *Prologue*. 332. See also Kuttner, 50.

[56] Somerville and Brasington, 133. Brasington in his singular analysis of the *Prologue, 325,* attempts to trace the formal sources of Ivo's work, i.e. who was the channel conveying the material sources to Ivo? He explains that it is very difficult to determine where Ivo obtained his education and knowledge of the canons because during World War II, in June of 1944, the great municipal library of Chartres was destroyed, so we only have hints of what may have been available as sources to Ivo.

[57] Somerville and Brasington, 133.

[58] Yves de Chartres, 75, 9 to 83, 18 and Somerville and Brasington, 137-142. Ivo's method for reconciling conflicting canons is founded on this particular distinction.

Contradictions and Distinctions

Faced with contradictions the reader should give serious consideration to "what pertains to rigor, to moderation, to judgment, or to mercy."[59] Ivo attempted to establish a "hierarchy of jurisdictions within the church" for the reconciliation of discordant laws. Canons originating with higher authorities (popes and general councils) took precedence over canons adopted by lesser authorities (provincial councils and diocesan synods.)[60]

Pay attention, taught Ivo, to the distinctions between general canons applicable to all Christians and particular ones, limited to specific regions, situations or classes of persons. Distinguish between variable laws and invariable laws. The variable ones may be able to be dispensed by the appropriate authority.[61] Ivo believed that any confusion was only apparent when considering the force and limits of individual canons.

Rooting his various divisions of canon law in the Scriptures and drawing liberally from the New Testament revelation for examples, Ivo made distinctions among admonitions[62] which neither compel nor threaten but, as in his example of a voluntary vow, promise a reward to those who maintain it but a penalty to those who do not; and indulgences[63] as again with a voluntary vow, when observed, results in a remedy or a reward and when not observed merits instead eternal punishment; precepts, immutable when sanctioned by the eternal law and, when observed, one is worthy of salvation and mutable, because of changing needs and circumstances, when discovered by tradition as useful in guarding more securely the acquisition of salvation;[64] and prohibitions, immutable when they speak out against vice, mutable when sanctioned by tradition in order to protect salvation. In the latter category a dispensation by the

[59] Somerville and Brasington, 133.
[60] Brundage, 39.
[61] Ibid.
[62] These are counsels of Christian perfection, observes Sorensen, 88.
[63] A safety net for human weakness, Ibid.
[64] Ibid., 90.

authority of the one in charge takes precedence if an honest and useful compensation follows.

The Theory of Dispensations

Ivo wrote for ecclesiastical doctors[65] and was a practical realist. He was the first author to formulate a general theory of dispensation[66] which he saw as "the mitigation of the rigors of the law for the needs of the times and the utility of the Church."

He concluded his *Prologue* with a number of actual historical case studies related to the subject of dispensation in various situations where, e.g., contrary to canon 15 of the Council of Nicea,[67] bishops were translated (transferred) from one city to another because of necessity or utility of the times and other situations where many deposed bishops had been restored to their sees by the apostolic see.[68] Additional examples are offered of clerical marriages being tolerated. Both priests and their sons were able to enter Holy Orders (Ivo notes several who had served as popes) and, according to a text from Pope Gregory the Great, the lower clergy were allowed to marry. [69]

Stephan Kuttner observed that the *Prologue* of Ivo of Chartres

> ...was a milestone in the history of the art of interpretation, in that it transferred certain principles of biblical and rhetorical hermeneutics to the field of the sacred canons, enriching the traditional commonplaces with new ideas which were to prove of considerable consequence both in scholastic theology and the nascent canonical science of the twelfth century.[70]

---

[65] Ibid., 91.

[66] Dispensation was "a hermeneutical tool for resolving perceived conflicts," ibid. 93. Brasington in his dissertation, *The Prologue*, understands dispensation as the "legal, historical expression of *caritas*." 555.

[67] "Neither bishops nor presbyters nor deacons shall transfer from city to city." Tanner, 1, 13. It was the canons of the Council of Sardica (especially canon 3), held some seventeen years after Nicea, that represent the classical opposition to the translation of bishops. Hamilton Hess, *The Canons of the Council of Sardica* (Oxford: Clarendon Press, 1958) 71-82.

[68] Somerville and Brasington, 151.

[69] Ibid, 156.

[70] Stephen Kuttner, "Harmony from Dissonance. An Interpretation of Medieval Canon Law" in Stephen Kuttner, *The History of Ideas and Doctrines of Canon Law in the Middle Ages* (London: Variorum Reprints, 1980) 4. See also p.8 for more on Ivo. In the same book see "Pope Urban II and

In any study of the evolution of canonical jurisprudence, of paramount importance are the impact and influence of Ivo's *Prologue* which spanned the jurisprudence of the twelfth century like no other text. Evidence of its weight as a formal source can be found in the writings of Gratian and of the decretists.[71]

The Problem of Lay Investiture

From approximately the ninth century there had been a nettlesome problem that consumed much of the energy of both the papal and secular rulers. It was a practice that had become somewhat firmly established as an integral part of the feudal system, viz., the appointment of bishops and abbots by secular authorities or lay investiture.

The investiture conflict arose over the questions, 'Who has the authority to grant clerical office?' and 'Who has the right to invest a church official with the symbols of his spiritual office, church authorities or lay authorities?' The bishops found themselves caught in between 'God and mammon,' or at least between the popes and the princes. The latter were watching carefully over the bishops' shoulders because many of the bishops enjoyed special status in addition to favors and rights, courtesy of the secular rulers. These would be endangered if the bishops embraced too lovingly the papal favoritism shown to the new law prohibiting lay investiture.[72]

In the lifetime of Ivo of Chartres this practice produced one of the most explosive conflicts in medieval history when the eleventh century reform popes, taking advantage of a weak child, the German King Henry IV, stripped the lay

---

the Doctrine of Interpretation." 55-86. A further study of the scope of Ivo's influence on canon law may be found in Paul Fournier, "Un tournant de l'histoire du droit: 1060-1140," in *Nouvelle Revue Historique de droit Français et Etranger*, 41(1917) 129-180.

[71] Brasington, 914. Among the twelfth and thirteenth century decretists (those canonists who commented on Gratian's *Decretum)* were Paucapalea, Rolandus Bandinelli, (later Pope Alexander III) Rufinus, Stephan of Tournai, Sicardus of Cremona, Huguccio (Hugh of Pisa) and Joannes Tetonicus (John Zimeke).

[72] Kuttner, 48.

powers of ceremonially investing clerics with churches and attempted to eliminate all forms of lay control over church offices. When King Henry IV came of age, he was determined to regain what he believed was a king's right and his actions quickly produced bitter words and condemnations, stubborn and unbending hostilities, even military battles.[73] The conflict of empire versus papacy had serious effects on the history of Western Europe in the eleventh and twelfth centuries.[74] Its consequences were grave especially in the area of simoniacal trade and the resurgence of Nicolaitism or clerical immorality and concubinage.

Ivo seems to have been the first to ponder over the investiture question and arrive at some kind of solution. During the twelfth century various compromises were agreed upon in this matter of lay investiture in France, England and Germany. The secular powers were willing to renounce their role in bestowing the honor on new bishops but still they required from them an oath of fealty and homage after their election and institution. This was due less to any weakness on the part of the papacy than to the politically adept bishops not wanting to lose their positions in the eyes of the secular princes. It was into this situation that the bold and forthright Ivo of Chartres, "a man of practical solutions, of compromise"[75] offered his help as a mediator. It is thought by some that Ivo contributed the distinction between *regalia* and *spiritualia* that eventually led to the compromise at Worms in 1127.[76]

Joseph Ryan notes that

> Ivo based his stand on a more precise delineation of the bishop's dual role as spiritual ruler and temporal lord and denied any sacramental meaning to the feudal ceremony, however it was

---

[73] For a brief overview of some of the principal players during this most inflammatory period of history, viz., Henry IV, Pope Gregory VII and the Countess Matilda of Tuscany, see Richard Cunningham, "The Law and the Lady," *The Jurist* 53 (1993) 62-103.
[74] Robert Lerner, "Investiture Conflict," *Dictionary of the Middle Ages*. 6, 498-500.
[75] Kuttner, 48.
[76] The question of just how much influence Ivo actually had in this investitutre controversy is challenged by Norman Cantor, *Church, Kingship and Lay Investiture in England, 1089-1135,* Princeton Studies in History, n. 10 (Princeton: Princeton University Press, 1958) 202-216 and by Uta-Renate Blumenthal, *The Investiture Controversy,* 158, 163-164. See also Barker, 33-34.

> conducted. He held that it could be tolerated to preserve peace, provided that free canonical election and consecration were observed.[77]

Ivo helped to integrate the law of the past with the law of his own day by using his method of interpretation.

Cornelius Van de Weil has written:

> Ivo defended the superiority of the spiritual power, but held that the salvation of mankind could only be achieved, through good cooperation between Church and State *(le monde bien gouverne)* and in the unity of Church and State . . . (H)e did not hesitate to give the decrees of Christian princes the force of law on the condition that they were not in conflict with the doctrine of the Church . . . In (Ivo's) works . . . he emphasized . . . the necessity of cooperation and unity between Church and State, and the fervant bond between jurists and canonists.[78]

Ivo believed that simony is not heresy and that no one had ever regarded the royal investiture as a sacrament. He emphasized the reality of the distinction between the bishop's religious authority and powers and his temporal rights, duties and properties. In all that belonged to the feudal side of the bishopric, "(Ivo) firmly supported the legitimate rights of the monarchy despite a decade of strained church-state relations and stressed the necessity that both parties collaborate for social harmony."[79] Only then could Christian society flourish.[80]

The king had rights, but in what belonged to the spiritual the king could have no rights at all. It may have been Ivo's way of looking at the embittered problem which had produced the pact of 1106 that ended the conflict in England between Henry I and his archbishop, St. Anselm.[81]

Ivo recognized the primacy and absolute rights of the Roman See but was opposed to the full power of the papal legates. He made a compromise between the *sacerdotium* and the *imperium,* the first power in the world.[82] The bishopric

---

[77] Joseph Ryan, "Ivo," *Dictionary of the Middle Ages,* 21.
[78] Cornelius Van de Weil, *History of Canon Law* (Louvain: Peeters Press, 1991) 97.
[79] Joseph Ryan, 21.
[80] Lynn Barker, 33.
[81] Philip Hughes, *The Church in Crisis. A History of the General Councils. 325-1870* (Garden City, NY: Hanover House, 1961) 191-192.
[82] See footnote 12.

is given by the Church but the investiture of the *temporalia* is made by the king. It is characteristic that he quotes the 1102 letter of Paschal II, (1099-1118),[83] viz., if the abuse of investiture can be destroyed without a schism, let it be destroyed; otherwise it is best to protest discreetly.

Friedrich Kempf observes that

> [T]he handing over of the episcopal office, so (Ivo) explained, was certainly to be refused to the laity, since it implied a sacramental act; on the other hand, the *concessio* of the temporalities could be granted by the King without difficulty, for it was a purely secular act, to be performed in any desired manner, to which the King could make a certain claim, in so far as, according to Augustine, property is based on constitutional law and hence the churches owed their goods to distribution made by the King.[84]

Ivo, in a 1097 letter to Hugh of Lyons, the papal legate, expanded his idea. It may have influenced the settling of the problem in France and, thanks to Ivo's pupil, Hugh of Fleury, in England as well.[85] Ivo further argued in his letter to Hugh of Lyons that Pope Urban's decree at Clermont in 1095 was not intended to forbid lay rulers granting temporal possessions to a new bishop. He wrote:

> What does it matter how this grant is made - by hand, or nod, or word, or staff – provided that kings do not intend to give anything spiritual, but only to assent to the request of the petitioners or to concede to the bishops-elect the . . . external properties which they receive from the generosity of kings?[86]

---

[83] For the text, see Uta-Renate Blumenthal, *The Early Councils of Pope Paschal II, 1100-1110* (Toronto:Pontifical Institute of Medieval Studies, 1978) 17-20.

[84] Friedrich Kempf et al., "The Church in the Age of Feudalism," *Handbook of Church History*,. eds Hubert Jedin and John Dolan, vol. III (NY: Herder and Herder, 1969-1970) 394.

[85] This is a theory questioned by, among others, Norman Cantor, *Church, Kingship and Lay Investiture*, 202-217. See footnote 77.

[86] Ivo of Chartres, ep. 60 *PL* 162, 73 BC and *Epistola ad Hugonem Archiepiscopum Lugdunensem* (1097) ed. E. Sackur, *MGH Libelli de Lite* II, Hanover: 1892, 644-646. English translation by Brian Tierney, 82. New York University professor Norman Cantor in his work, *Medieval Lives* (NY: Harper Collins, 1994) 73-74, invents an imaginative conversation, based on original sources, between Cardinal Humbert Silva Candida, the chief political theorist of the medieval papacy and one of the principal players in the disastrous Eastern Schism of 1054, and the Abbot Hugh of Cluny, on the need for the papacy to be entirely free of lay interference. Humbert acknowledges his respect for Ivo of Chartres' scholarship but also proclaims his disappointment in learning that Ivo believed that the Church and society are now so conjoined that the Church cannot be withdrawn from the control of kings and the interests of the nobility.

This was Ivo's interpretation of the Clermont decree which became widely known and in which he made familiar the distinction between the bishopric itself and the *regalia* attached to it.[87] It would take more than a score of years however for the matter to come to an end in Germany thanks to the Concordat of Worms.

The Conciliator

As part of Ivo's policy of mediation and with a view to the reform of the Church, Ivo, the conciliator, favored a compromise. He brought about the acceptance of the distinction between spiritualities, the purely religious functions such as the election of bishops, which was to be free and clerical, and the temporalities, the purely secular functions, handing over property and the investiture of the new bishop by the king bestowing the scepter. This was to take place only afterward and to be of limited significance. Ivo certainly respected the papacy and struggled to protect the rights of the Church against kings, but at the same time his loyalty and devotion to the king is very evident in his writings.

His moderate approach appeared to bear fruit, possibly settling the disputes in England, where the king renounced investiture while still requiring homage from bishops before consecration and more probably in France where the king also renounced investiture but required an oath of allegiance.

The Concordat of Worms and the First Lateran Council

These distinctions, actually compromises, developed by Ivo and approved by the pope, found a place in the Concordat of Worms in 1122 bringing an end to the investiture struggle with a compromise that saved face for both the Church and the King, bringing almost a half century of peace between the papacy and the empire.[88]

Brandeis University Professor Geoffrey Barraclough observed that the 1123 Lateran Council ushered in the post-reform period. He noted it was the first

---

[87] Colin Morris, 156-157.
[88] Jean Leclercq, "Ivo of Chartres, St." in vol. 7 - *New Catholic Encyclopedia* , 1967 ed., 7, 777-778.

ecumenical council since the council of Constantinople in 869, the first to be held in the west under the aegis of the pope and the first to have its decrees promulgated by the pope in his own name.

He wrote:

> With the conclusion of the Concordat of Worms the papacy had emancipated itself from imperial control and asserted its position as an independent political power. The purpose of the (Lateran) council was to celebrate this triumph. It also registered the papacy's success in establishing universal dominion over the Catholic church. The independence of the great metropolitans was broken.[89]

Conclusion: Ivo the Interpreter

More than a century after the death of Ivo, Gratian, quoting St. Isidore of Seville, wrote "Law shall be clearly expressed lest by its obscurity it lead to misunderstanding."[90] This ideal of clarity is not always attainable by human beings, hence the need for those who are expert in the art of interpretation.[91]

According to Ladislas Örsy, interpretation is a "clarification of the meaning of the law by diverse means and by various persons."[92] He finds it wiser to follow the tradition of the Roman *jurisprudentes* who avoided a precise definition of a word so as not to wrap it in a straitjacket and hamper its development.

Lawrence Wrenn offers as a definition of interpretation: "a declaration or an explanation of the true sense already contained, at least obscurely, in a law."[93]

---

[89] Geoffrey Barraclough, *The Medieval Papacy* (NY: W.W.Norton, 1968) 101-102.

[90] C.2, D, 4. Even our 1983 code's canon 17 commands that canon laws must be understood "in accord with the proper meaning of the words considered in their text and context."

[91] See John Huels, "Book I: General Norms" in John Beal, James Coriden and Thomas Green, *New Commentary on the Code of Canon Law* (New York, NY/ Mahwah, NJ: Paulist Press, 2000) 73-80. See also Wojiech Kowal, "Some Remarks on Understanding the Concept of *Propria Verborum Significatio," Studia Canonica* 34/2 (2000) 489-504.

[92] Ladislas Örsy, "The Interpretation of Laws: New Variations on An Old Theme," in *The Art of Interpretation, Selected Studies on the Interpretation of Canon Law* (Washington, DC: Canon Law Society of America, 1982) 47.

[93] Lawrence Wrenn, *Authentic Interpretations on the 1983 Code* (Washington, DC: Canon Law Society of America, 1993) 1. This booklet, together with the one mentioned above, contain much useful information on the subject of interpretation.

Ivo was one of those persons who tried to find a solution to the problem arising from contradictory texts in the laws of the Roman reform and the traditional Germanic canon law. His method for understanding contradictory texts, resolving discrepancies and restoring some harmony among them was to utilize a method of interpretation.[94]

For Ivo the key to interpretation is to understand the nature of the law as it relates to justice and to mercy. The proof of this for Ivo lies in history and so he provides the reader with many examples from the Church's historical past.

An influential supporter of legal reforms, Ivo's importance as the most celebrated canonist of his day is evident in his works, which comprised the last significant canonical collection in the period that ended the Gregorian Reform. In turn, he was much influenced by the new systematic arrangement of law according to themes and subjects, characteristic of the more advanced legal thought of the late eleventh century. He was the greatest canonist before the time of Gratian whose twelfth century's authoritative work owed much to Ivo's writings.

Desiring a method of concordance in examining and interpreting the laws, Ivo and other canonists worked on a set of rules for textual criticism and in time utilized the dialectical method to solve the contradictions they found with distinctions and sub-distinctions.[95] He was one of the pioneers of the dialectical form of textual analysis.[96] The science of canon law was being born and would later begin to mature in the twelfth century under Gratian. Eventually, a universally accepted juridical order took precedence over particular customs and privileges.[97]

It was Ivo of Chartres who was the first who tried to find a solution for what to do when texts are contradictory. He had to find a method for conciliating

---

[94] Stephan Kuttner, 50.
[95] Friedrich Kempf *et al.*, III, 427.
[96] Somerville and Brasington, 117.
[97] Friedrich Kempf *et al.*, IV, 50.

them. For Ivo that method was interpretation.[98] For this contribution he may be looked to as the first master of interpretation.

[98] Stephen Kuttner, 50.

Nullity of Marriage by Error of Quality

Luigi de Luca

The problem of error in matrimonial consent has always interested canonical doctrine, and there have been numerous writings and decisions regarding this topic in an effort to define the limits of such error both in law and in fact.

"Nothing is as contrary to consent as error."[1]

Here I will not consider the historical evolution of the doctrine concerning error of fact in which I had the occasion of being interested already many years earlier in another article.[2] (I also want to make reference to a paper given at the 10th International Congress of Canon Law, organized by the *Consociatio Internationalis Studio Iuris Canonici Promovendo,* Pamplona, September 14-19, 1998). In this paper I intend to limit myself to expressing my opinion on the interpretation which, in my view, must be given to canon 1097, §2 in the 1983 *Code of Canon Law.* In regard to this canon, it is well known how doctrine and jurisprudence with a certain intensity have sought to define how and when an error about a personal quality of the other spouse can establish

[1] *Johannes Teutonicus, Gloss,* quod autem *(at the end) on Ca. XXIX, q.1; see also Gloss,* Consensus, *quodam.*

[2] *L. de Luca, "Considerazioni in tema di errore nella persona nel matrimonio civile e canonico," in* Rivista di Diritto Civile *(1940) 52ff., and in L. de Luca,* Scritti vari di diritto ecclesiastico e canonico, *vol. 1 (Padova, 1997) 1ff.*

a reason for the nullity of marriage and also wondering whether such nullity is of ecclesiastical law or actually of natural law.

In view of the text of canon 1083 of the *Code of Canon Law* of 1917, it is known that for years both doctrine and, above all, jurisprudence have remained faithful to the theory that only an error about the physical identity of the other spouse would have the ability to produce the nullity of marriage.[3] There has been, however, no lack of attempts in both doctrine and jurisprudence in support of the conclusion that an error about personal qualities of the other spouse should also be given relevance even when it is not a question of *determinative qualities of the person*, which is in substance an error about the physical identity of the other spouse.[4]

The best example I can recall is a rotal decision *c.* Wynen of 28 March 1939 which affirms: "It can happen that when someone enters marriage, the person so wants this or that quality that, if this quality is lacking, *it can be said*, that matrimonial consent is also lacking."[5] Thus, the way was opened for the well-known decision of Canals of 21 April 1970,[6] which states that, in order for juridical relevance for an error about the person to be recognized, one must consider this person in a "more complete and integral sense." In other words, while not foreseeing the 1983 code's explicit hypothesis about error of quality, the only possible method of giving relevance to such qualities in cases where they had exercised a decisive role in the determination of matrimonial consent, one had to abandon the reference to the person understood exclusively as physical identity and, instead, consider the person in a more integral manner, that is, to have a concept of the person as endowed with determined qualities. In this way, little by little, jurisprudence had practically arrived at maintaining that a marriage must be considered null in case of an error on the part of one

---

[3] Sanchez has expressed this idea in *De S. Matrimonii Sacramento Disputationes* (Lyon, 1625) lib. VII, XVII, n. 27, and this has, as is known, exercised a decisive influence on subsequent doctrine.
[4] L. de Luca, s.v., "Marriage," "Canonical Marriage" in *Enciclopedia Giuridica*, vol. XIX (Rome, 1988) 12 of the abstract.
[5] *C.* Wynen, 28 March 1939: *RRDec* 31: 179.
[6] *C.* Canals, 21 April 1970: *RRDec* 62: 370 ff.

contractant about the other contractant's personal qualities which were held to be essential.[7]

However, such a prevailing orientation of jurisprudence was kept in check by an equally well-known sentence *c.* Pompedda in a case from Calcutta of 6 February 1992[8] (which was not published until 1994). This was a sentence which drove home the point that §1 of canon 1097 refers solely to the physical identity of a person. Nevertheless, as is known, the legislator of the 1983 code explicitly recognized that cases can exist in which the nullity of a marriage can be declared if one of the two spouses had fallen into an error about "a quality of the person," but with the qualification that this can occur only if such a quality is "directly and principally intended."

Therefore, in doctrine and jurisprudence, there has been an effort to define what must be understood by "a quality directly and principally intended." Some have held that there should be recourse to this hypothesis when a contractant intends one or more qualities of the person s/he wants to marry more than the physical person.

The more rigorous opinion is the one which was clearly formulated by Orio Giacchi, a professor of Canon Law at the Catholic University of Milan. Already before the definitive redaction of the present code when reference was still being made to the hypothesis of the *error redundans* of St. Alphonsus of Liguori, who had taught that such an error in its third meaning must be maintained as operative when "consent is given directly and principally to a quality, and less principally to a person." He goes on to write: "in the case of *error redundans,* the contractant wants to marry, as it were, *the quality* considered or, to say it better, *an abstract type of person* who is constructed from the concept of that quality."[9] One cannot deny that such an hypothesis is

---

[7] L. de Luca, "Matrimonio canonico," cf. p. 13, footnote 4.

[8] *In Diritto Ecclesiastico*, (1995):2, 223ff.

[9] O. Giacchi, *Il consenso nel matrimonio canonico* (Milan, 1968) 71 ff. It is very probable that, on the basis of Giacchi's authority in matrimonial matters, the *Plenaria* of the Code Commission welcomed the formulation proposed by the *coetus consultorum* and definitively included it in the text of §2 of c. 1097 (cf. *Communicationes,* vol. XV, N. 2, [1983]: 232).

possible, but it seems truly to be outside of the concept of marriage intended as an union of two persons *in their totality*, in order to give life, as has been effectively stated, to a communion of destinies (*Schicksalsgemeinschaft*).[10]

There is an expression found in the Allocution to the Roman Rota of 30 January 1993 by Pope John Paul II which is applicable to canon 1097, §2, namely, "when the quality is intended before the person." This remark cannot be understood in the sense that this canon is applicable only if a contractant intends to marry an abstract will *prescinding from the person of the spouse,* but can mean only that without the existence of such a quality, considered as *essential* by the contractant, the marriage does not exist, as will shortly be better shown.

The expression contained in canon 1097, §2 of the *Code of Canon Law* in which an error about a quality of a person is irrelevant even if it "was the cause for the contract" was already contained in canon 1084 of the old code, which endorsed the irrelevance of a simple error regarding the unity or indissolubility of marriage even if it "was the cause for the contract." The Legislator decided to modify this expression by specifying in the present canon 1099 that such an error of law (in addition to that of the sacramental nature of marriage) can invalidate matrimonial consent if this error *determined the will.* This modification of the formula actually has no important significance and, therefore, both the formula contained in canon 1099 and the one contained in canon 1097, §2 must be seen as equivalent in their substance. In fact, even in the latter case, it is established that error about qualities of a person has relevance for validity only if the quality in question was directly and principally intended.

This then means that in the hypothesis envisaged in canon 1097, §2 as well as in that envisaged in canon 1099, one cannot consider as invalidating an "error which is the cause for the contract" if it is actually only a question of an

---

[10] Cf. in particular, K. Lüdicke, "Matrimonial Consent in Light of a Personalist Concept of Marriage: On the Council's New Way of Thinking about Marriage," *Studia Canonica* 33 (1999:2) 473ff., and especially 489 where he approves the expression *Schicksalsgemeinschaft* used by Norbert Ludeck in his book *Eheschließung als Bund. Genese und Exegese der Ehelehre der Konzilskonstitution 'Gaudium et spes' in kanonistischer Auswertung* (Würzburg: Echter, 1989): 960. This expression is substantially equivalent to "*comunanza di sortes*," used by Giacchi in his book (cf. footnote 9) 353f.

"interpretative will," that is, of a will which, for example, in the words of Ferraris is "[a will] which the person never had; yet [the error] is so ready in the mind, that s/he would have had [the will] *if s/he had thought of it*."[11] In other words, there would be irrelevance of error only when the contractant, in the process of forming his/her will, had not fixed his/her consent on these circumstances which s/he would have otherwise considered essential if the problem had presented itself. Therefore, one can speak of "interpretative will" only when such a will "does not have any influence upon the operation" [of the will].[12]

On the other hand, one must come to the opposite conclusion if the contractant, in the process of forming the matrimonial will (on the basis of the assessment done by the judge by considering all the objective and subjective circumstances), has been shown to have regarded the circumstances envisaged in canon 1097 (error of fact) or in canon 1099 (error of law), as essential circumstances, as elements, that is, of the object of his/her matrimonial consent.[13]

In my opinion, it is only by keeping in mind the principles of modern juridic science that one can identify the true idea of the affirmations by which

---

[11] Ferraris, *Prompta bibliotheca canonica, iuridica, moralis, theologica* (Montecassino, 1848) vol. IV, 440.

[12] This expression is also used by Prümmer, *Manuale Theologiae moralis* (Freiburg i/Br., 1933) vol. III, 51.

[13] It seems that P. Moneta ("Un intervento risolutivo della Rota Romana in tema di errore sulla persona?" in *Il Diritto Ecclesiastico* 106:2 [1995]: 242ff.) would fully agree with what has been explained in the text above when he writes that the figure of an error of quality which invalidates a marriage cannot ... be applied in those cases ... where the contractant simply intends ... to unite him/herself with the person whom s/he loves accepting this person in his/her entirety just as s/he believes to know him/her, without seeing any problem regarding possible specific requirements that s/he should possess."

The thesis explained in this article is also confirmed in doctrine. For example, Juan Ignacio Bañares ["Error 'causam dans' y error en cualidad directa y principalmente pretendida" in *Ius Canonicum* 35, num. 69 (1995): 110f.] affirms that the nullity of marriage through an error about personal qualities of the other spouse is due "to the non-existence of the object of consent because the quality which the subject included as a part of it [the consent] did not exist. I think also that, for this reason, such nullity is rooted in 'natural law' itself, and not in an intervention of the legislator."

Recently, A. Mendonça in "Error of Fact: Doctrine and Jurisprudence on Canon 1097" in *Studia Canonica* (2000): 23-74, after having throughly analyzed doctrine and rotal jurisprudence since 1984, also comes to the same conclusions referring to the general principle dictated by c. 126 CIC (See 73f.).

the one who marries, taking for granted that the spouse possesses certain qualities or that the marriage would not have the character of unity or indissolubility or would not have a sacramental nature, converts it into a simple virtual intention which is irrelevant.

The expression used by the canonical legislator in canon 1097, §2, by which relevance is given to an error about personal qualities only when they were intended directly and principally, in my opinion does not mean anything different than what the same legislator affirms in canon 1099, namely, that the errors envisaged there produce the nullity of the marriage, if those qualities have *determined* the will of the one marrying. Only in this sense can we hold as correct what some authors affirm, namely, that an error about personal qualities of the other spouse becomes invalidating when it concerns qualities which may be posited by the contractant as "*at the foundation of his/her consent.*"[14]

Actually the problem regarding error, just as regarding simulation or condition (and also, as Pompedda holds also regarding the existence of *fear*),[15] is a problem which reduces itself to the general problem of the relationship between intellect and will.[16] In fact, in order that what is known to have juridical relevance in all cases it must "unite in operation the will," or, as I have already said in another article, "that [what is known] becomes an essential element of the consent and, thus, of the contract, or, as we read in a rotal sentences, 'if it truly enters into the consent' and not only 'accompanies' it."[17]

In the same article I emphasized the significant contribution which Msgr. Pompedda, in his role as dean of the Rota, made by addressing with courage the question of the "relationship between intellect and will" and by affirming that "for this purpose it is now time to heal the rupture which occurred ... between the two faculties; though they are distinct in form and reality, they

---

[14] Cf. Vitali – Berlingò, *Il matrimonio canonico* (Milan, 1994): 96.
[15] M. F. Pompedda, "Prolusione letta allo 'Studio Rotale' il 10 novembre 1998 in occasione della Inaugurazione dell'anno Accademico 1998-1999," 20, also in *Ius Ecclesiae*, 11:3 (1995): 679.
[16] Pompedda, "Prolusione," note 15. In this matter I also refer to my article cited below.
[17] Luigi de Luca, "Giurisprudenza della Rota Romana: Sguardo verso il futuro" in *Il Diritto Ecclesiastico* 110:1 (1999:1) 12.

are nonetheless operationally unified in every rational human deliberation." And he affirmed: "yes, it is high time to redirect and therefore to show forth the human person in its unity in a synthesis of the two rational faculties ... and so an act of choosing – precisely as a human act – must be attributed to the entire person, that is, to that spiritual entity in which, as a summit, the operations of the intellect and the will take the first place and in which, therefore, the unification of the different human faculties is realized."[18]

In the final analysis, by keeping in mind this "unification of the diverse faculties of the human person," one resolves the concept of "the positive act of the will." This expression, therefore, means nothing other than the existence of a clause which is essential for a transaction. In its substance, canon 1097, §2 must be interpreted in the sense that a marriage is null for a person who, in the process of forming his/her matrimonial will, kept directly in mind a determined quality of his/her future spouse and for this quality (or *even* essentially for it) s/he decided to marry even though there was no explicit condition. Lawrence G. Wrenn, to whom this article is dedicated with the expression of my longtime and deep affection, has specified precisely this, namely, that one should not say that the person "explicitly" kept a quality in mind.[19]

Msgr. Pompedda has affirmed exactly the same thing in his well-known sentence in a case from Calcutta of 6 February 1992, namely, that canon 1097 must be understood in the sense that "the quality itself can have an impact on the

---

[18] In the article cited in footnote 41 pointed out that Msgr. Pompedda expressed this idea already many years ago. In fact, I remember that in a case from Catania of 1 July 1969 (in *RRDec* 61: 691, n.3) he already wrote: "It is to be recalled that the superior faculties of the human person cannot be so separated between themselves that they alternately evade or find each other. Just as there is nothing in the intellect which was not first in the senses, so a fortiori, nothing is willed which was not first known and a person's will always desires the objects as they are offered and presented by the intellect."

[19] Wrenn, in fact, counts among the "intentions that are not required ... an explicit intention – which expresses a condition in clear and definite terms. e.g., 'I intend the validity of this marriage to hinge on the condition that John is a practicing Catholic'," L. Wrenn, *Annulments*, 6th edition (Washington, DC: Canon Law Society of America, 1996): 101.

consent invalidating it through an error insofar as [this error] *through an intention* constitutes the object of the contractant's will."[20]

The most recent canonical legislator in formulating canon 1097, §2 intended to reassess the personalist significance of marriage,[21] and above all, the freedom of the contractants in that act which has such decisive value for their entire lives, that is, marriage. This is also confirmed by another consideration, namely, that the canonical legislator has not followed the accepted system: according to art. 122 of the Italian Civil Code the judge must ascertain that the spouse would not have given consent if "s/he would have known exactly" the conditions of the other spouse, *while still providing taxative list of indications* about cases in which error can be relevant. Moreover, this article sets a time limit within which a petition to impugn the marriage can be made.

According to this above-mentioned consideration I believe that the expression contained in canon 1098 regarding a *fraudulent error* through which the error about personal qualities is caused by deceit is relevant if it is a question of a *quality* " which by its very nature can gravely disturb the partnership of conjugal life,"[22] understood not in a rigidly objective sense but in the sense that the quality is evaluated as suitable to cause the wreckage or a "grave disturbance" of the conjugal life, keeping in mind the mentality, the formation, and the milieu to which the *deceived* person belongs as well as his/her deepest concept of marriage.

And indeed, even in a case of fraudulent error, the effect which fraud produces in the mind of the contractant is nonetheless an *error*. In my opinion,

---

[20] In *Il Diritto Ecclesiastico*, vol. 106:2 (1995): 225.
[21] See the recent article by K. Lüdicke, cited in footnote 10 above, especially on p. 496 where he writes: "The fundamental contractual principle that a declaration of the will has been made to the wrong person is not valid, has been intensified through the personal relation of matrimonial consent." Therefore he rightly affirms: "Whenever someone forms his or her will to marry in such a way that the quality of a person is directe et principaliter intended, it in no way involved the acceptance of the gift of the other and the self-giving intended by c. 1057, §2. Moreover, the consent to the individual person of the partner is required to relate to, and affirm, the real being of the other in all its dimensions, and not simply a quality of that person. More directly, one cannot marry a quality."
[22] de Luca, "Giurisprudenza della Rota Romana: Sguardo verso il futuro," 20.

what the canonical legislator wants to guarantee is not so much the fact that the contractant not have been deceived, but rather the effective will of the contractant him/herself. In fact, I am convinced that the circumstance that made it necessary to have recourse to deceit in order to obtain the matrimonial consent of the contractant is only an element confirming the so-called "great price" which the quality had for the contractant so that the one involved in deceit realized that without deceit the marriage would not have been celebrated.

Therefore, I believe that even in the hypothesis envisaged in canon 1097, §2 the quality which is the object of the error must be of such gravity for the one in error that it would bring serious harm to the conjugal life.

(Translation by Marianne Burkhard, OSB)

PROBING THE BOUNDARIES BETWEEN INCAPACITY FOR CONSENT AND OTHER DEFECTS OF CONSENT

FREDERICK C. EASTON

Introduction

Those who labor in tribunal ministry know well the value of research and study in enabling them to better address the task of adjudicating a marriage case which has the overarching goal of determining how to reconcile a person's status with our Catholic understanding of marriage. This task has been underway in the Church since St. Paul faced the situation of the recent converts to Christianity in Corinth and St. Matthew faced a similar situation in Antioch.

Throughout the centuries many others have addressed these difficult questions. The one who is honored in the publication of this volume has made his own contribution. His writings have assisted so many in the ministry of the tribunal. Therefore, in honor of Lawrence Wrenn this author wants to offer his own ruminations.[1]

Evolving Jurisprudence

In their study, deliberation and discussion of individual causes of nullity of marriage which come to their attention, tribunal judges are charged not only with determining if the marriage is null and void but are required also to explain the cause of nullity according to the law and jurisprudence of the

[1] This article is an edited version of an address given by this author at Saint Paul University, Ottawa,

Catholic Church. The jurisprudence as well as the law of the Church has changed and developed over the centuries. In the memory of many ecclesiastical judges of today are their struggles to find a way to explain their conviction that certain marriages were invalid, when the so-called traditional grounds, especially that of either partial or total simulation, did not seem to be adequate. Nonetheless, they continued to try to explain why they felt a marriage was invalid on the basis of the grounds of grave force and fear and exclusion of one of the traditional three *bona – bonum sacramenti, bonum fidei* and *bonum prolis*.

At the same time the judges of the Roman Rota were addressing this same situation as well. They began to acknowledge there were situations wherein persons were evidently not capable of marriage even though one could not say they were insane in the common understanding of the word. Without claiming that I have researched all of the sentences of the Rota from 1950 until 1983, I think it is safe to say that out of many years of working with these cases there came to be some constancy in the rotal jurisprudence on this point. Out of this wealth of growing jurisprudence, the framers of the 1983 *Code of Canon Law* formulated the now famous canon 1095. This process developed for the tribunal practitioners another "arrow" in their "canonical quiver."

As we all know, since the advent of the use of these "psychological grounds" of canon 1095, the Supreme Tribunal of the Apostolic Signatura began pointing out that many if not most, tribunals especially in this part of the world were using this new "arrow" almost exclusively. The published observations of the Signatura as well as anecdotal evidence would seem to suggest that if tribunals felt there was a good case for nullity, the reason for that nullity must be because one of the parties was not capable of marriage. In a sense, we moved from a time during which we tried to "force-fit" certain case facts into the categories of simulation and force and fear to a situation in which we *may* now be "force-fitting" case facts into the category of incapacity for consent.

Canada in February 1999 when he was President of the Canon Law Society of America.

When this author first examined the *Rotal Anthology* done so well by Augustine Mendonça[2], something surprising caught his attention. It seemed from looking at the data compiled in the *Rotal Anthology* that while many tribunals were going on their "merry way" judging cases on the grounds of incapacity for consent, the Roman Rota was developing a deeper understanding of the so-called traditional grounds. This conclusion is to be found as well in an article by John Beal in *The Jurist.*[3] We might say, regarding the present time, that we are using the so-called traditional grounds again, for the first time. The "cutting edge" of jurisprudence in this part of the world, at least, has for some time been moving into taking a fresh look at these long-established grounds.

With this approach, there is some observable connection between these grounds and the grounds of incapacity for consent. It is further noted that whether a marriage is invalid from either perspective, what is always missing is the commitment to the essential marital rights and obligations. This leads me to what may be for many tribunal practitioners a burning question: *How does one decide whether the presented facts and proofs establish incapacity for consent as opposed to another more traditional defect of consent?*

Therefore, what is the boundary between incapacity and other defects of consent? Or, perhaps, the question might be posed: *Is there a true boundary?* At the very least we must ask the question of what are the criteria for a more accurate analysis of the evidence and of its import.

Let us consider the case in which Mary, a Catholic, married Andrew, a well-established Catholic doctor, on August 13, 1958 in a Catholic church. However, she had for some time associated with Benjamin, a non-Catholic medical student at the same school which she herself was attending. She had also known Andrew for some time, and she found him likeable. Her mother was very much interested in her daughter not continuing her relationship with

---

[2] Augustine Mendonça, *Rotal Anthology: An Annotated Index of Rotal Decisions from 1971 to 1988.* (Washington, DC: Canon Law Society of America, 1992).

[3] John Beal, "The Substance of Things Hoped For: Proving Simulation of Matrimonial Consent," *The Jurist* 55 (1995): 749-775

Benjamin, because he was not a Catholic and not yet well established as a doctor. Eventually, upon receiving some advice from a priest, she accepted Andrew's offer of engagement. Four months later they married. Their union was extremely short-lived: only two weeks. Andrew submitted a libellus to his diocesan tribunal on November 5, 1958 because he believed Mary had either intended no marriage at all, or she excluded a permanent commitment. An affirmative sentence was finally reached on December 14, 1961 in which the judges resolved the question as follows: "either the respondent intended no marriage at all or at best she intended to enter a union which she could dissolve at will."

The principal facts upon which the judges based their conviction were these: "the abandonment of the plaintiff by the respondent, occurring only ten days after the wedding, seems to indicate that she had no intention to enter the marriage; ...her trip to New York (to resume first-hand association with Benjamin) just a week after the marriage is indicative of that same intention...her filing for a divorce just a month after her wedding to Andrew and her civil marriage (to Benjamin) just six months after her first wedding give the same indication; [one witness] tells us that Mary on the day before the wedding after the wedding practice said she still loved Benjamin; ...her refusal of intercourse after the first night; [two other witnesses] testify that the respondent associated with Benjamin during the time of her engagement to Andrew."

The tribunal of second instance reversed the first instance sentence. The principal arguments behind the reversal were these: Although many of the circumstances mentioned in the first instance sentence supportive of nullity were accepted as proven by the second instance judges, they saw that the woman respondent was denying any simulation of consent in the statements she made prior to publication of the process. She had stated: "You would not go through a marriage ceremony unless you had the intention of getting married." "There was a great deal of doubt but I decided that I could go ahead and marry." The second instance judges rejected as worthless the following statements made *in tempore suspecto* by the respondent after publication of the process in which she stated: "Circumstances were such that I went through the ceremony, but I did not want to marry Andy either before, during or after the wedding." Although these appellate judges acknowledged the pressures suffered by the respondent in making a decision to marry, they concluded that the nullity had not been proven.

At the level of third instance at the Apostolic Tribunal of the Roman Rota, the advocates for the petitioner asked for the addition of the grounds of fear as if in first instance. The Dean of the Rota granted this, and the issue was eventually joined. Later, as the judges convened, they deferred their decision in order to investigate a psychological condition of the respondent which had been mentioned in the testimony. They asked one of the judges of the *turnus* who was more conversant with English to select an American psychological expert who would be better able to understand the situation. A well-known psychiatrist in the United States at the time was selected and submitted his *votum*.

Msgr. Arthur De Jorio,[4] as *ponens*, stated the rotal auditors *de turno* did not see the fear or pressure present in the respondent at the time of the marriage as coming from outside her and, hence, the existent fear did not qualify under the terms of the canon. They likewise did not see the grounds of exclusion of indissolubility as proven because the best indications of the respondent's unwillingness to enter the marriage came from her statements expressed only *after the marriage was breaking up*. Further, the respondent had an interest in a declaration of invalidity. Finally, there were the statements, which she made at the beginning of the process in first instance, which seemed contradictory to her later statements in the process in first instance.

The rotal judges noted the above referenced psychological expert had stated in his *votum* that at the time of the marriage the respondent was suffering from an inner conflict which would have significantly disturbed even a normal young woman. Intellectually, it made sense for her to marry someone of her own religion who possessed the same socio-economic position as the petitioner.

However, at the emotional level she was still feeling love for Benjamin and wanted to marry him. In her own testimony she stated that she did not want to embarrass her parents by canceling the wedding, but after the wedding plans were set she did not want to marry Andrew. She did not want to abandon the Catholic Church by marrying Benjamin which she must have felt would necessarily happen if she were to marry him. The judges saw the situation of the respondent as one in which she was laboring under a condition which did not allow for "that greater liberty and deliberation which is required in entering marriage than in entering other contracts."[5] They saw the respondent in a state of both "not wanting the marriage and wanting it … which rendered her absolutely incapable of making valid consent to the very matter about which she was disturbed."[6] Thus, the *turnus* of judges declared the nullity of the marriage was proven on the grounds of incapacity of the respondent of issuing valid consent, which is both conscious and free.

The Rota upon further investigation saw rather as a lack of the *capacity* for a valid decision to embrace marriage what the first instance tribunal saw as exclusion of indissolubility. In a small work of the selected sentences of Msgr. De Jorio published after his death, this particular rotal sentence was listed under the grounds of grave lack of discretion of judgment.[7]

The rotal defender of the bond appealed this sentence not *ex conscientia sua* but *pro forma* because he judged the sentences to be non-conforming. Of importance is the argument of this Defender. He saw the affirmative first instance sentence on the grounds the respondent had excluded indissolubility as affirming her capacity for consent. He argued further that the Rota's affirmation that she was incapable of consent at the time established not only a juridic contradiction but also an ontological contradiction because the two

---

[4] *Coram* De Jorio, July 19, 1977: *RRDec* 59, 598-612.
[5] *C.* De Jorio, 611.
[6] *C.* De Jorio, 612.
[7] "La Giurisprudenza sull'Incapacità Psichica," in *Coram De Jorio, Decano: Sententiae Selectae*, (Roma: Monitor Ecclesiasticus Supplementum, 1985): 123-127.

sentences were in disagreement precisely about the very relevant juridic fact in the case and so could in no way be considered conforming sentences.[8]

However, the second rotal *turnus* disagreed with the defender. The *ponens* at this level, Msgr. Charles Lefebvre,[9] stated for this *turnus* that the Defender's difficulty was that he saw the first instance sentence and the rotal sentence as too distinct from one another to be concordant. He said the judges of this second rotal *turnus* looked at the following statements of the first instance sentence: "Mary had not intended a marriage" and "the respondent had no marriage in mind or had in mind only entering a union which was dissoluble at will," and then the statement of the earlier rotal sentence which had stated that the marriage nullity had been proven in this case "on account of a defect of consent in the respondent." Seeing these statements together, the second rotal *turnus* concluded that it was evident that there was "no real independence" (as they worded it) of the factual bases of the two sentences and as a consequence between the first instance sentence and the sentence *coram* De Jorio were concordant.

A Case from Bologna Heard Three Times at the Roman Rota

Dr. Lynda Robitaille has traced a case of nullity of marriage judged in the negative in first instance in Bologna through three subsequent instances at the Roman Rota.[10] The marriage in question was between a nineteen year-old young man named George and a seventeen year-old girl named Sandra. George had left the practice of the Catholic faith when he was twelve and grew into a "hippie" lifestyle and professed a disbelief in the institution of marriage. He nonetheless wanted to avail himself of some of the aspects of married life by having sexual relations with Sandra who subsequently became pregnant. He did

---

[8] From the acts of the case published to the diocesan tribunal of first instance.
[9] Ibid.
[10] Lynda Robitaille, "Simulation, Error Determining the Will or Lack of Due Discretion? A Case Study," *Studia Canonica* 29 (1995): 397-432.

not want to marry her but eventually did so in the Catholic Church at the instance of Sandra's parents when the girl was already eight months pregnant. George did not stay long in the common life; he left after five months.

In the regional tribunal in Bologna, a negative sentence was issued on the grounds of exclusion of indissolubility. After an appeal to the Rota in second instance, the grounds of total simulation were entered as if in first instance and an affirmative sentence was issued. Writing for this rotal *turnus*, Msgr. Stankiewicz clarified that George's adherence to the "hippie" lifestyle amounted not only to a deeply-rooted error regarding the whole institution of marriage but an implicit intention to totally reject marriage in this case.[11]

The cause was automatically appealed to another *turnus* at the Rota. At this level there was introduced another ground as if in first instance, namely, grave lack of discretion of judgment on the part of the respondent. In the affirmative sentence Msgr. Davino[12] argued that the deeply-rooted error considered proven in the previous sentence could not only be a foundation for establishing implied simulation but also can be a cause of grave lack of discretion of judgment which he believed was the truth about this case. It is important to observe that Msgr. Davino noted that since there was no mental illness as such, that an expert would not be needed especially since such would unduly prolong the case.

There was, of course, a *pro forma* appeal by the defender of the bond since he saw the grounds as obviously not concordant. However, writing the decree for the third rotal *turnus* Msgr. Serrano declared the two prior rotal sentences to be equivalent in substance and declared the affirmative sentence to be executive.[13]

What we have seen in this brief narrative of two cases is strong evidence for the difficulty to distinguish at the practical level the grounds of

---

[11] *Coram* Stankiewicz, July 23, 1982: *RRDec.* 84, 421-432.
[12] *Coram* Davino, March 10, 1985: *RRDec.* 87, 180-188.
[13] *Coram* Serrano, October 24, 1986: *RR Decreta* 4 (1986) 143-156; also found in *Monitor Ecclesiasticus* 114 (1989): 283-297.

incapacity for consent from other grounds such as deeply rooted error and especially the forms of simulation. I believe it very significant in the context of this discussion that Msgr. Davino determined that it is not necessary to use an expert as proof for grave lack of discretion of judgment when there is no question of an illness of any kind. Canon 1608 states the age-old principle that a judge is not to pronounce in favor of invalidity unless there is moral certitude the marriage in question is invalid. However, canon 1680 further directs that the judge is not to pronounce a marriage invalid by reason of incapacity for consent without the assistance of an expert appropriate to the case at hand "unless it is obvious from the circumstances that it would be useless." But when would it be obviously useless?

Apostolic Signatura and the Use of Experts

This very question of when experts are require and when they are not was addressed to the Apostolic Signatura on 13 August 1997 and a reply was given on 16 June 1998.[14] The Signatura declared that the services of experts in these cases are required not only by law but because these reports are "an instrument of proof" and hence, one source from which the judge derives moral certainty. Such expert reports (*vota*) or expert advice based upon psychological interviews and testing (*peritia*) may be evidently useless when "in the acts there exists a document or testimonial, which is so qualified, that it provides sufficient relevant proof to the judge" or "when from the proven facts and circumstances, without any doubt, there appears either a lack of sufficient use of reason or a serious lack of discretion of judgement or an incapacity to assume the essential obligations of marriage." The following continuation of the Signatura's declaration seems to capture the crux of the matter: "The reason is that in this case the nullity of the marriage can be declared on account of an evident lack of

---

[14] Supreme Tribunal of the Apostolic Signatura, Prot. N. 28252/97 VT in *Forum* 9 (1998): 35-38. See also Augustine Mendonça, "The Apostolic Signatura's Recent Declaration on the Necessity of Using Experts in Marriage Nullity Cases," *Studia Canonica* 34 (2000): 33-58.

consent, without the need of a carefully drawn up diagnosis of the psychic cause due to which there exists that defect."

The Signatura's declaration is at pains to point out the exceptional character of the two situations it gives as occasions when the expert's report may be omitted. Yet, the exception provided in canon 1680 coupled with the Signatura's explanation on how it views the canonical exception sheds light on the identification of the juridical facts relevant to the various types of defect of consent. It suggests that the judge can legitimately infer the existence of psychic incapacity when the evidence for lack of consent is so flagrant. In other words, the tribunal can posit the existence of the cause when the effect is so evident.

The Bologna Case in Light of the Apostolic Signatura's Declaration

In the first instance case the judges of first instance were convinced that "the respondent had no marriage in mind or had in mind only entering a union which was dissoluble at will." The Rota in third instance was convinced even before they used their expert that there was some "defect of consent in the respondent." In the Bologna case the judges who voted in favor of grave lack of discretion of judgment did so without having an expert because, as Dr. Robitaille noted, "Since in this case there is no question of illness of any kind, it seemed to the judges that in order to avoid delays, it was better simply to come to a decision. Thus, the judges found the marriage was null because of a defect of discretion in the petitioner at the time of the marriage."[15]

In thinking about these two cases as well as others which have been addressed in the various canonical journals over the years, a conclusion arises that the boundary between incapacity for consent and the other defects of consent is murky at best. There is, of course, no lack of clear definition in the theoretical order, but there is "murkiness" when one tries to argue and adjudicate cases in the jurisprudential arena. Rotal judges seem to disagree on what should be considered sufficient evidence for incapacity, albeit transitory,

---

[15] Robitaille, 'Simulation," p. 427.

versus sufficient evidence to prove substantial error or simulation, whether partial or total.

A Look at the Role of the Diagnostic and Statistical Manual of Mental Disorders

The Roman tribunals continue to emphasize that proving someone incapable of matrimonial consent is more difficult than the experience of many tribunals in the United States and Canada would lead one to think. The allocutions of Pope John Paul II to the Roman Rota have addressed the problem of judges too facilely concluding to a true incapacity for consent based upon a proven psychic limitation which may even be classified in *the Diagnostic and Statistical Manual of Mental Disorders.*[16] In other words, simply establishing without any significant clinical doubt that a person was suffering from a certain mental disorder does not solve the problem of establishing that the cause or even the existence of a defect of consent is attributable to incapacity. The allocutions of the pontiff caution judges not to argue from the existence of difficulty to the existence of an incapacity for an activity which is natural to the human being. Perhaps, we should give some consideration to the limits of psychology in our deliberations.

In his presentations at the Third Gregorian Colloquium held in 1986 at what was then St. John's Provincial Seminary in Plymouth Michigan, Father Giuseppe Versaldi, professor of psychology and of canon law at the Gregorian University, observed that modern psychology has benefited the world by pointing out the impact of "the unconscious" upon the human individual. He cautioned from what is a more metaphysical basis that all unconscious influences do not render a person incapable. However, some unconscious influences actually destroy human freedom but only if they influence the very psychic structure of the human person and in particular those operations of intellect and will pertinent to the act of consent or fulfilling the obligations of marriage.[17]

Versaldi's presentation was based heavily on the more Freudian conceptions behind mental disorders which approach has clearly begun to fall in some disfavor in the field of psychology. Yet, what seems to remain true is that not every disorder destroys the human ability to function naturally.

The fourth and most recent edition of the *Diagnostic and Statistical Manual of Mental Disorders* gives its own cautions regarding the application of its classifications in the forensic sphere.

> In most situations, the clinical diagnosis of a DSM-IV mental disorder is not sufficient to establish the existence for legal purposes of a "mental disorder," "mental disability," "mental disease," or "mental defect." In determining whether an individual meets a specified legal standard (e.g., for competence, criminal responsibility, or disability), additional information is usually required beyond that contained in the DSM-IV diagnosis. This might include information about the individual's functional impairments and how these impairments affect the particular abilities in question.

It also cautions: "Neither deviant behavior (e.g., political, religious, or sexual) nor conflicts that are primarily between the individual and society are mental disorders unless the deviance or conflict is a symptom of a dysfunction in the individual, as described above." [18]

The authors of DSM-IV also give this caveat:

> ...Although this manual provides a classification of mental disorders, it must be admitted that no definition adequately specifies precise boundaries for the concept of "mental disorder." The concept of mental disorder, like many other concepts in medicine and science, lacks a consistent operational definition that covers all situations. All medical conditions are defined on various levels of abstraction – for example, structural pathology (e.g., ulcerative colitis), symptom presentation (e.g., migraine), deviance from a physiological norm (e.g., hypertension) and etiology (e.g., pneumococcal pneumonia.) Mental

---

[16] Here the reference is to the series rather than to one of the versions in the series.

[17] Giuseppe Versaldi, "The Dialogue between Psychological Science and Canon Law," *Incapacity for Marriage: Jurisprudence and Interpretation – Acts of III Gregorian Colloquium*, Robert M. Sable, ed. (Romae: Pontificia Universitas Gregoriana, 1987): 25-78.

[18] American Psychiatric Association, *Diagnostic and Statistical Manual of Mental Disorders-Fourth Edition* (Washington, DC: American Psychiatric Association): xxi-xxii.

> disorders have also been defined by a variety of concepts (e.g., distress, dyscontrol, disadvantage, disability, inflexibility, irrationality, syndromal pattern, etiology and statistical deviation.) Each is a useful indicator for a mental disorder, but none is equivalent to the concept, and different situations call for different definitions.[19]

The point of this seeming digression into clinical psychology is to emphasize a need for caution to those who argue and judge marriage cases not to attribute too much to a diagnosis by the psychological expert. These diagnoses cannot by themselves give the judge the certainty needed to pronounce that one of the parties was incapable of marriage. Further, the expert's report might surface for the judge additional evidence useful for becoming certain of other defects in consent.

If certain mental disorders merely influence a person without taking away freedom, is it not also important to ask the question how the person is influenced by such disorders? From practical experience an ecclesiastical judge often sees genuine lack of marital commitment on the part of one of the parties. What, therefore, the judge asks is the cause of this evident deficiency? Would it be methodologically more honest and congruent with our Christian anthropology to begin by ascribing the cause to free human choice than to jump so quickly to the assumption that only an incapacitated person would act in such a fashion?

We must assume that the words and signs used in the wedding ceremony correspond to the inner assent of the bride and groom at the wedding. Canon 1102 points out that there may be a case where there is a positive act of the will to exclude one of the essential elements or properties of marriage and so the marriage consent is deficient. However, when we read the canon perhaps we may be led to envision two acts of the will: one to enter marriage and another to exclude something, even marriage itself. In reality there is only one act of the will; it is the act of the will by which at least the act of consent is expressed.

---

[19] Ibid., xxi

However, when there is an exclusion or total simulation, this one act of will – this one human choice – will contain contradictory elements. For example, a person may want to be viewed by others as married and perhaps to a particular person. However, at the same time this person may not want to be obliged to one or the other duties of the married state. It is well known how complicated and involved are the motivations behind the actions of human beings including the action of getting married! Is it assumed that because all of these motives are not so immediately conscious to the person or openly expressed that they are arising from some mental disorder, which incapacitates the person from giving true consent? The Rota has often argued that the existence of a person's intentions can become known through his or her actions. It would seem more in keeping with our belief in the essential human freedom of the individual to presume the person was acting out of that essential freedom and was nonetheless deficient in marital consent rather than jumping to the conclusion of incapacity.

Consent to marriage is always itself a positive act of the will. As one listens to practitioners who want to conscientiously consider the "so-called traditional grounds," they immediately state the difficulty in knowing when there exists a 'positive act of the will' to simulate consent. It may be that there is much misunderstanding of what constitutes such a positive act of the will. Perhaps, some may be unconsciously requiring an *explicit* act of the will in order to be certain of simulation.

It would seem logical that if that positive act of the will did not include the *content* of the essential rights and duties of marriage then this complex act of the will positively excluded what it did not include. I am not intending to state here that a person must consciously advert in detail to all of the rights and duties at the time he or she is choosing to marry. For example, how would one assess the case of a perfectly capable person who entered marriage flippantly and failed right from the beginning to fulfill the obligations of marriage? Did the person simply fail to exercise due discretion in getting married? However, if this flippant behavior was simply the result of believing it really was not necessary to take the step seriously or the belief that there was really no enduring obligation beginning at the time of entrance into the marriage, then it would seem sufficiently evident this person essentially had a positive act of will to exclude an essential property or element according to canon 1102, §2.

This type of approach seems to be followed by Peter Kitchen in a 1994 article.[20] Here the author is giving the main thrust of his doctoral dissertation at the University of St. Thomas Aquinas in Rome (Angelicum), entitled, *The Presence and Absence of the Essential Elements of the 'mens matrimonialis': A Juridical Analysis Concerning the 'intentio nubendi' Through the Jurisprudence of the Cases of Simulation with Reference to the English Common and Criminal Law.*[21]

Peter Kitchen notes that the Rota's experience in dealing with cases submitted on the grounds of incapacity for marriage in accord with canon 1095 has shaped its understanding of the concept of the rights and duties to be exchanged in marriage. Persons may not be capable of consent precisely because they gravely lack discretion of judgment concerning the rights and duties to be exchanged in marriage. However, if they are capable of consent, they then have the obligation to exercise the minimal discretion for making the marital commitment. Peter Kitchen notes that not only do the forms of simulation require a positive act of the will, so also does consent itself. Consent is not simply a subjective negative act of the will in the face of the objective institution of marriage. In other words, one cannot be totally passive and enter a marriage like a person simply entering a fog. The person who consents has the obligation of discerning the scope of the commitment to marriage as the Creator intended it. One who is capable of so doing and fails to do so may have culpably neglected a duty and by implication may have excluded an essential element of consent.

[20] Peter Kitchen, "Matrimonial Intention and Simulation," *Studia Canonica* 28 (1994): 347-406.
[21] Peter Kitchen, "*The Presence and Absence of the Essential Elements of the 'mens matrimonialis': A Juridical Analysis Concerning the 'intentio nubendi' Through the Jurisprudence of the Cases of Simulation with reference to the English Common and Criminal Law,*" Pontificia Studiorum

Such an implied exclusion might be evident if there are clear signs in the evidence that the person quickly failed in his or her essential marital obligations in some way and this failure itself was not effectively the result of a change of mind after the wedding. What reasonable explanation can we give to explain the cause of this failure? If there are no signs which justify the conclusion of incapacity, then the person must not have felt obliged. Such persons by their failure to discern properly the seriousness of the marital commitment quickly turn away from the fulfillment of obligations and the nurturance of the *consortium vitae* because they implicitly did not commit to this personal orientation of life when they exchanged consent. Actions reveal an intent *not* to be obliged precisely in a context wherein the *accepting* of rights and duties is of the essence.

Peter Kitchen's article does not thoroughly develop the connection between certain types of "mental disorders" and establishing the proof for implied simulation, but what he has written suggests this study is necessary. The author makes this point when in a footnote in the article, he refers to his own dissertation where he quotes Msgr. Serrano as saying: "The development of jurisprudence requires that the subject of 'exclusion' be treated with the same profundity that has produced the developments in the handling of the cases of 'incapacity'."[22]

Many ecclesiastical judges can recall being totally convinced that a marriage was invalid and that the consent was certainly not present at the time of the wedding. An expert was assigned to the case who provided a certain diagnosis of a mental disorder. As a consequence, the marriage was declared invalid on the grounds of one of the numbers of canon 1095. In this connection it is well to recall that many rotal sentences admit that these mental or emotional difficulties do have some effect upon a person but do not necessarily rob the person of his or her native and radical capacity for marriage consent. Should

---

Universitas A S. Thoma in Urbe, Roma, 1989.

[22] Kitchen, "Matrimonial Intention," *Studia Canonica* 402, n. 171.

some cases be examined for the presence of such disorders as figuring in the cause of some form of simulation of consent? Therefore, could not the expert's report also give the judge some assistance in determining the existence of a positive will to exclude an essential of marriage?

Certain mental disorders like those in the psychotic classification are as likely as not to be a cause of a person's inability to either give consent or assume the essential marital obligations. The DSM-IV clearly distinguishes these psychotic disorders from the personality disorders. The evidence of delusions and hallucinations characterizes the psychotic disorder.[23] Psychotic disorders can easily be the psychic cause for either the inability of the person for a human act or decision or specifically for that discretion of judgment proportionate to the rights and duties to be exchanged in marriage consent" (c. 1095, 1°or 2°).

Personality disorders are not characterized by a focus on the deterioration of the thought processes of the person even though they have some impact on those thought processes and their outcome. Nonetheless, the DSM-IV states that the "essential feature of a Personality Disorder is an enduring pattern of inner experience and behavior that deviates markedly from the expectations of the individual's culture and is manifested in at least two of the following areas: cognition, affectivity, interpersonal functioning or impulse control."[24] When the DSM-IV speaks of "inner experience" it makes no attempt to focus its attention on phenomena suggestive of disorders in thought. Rather, by classifying these disorders separately from the psychotic disorders, the authors draw attention to the outward behavior of a person but at the same time recognize there must be some corresponding "inner experience" which is essentially congruent with the outward behavior.

When it is a matter of judging questions of alleged invalidity of marriage, it is the working presumption that a Catholic person is presumed capable of the act of consent once he or she has reached the canonical age. One

---

[23] "Schizophrenia and Other Psychotic Disorders" in *DSM-IV*, 273.
[24] *DSM-IV*, 630.

can also be safe in assuming the same capability for *all* persons at those ages. Thus, before the natural law all persons, even those with true mental disorders, must be presumed capable of matrimonial consent until proven otherwise.

It would seem that the presumption in favor of capacity for consent could more easily fall for persons affected by psychotic or thought disorders since this disorder is seen as more directly attacking those human faculties which are the very structure of the process of decision-making.

Persons with personality disorders could also be incapable of consent. At the same time, depending on the state of knowledge establishing any impairment of the decision-making process or of the person's ability to assume the essential marital obligations, it might be easier to establish such a person was more likely to have simulated consent. Let us return to what the DSM-IV states about the defining characteristic of personality disorders.

The *Manual* stated: the "essential feature of a Personality Disorder is an enduring pattern of inner experience and behavior that deviates markedly from the expectations of the individual's culture."[25] It is this marked deviation "from the expectations of the individual's culture" which might be worthy of a deeper look.

This definition of the DSM-IV is very generic. The "individual's culture" is a term wide enough to include any of the values, social or religious, which might make up a person's culture. Among these could certainly be elements which could encompass the content found in the essential properties and elements of marriage. A person with a personality disorder might very well be capable of exchanging valid marriage consent. At the same time, however, the "enduring pattern of inner experience and behavior" of that person prior to and at the time of the marriage was such as *to be in dissonance* with such values as the indissolubility of marriage or fidelity in marriage.

One cannot oversimplify the reasoning process in these matters. The "truth is in the details" when it comes to marriage cases. However, if one can find in the evidence that one of the parties clearly had some mental disorder and at the same time seemed clearly not committed to the marriage or its obligations, it may *not* be the truth of the matter to conclude the person was not capable of being committed. Rather this failure to accept being committed or being obligated may arise from the habitual way this person acts. He or she wanted to be married. Such persons may deny under oath that they were uncommitted to the marriage from the beginning. However, their behavior throughout suggested just the contrary and the "inner experience" of such persons would be presumed to be consistent. Further, if this behavior pattern seemed in the view of a psychologist to be indicative in light of other factors to arise out of a personality disorder, then there is no doubt that the motivators for simulation most likely arose prior to marriage. This conclusion is supported by the fourth criterion for the establishment of a personality disorder according to the DSM-IV, namely, that the "pattern is stable and of long duration, and its onset can be traced back at least to adolescence or early adulthood."[26]

A canonist could well look at the features of the various personality disorders to see how plausible it might be that the very disorder itself is the foundation or motive of either partial or total simulation. Of course, the ecclesiastical judge in a given case may well use a psychological expert to be of assistance since the judge cannot truly diagnose mental illnesses. However, with this necessary *caveat* let us look at some of the descriptions of personality disorders in the DSM-IV.

> The essential feature of the Paranoid Personality Disorder is a pattern of pervasive mistrust and suspiciousness of others such that their motives are interpreted as malevolent.[27]

A person with such a "pervasive mistrust" of others might be so affected that he or she would never even think of getting married or would always break off the association prior to any engagement or marriage. However,

---

[25] "Personality Disorders" in *DSM-IV*, 630.
[26] Ibid., 630.
[27] Ibid., 634.

depending on the severity of the disorder and what elements of the person's psychic structure are affected, such a person might or not be capable of consent.

However, if capable, such a person might marry but always very intensely reserve the right to leave the marriage when and if the other partner exhibited that degree of "disloyalty" deemed unacceptable. In such a case, the characteristics of the disorder would clearly establish, that if the person was not proven incapable of consent, the person was nonetheless committed to dissolving the marriage if things did not go his or her way.

> The essential feature of the Schizoid Personality Disorder is a pervasive pattern of detachment from social relationships and a restricted range of expression of emotions in interpersonal settings.[28]

With this deeply pervasive lack of desire for intimacy, such a person, too, might never choose to marry. However, he or she might agree to marry but with certain very definite restrictions regarding intimacy. In given cases, it is easy to see how such a person might simply not give enough of the self to create a minimal *consortium vitae*. Likewise, such a person might enter a "trial marriage" based on the idea that if the intimacy becomes "too much" he or she would terminate the marriage and perhaps try again with someone less "threatening." In some instances, such an affected person might simply assume as natural and expected that he or she would regard marriage as merely having a roommate or a housekeeper. In such instances, the lack of marital commitment might be the result of deeply rooted substantial error.

> The essential feature of the Narcissistic Personality Disorder is a pervasive pattern of grandiosity, need for admiration, and lack of empathy that begins by early adulthood and is present in a variety of contexts.[29]

Such persons are so self-centered that "re-writing the definition of marriage" for their own purposes would not be extraordinary. Implied in such person's way of life is the idea that if something or someone does not suit them, the thing or the person can be jettisoned from their life. What would such

---

[28] Ibid., 638.

persons do in the face of a decision to enter marriage? Would they advert to being obliged to something which they would habitually never choose to fulfill?

> The essential feature of the Obsèssive-Compulsive Personality Disorder is a preoccupation with orderliness, perfectionism, and mental and interpersonal control, at the expense of flexibility, openness, and efficiency.[30]

Everyone knows that living in marriage is often a "messy business." One must live with at least a modicum of uncertainty. The judge might expect to find in the obsessive-compulsive person at least a virtual intention to demand such conformism with his or her views that the other partner would not truly be a partner but a slave. If the obsessive-compulsive person were not so assertive and dominant over the partner, the desire and demand for unrealistic orderliness might easily be the foundation for an implied intention to break the marriage bond if his or her needs were not met.

Conclusion

The purpose of this brief presentation is simply to continue the discussion which has begun about revisiting the so-called traditional grounds. It is hoped that there will be a continued dialogue on this topic. Tribunal practitioners and jurists must spend time and energy on delving into the human psyche but not simply from the point of view of establishing incapacity for consent but also from the perspective of seeing how we humans come to choices as well as how and why we are held accountable for the choices we make. A part of this project will inevitably involve a re-visiting of the skills of close reasoning and logic. At the same time, it will likely call us to take a fresh look at what the psychologists can offer us when their reports do not serve as proof of incapacity for consent.

---

[29] Ibid., 658.
[30] Ibid., 669.

PROCEDURAL LAW: SOME COMPARATIVE REFLECTIONS ON THE LATIN AND EASTERN CODES

THOMAS J. GREEN

Introduction

In the October 1990 apostolic constitution *Sacri canones* promulgating the *Code of Canons of the Eastern Churches* (*CCEO* or Eastern code), John Paul II stated that: "...the Church, gathered in the one Spirit breathes as though with two lungs – of the East and of the West – and it burns with the love of Christ in one heart having two ventricles."[1] In presenting that code to the synod of bishops on October 25, 1990, the pope indicated that this new legal document, together with the 1983 Latin code[2] and the 1988 apostolic constitution on the Roman Curia *Pastor bonus*, constituted one *Corpus Iuris Canonici* of the universal Church. The promulgation of the Eastern code completed the revision of universal law that had been underway for twenty-five years following the close of Vatican II. The pope chose the synod to announce the promulgation of the Eastern code because he wanted it to be received by the whole Church, East and West, as an extremely important ecclesial development.

In announcing the promulgation of the Eastern code, the pope also called for serious comparative study of both codes in all canon law faculties even if they focused their primary attention on one code or the other, e.g., Latin

[1] *Code of Canons of the Eastern Churches Latin-English Edition* (Washington, DC: CLSA, 1992) xiv. For a critique of certain aspects of this translation, see George Nedungatt, *A Companion to the Eastern Code* (Brooklyn, NY: Saint Maron Publications, 1994). The Eastern canons will be cited as *CCEO* and the pertinent canon number(s).

[2] For the canons of the Latin code the author uses *Code of Canon Law Latin-English Edition New English Translation* (Washington, DC: CLSA, 1999). The Latin canons will be cited as *1983 CIC*

code (most faculties), Eastern code (Pontifical Oriental Institute in Rome and India).[3] The pope renewed this invitation to comparative canonical study a few years later on April 23, 1993 at an international canon law meeting in Rome celebrating the tenth anniversary of the promulgation of the Latin code.[4] Interestingly enough he took the occasion of two international church assemblies to highlight the promulgation of the 1990 Eastern code and call for comparative canonical studies that at this point in time are still somewhat rare but slowly increasing.[5]

Canonical science will be advanced to the extent that canonists, Latin and Eastern, understand better the legal traditions of the various churches in the Catholic *communio*. This should expand their theoretical and practical horizons and foster a more refined appreciation of the legitimacy and advantages of canonical as well as theological, liturgical, and ascetical pluralism in the Church. The present collection of studies is dedicated to Lawrence Wrenn, one of the most distinguished postconciliar specialists in procedural law.[6] It seems only fitting then to reflect briefly on some comparative procedural law issues.

The author, a Latin canonist, writes primarily for his fellow Latin canonists, especially those in tribunal and chancery practice. However,

---

and the pertinent canon number(s).

[3] See *Nuntia* n. 31 (1990) 13 (Latin text); 20 (Italian text). (Rome: Pontificia Commissio Codici Iuris Canonici Orientalis Recognoscendo).

[4] See "Discorso del Santo Padre Giovanni Paolo II," in *Ius in Vita et in Missione Ecclesiae* (Città del Vaticano: Libreria Editrice Vaticana, 1994) 1264-1265. Also *Communicationes* 25 (Città del Vaticano: Libreria Editrice Vaticana, 1993) 13-14.

[5] The author of this article has attempted such comparative studies in several areas of church law. See Thomas Green, "Penal Law in the Latin Code and in the Code of Canons of the Eastern Churches," *Studia Canonica* 28 (1994) 407-451 (hereafter cited as Green, "Penal Law"); idem, "The Teaching Function of the Church: A Comparison of Selected Canons in the Latin and Eastern Codes," *The Jurist* 55 (1995) 93-140; idem, "Diocesan and Parish Structures: A Comparison of Selected Canons in the *Codex iuris canonici* and *Codex canonum Ecclesiarum orientalium," Studia Canonica* 33 (1999) 349-397. The canonist who thus far has provided the most extensive series of such comparative studies in English is Jobe Abbass. See, for example, idem, "Two Codes in Comparison," *Kanonika* 7 (Rome: Pontificio Istituto Orientale, 1997) (hereafter cited "Two Codes").

[6] See, for example, his work entitled *Procedures* (Washington, DC: CLSA, 1987). More recently see his commentaries on Book VII in *The Code of Canon Law: A Text and Commentary*, ed. James Coriden et al. (New York/Mahwah: Paulist Press, 1985) 949-1022 and in *New Commentary on the Code of Canon Law*, ed. John Beal et. al. (New York/Mahwah: Paulist Press, 2000) 1607-1654.

hopefully, Eastern canonists may find these observations helpful while offering appropriate critical comments.

Limitations of space and the complexity of the issues raised by the numerous procedural canons in both codes preclude the author's doing anything more than offering a general overview of some significant similarities but *especially procedural differences* between the codes, using the Eastern code as the primary frame of reference.[7] One fundamental *datum* that will soon become evident is the *notable similarity* between the codes in this general area, the result of a conscious Eastern code commission decision to be mentioned later. The aforementioned overview will be organized as follows. After reflecting on contemporary Eastern procedural law developments, the author will consider the canons on trials in general (*CCEO* cc.1055-1184; 1983 *CIC* cc. 1400-1500) and then only briefly mention those on contentious trials (*CCEO* cc. 1185-1356; 1983 *CIC* cc. 1501-1670). Subsequently he will examine certain special procedures, e.g., marriage nullity norms (*CCEO* 1357-1400; 1983 *CIC* 1671-1716; 1740-1752), and finally pertinent canons on penal sanctions (*CCEO* cc.1401-1467; 1983 *CIC* 1311-1399) and penal procedures (*CCEO* cc. 1468-1487; 1983 *CIC* cc. 1717-1731).[8]

---

[7] For more detailed analyses of procedural law in the two codes see Abbass, "Trials in General," in *Two Codes*, 209-249; idem, "Contentious Trials," in ibid., 251-278. This author found Abbass particularly helpful in preparing these reflections. The latter's analyses are organized as follows: (1) concerns for uniformity of the two codes, (2) Latin canons without Eastern counterparts, (3) Eastern norms without Eastern counterparts, and (4) parallel norms in the two codes that differ significantly.

[8] Because of the aforementioned limitations, the author will not address a couple of procedural issues outside of the primary Eastern titles on procedures and sanctions. He will deal neither with the canons on administrative recourse (*CCEO* cc. 996-1006; 1983 *CIC* cc 1732-1739) nor with those on the dismissal of monks or members of orders, congregations, societies of common life, or secular institutes (*CCEO* cc. 497-503; 551-553; 562, 3; 568, 2; 1983 *CIC* cc. 694-704; 729; 742; 746). For some valuable reflections on the latter issue, see Rose McDermott, "Two Approaches to Consecrated Life: The *Code of Canons of the Eastern Churches* and the *Code of Canon Law*," *Studia Canonica* 29 (1995) 193-239, esp. 228-234; 237.

The Drafting of Eastern Procedural Law[9]

Establishment of Eastern Code Commission

On June 10, 1972 Paul VI established the Eastern code commission to revise the promulgated[10] and hitherto unpromulgated texts of legislation for the Eastern churches. His key concerns in this enterprise were ensuring fidelity to Eastern canonical traditions as well as to the spirit and directives of Vatican II with due regard for a sensitivity to contemporary legal-pastoral issues.[11] He formally inaugurated the commission's work on March 18, 1974 at its first plenary session which lasted for five more days. Nine principles were approved to guide the future revision process,[12] somewhat comparable to the action of the 1967 synod of bishops in approving ten principles for the revision of the Latin code.[13]

---

[9] For detailed and thoughtful observations on the drafting of the whole Eastern code, see John Faris, *The Eastern Catholic Churches: Constitution and Governance* (Brooklyn, NY: Saint Maron Publications, 1992) 67-106. For somewhat briefer comments on this process, see Thomas Green, "Reflections on the Eastern Code Revision Process," *The Jurist* 53 (1993) 18-37 (hereafter cited Green, "Revision"). For helpful comments on the whole process of the revision of Eastern procedural law, see Abbass, in *Two Codes*, 210-216; 252-255. For a useful report on the early stages of the drafting of procedural law by the *coetus relator*, see Youssef Sarraf, " Les canons *de processibus*," *Nuntia*, n. 5 (1977) 3-39.

[10] This refers to the four documents promulgated *motu proprio* by Pius XII between February 22, 1949 and June 2, 1957. See Green, "Revision," 20-21.

[11] See *Nuntia* n. 1 (1975) 11.

[12] For the text of a pertinent preamble and the nine (unnumbered) principles, see *Nuntia* n. 3 (1976) 18-24 (English version). For a brief background report on the principles, see ibid., 10. They had been initially prepared by the canon law faculty of the Pontifical Oriental Institute. See *Nuntia* n. 26 (1988) 100-113.

[13] See *Communicationes* 2 (1969) 78-85. Trans. Roger Schoenbechler, "Principles Which Govern the Revision of the Code of Canon Law," in *Readings, Cases, Materials in Canon Law: A Textbook for Ministerial Students*, ed. Jordan Hite and Daniel Ward (Collegeville, MN: Liturgical Press, 1990) 84-92 (hereafter cited as Schoenbechler). It would be useful to prepare a comparative examination of the two sets of code revision principles. For a critical examination of the implementation of the Latin revision principles, see J. Canosa, ed., *I principi per la revisione del Codice di Diritto Canonico La ricezione giuridica del Concilio Vaticano II* (Milan: Giuffrè Editore, 2000). Two of the essays are of significant procedural law interest although they do not notably address issues facing ordinary tribunals dealing primarily with marriage nullity cases: Zenon Grocholewski, "Il sistema dei ricorsi e la giurisdizione dei tribunali amministrativi," in ibid., 461-499; Joaquin Llobell, "Il sistema giudiziario canonico di tutela dei diritti. Riflessioni sull'attuazione dei principi 6° e 7°

As was true during the Latin code revision process, the comparable task of revising the Eastern code was entrusted to ten committees (*coetus*), one of which addressed distinctly procedural law concerns.[14] This *coetus* was to revise the 576 canons of the January 6, 1950 *motu proprio* of Pius XII *Sollicitudinem nostram*,[15] which had largely governed the Eastern churches in communion with Rome since January 6, 1951. This task was to be carried out especially in light of the aforementioned principles. Two seem particularly pertinent: principle two on the code's Eastern character, which obviously has no Latin counterpart, and principle eight on the canons *De Processibus.* While no Latin principle is explicitly entitled "canons *De Processibus*," several of them address procedural issues.[16]

Principles for Revision

First and foremost, the Eastern code was understandably to be an authentically Eastern canonical document, depending primarily on the apostolic tradition, Eastern canonical collections, and still operative Eastern customs (principle two).[17] Furthermore, a key concern in revising *Sollicitudinem nostram* was to ensure an administration of justice perfectly proportioned to the real state of things, i.e., the conditions of the individuals involved and the needs of the

---

approvati dal sinodo del 1967," in ibid., 501-546.

[14] See *Nuntia* n. 1 (1975) 13-18 at 18.

[15] See *Acta Apostolicae Sedis* 42 (1950) 5-120.

[16] One might note especially the Latin principle five on subsidiarity, which treats procedural law in some detail, expressing caution about too extensive decentralization in this area. It does so after differentiating the Latin church from the Eastern churches in principle regarding the legitimacy of broad particular law options. Among the stated reasons counseling such caution are the need to respect the right of all the faithful to bring their cases to the Holy See and the importance of facilitating the administration of justice. See *Communicationes* 2 (1969) 81-82; Schoenbechler, 88-89. The Eastern principle six on subsidiarity does not explicitly mention procedural law. However, it stresses the desirable limitation of the Eastern code to those matters common to all the Eastern churches. Authorities in the various churches should be empowered to regulate all other disciplinary matters not reserved to the Holy See. See *Nuntia* n. 3 (1976) 21-22. The Latin principles six and seven (especially) also address procedural issues given their primary focus on the importance of both affirming the existence of subjective rights and protecting their exercise especially but not exclusively in the administrative arena. This is the context in which the issue of administrative tribunals is briefly discussed. See *Communicationes* 2 (1969) 82-83; Schoenbechler, 89-91. See also Eastern principle eight in *Nuntia* n. 3 (1976) 23-24.

[17] See *Nuntia* n. 3 (1976) 19.

broader society. Despite the *motu proprio*'s technical excellence and its adaptability to the situation of the Eastern churches, certain changes were warranted to reflect better the distinctive structure of such churches and to simplify the pertinent legislation – a key concern also of post-conciliar Latin procedural reform.

Although the Eastern canons were to reflect distinctly Eastern traditions, principle eight[18] also called for the structuring of a largely uniform procedural law for all Catholics, probably to ensure impartial justice[19] but also to guarantee a possible recourse (*provocatio*) to the pope by any of the faithful (*CCEO* c. 1059; 1983 *CIC* c. 1417). For the Code Commission, any movement to enhance decisional options for Eastern tribunals (especially patriarchal ones) needed to be tempered somewhat by a respect for this procedural right of the faithful. As the Eastern revision process continued, this concern for procedural uniformity between the codes seemed to be an especially dominant motif. Although numerous canons in the two codes are similarly formulated, in no other part of the code does there seem to have been such a studied effort to ensure such uniformity.[20] Despite such concerns it was decided not to constitute a mixed procedural *coetus* with Latin canonists at a time when the original Latin procedural schema had almost been completed. However, this schema was made available to the Eastern procedural *coetus* to serve as a key point of reference in its work, which began in earnest at a meeting held December 2-7, 1974.

Drafting of Eastern Procedural Law: 1974-1990

On February 27, 1982 a schema of 398 procedural canons was forwarded to various consultative organs with a request that an evaluation of the

---

[18] See *Nuntia* n. 3 (1976) 23-24.

[19] Principle eight briefly mentioned concerns about removing suspicions of arbitrariness in church administration, improving systems of administrative recourse, and structuring administrative tribunals. See *Nuntia* n. 3 (1976) 23-24. However, the Eastern principles did not address issues of substantive and procedural rights quite as extensively as did their Latin counterpart. See *Communicationes* 2 (1969) 82-83; Schoenbechler, 89-91.

[20] It might be useful to examine the two codes to see how many canons are similarly formulated and

schema be submitted to the commission by September 30, 1982.[21] According to the *Praenotanda* of the schema,[22] the *coetus* revised and notably simplified *Sollicitudinem nostram,* however adding some new material, e.g., norms on separation and presumed death cases, administrative penal procedure, and administrative recourse. The schema lacked norms on the Holy See tribunals or on certain "Roman cases", e.g., non-consummation or privilege of the faith procedures because such provisions were deemed unnecessary given available Roman norms.

The *coetus* basically followed the aforementioned nine revision principles and was concerned especially that non-reserved cases be handled exclusively by patriarchal tribunals without appeals to the Roman dicasteries with due regard, however, for possible recourse (*provocatio*) to the pope. However, he alone would be competent to deal with all cases involving patriarchs and criminal cases involving other bishops. Efforts were made to ensure uniform formulations between the codes as much as possible. However, the Latin canons were not always adopted for various reasons: respect for a different Eastern tribunal organization, the relevance of particular personal statutes in effect in certain regions, a respect for the Eastern mentality and culture, an effort to assure an administration of justice appropriate to the means of communications available in various settings.

During May and October 1983 a special *coetus* of eight consultors reviewed the input received regarding the 1982 schema.[23] Once again, concerns were expressed regarding procedural uniformity in light of the recent January 1983 promulgation of the Latin code. However, certain differences between the codes were preserved in light of the distinct hierarchical configuration of the

---

why such is the case.

[21] For the text of the schema and its corresponding *Praenotanda*, see *Nuntia* n. 14 (1982) 3-109.

[22] See ibid., 3-4.

[23] Actually only about 40% of the consultative organs responded to the request for an evaluation of the schema.

Eastern churches and particular Eastern ecclesial conditions. Hopefully, this would facilitate a better understanding of the code by Eastern Catholics.[24]

After the various Eastern law schemata had been revised by the various *coetus*, a coordinating committee prepared a draft of what would ultimately become the Eastern code. On October 17, 1986 the so-called 1986 schema[25] (comparable to the Latin 1980 schema) was forwarded to the thirty-three members of the Eastern code commission for their appraisal with a covering letter and a brief *relatio* concerning the Eastern code revision process.[26] The commission members' animadversions were reviewed by a special *coetus, de expensione observationum*, which led to a new schema being presented to the second plenary session of the commission on November 3-14, 1984. This meeting was comparable to the October 1981 *Plenarium* towards the end of the Latin code revision process. After some further refinements, on January 28, 1989 the commission presented the *Schema novissimum* to John Paul II for promulgation. After examining this schema with selected advisors he promulgated the Eastern code on October 18, 1990.

Trials in General (CCEO *title 24: canons. 1055-1184;* CIC *canons. 1400-1500)*[27]

Not surprisingly the Eastern code on trials in general is greatly similar to, if not identical to, the Latin code. This corresponds to revision principle eight that all Catholics should observe the same procedural laws, which meant striving for maximal uniformity between the codes. Initially the Latin procedural law

---

[24] For a report on the work of this special *coetus*, see "Prospetto dello schema 'de Processibus' dopo la sua revisione," *Nuntia* n. 21 (1985) 40-65. For observations on modifications of the 1982 schema to ensure maximal conformity to the Latin code see Abbass, in *Two Codes*, 214-215.

[25] See *Nuntia* nn. 24-25 (1987) 1-278, especially 192-244; 255-258. Of particular procedural interest are the following titles and canons: trials in general (title 24: cc. 1070-1199); contentious trials (title 25: cc. 1200-1371); certain special processes (title 26: cc. 1372-1415); penal procedure (title 28: cc. 1483-1502).

[26] See *Nuntia* n. 23 (1986) 109-119.

[27] See Abbass, in *Two Codes*, 209-249, esp. 217-249. For a brief overview of the pertinent canons, see Victor Pospishil, *Eastern Catholic Church Law*, Revised and Augmented Edition (Staten Island, NY: Saint Maron Publications, 1996) 706-719 (hereafter cited as Pospishil).

schema and later Book VII of the Latin code served as key points of reference in drafting the Eastern code; hence, it incorporates the principal Latin canons. However, the Eastern code contains more canons on trials in general (130) than its Latin counterpart (110), and a fair number of these canons are distinctly Eastern in character. Many have no Latin code counterpart or somewhat differ from the comparable Latin text. As noted earlier, we will briefly highlight some *significant differences* between the codes.

Recourse against Administrative Decrees

The initial Latin canon 1400, §2 on administrative recourse mentions two options: either the higher administrative authority or an administrative tribunal; however, realistically speaking, at the end of the Latin revision process the only such tribunal was the second section of the Apostolic Signatura (see *Pastor bonus* 123, §1). The Eastern code does not mention such tribunals, simply alluding to the canons on administrative recourse (*CCEO* cc. 1055, §2; 996-1006).

Roman Rota and Apostolic Signatura

Unlike the Latin code, the Eastern code mentions neither the Roman Rota nor the Apostolic Signatura and does not specify their competencies (1983 *CIC* cc. 1444-1445) but simply refers generically to the law governing the Roman dicasteries (*CCEO* 1056).[28]

[28] See, e.g., *Pastor bonus* 121-125 on the Rota and 126-130 on the Signatura. It is noteworthy that the Eastern code significantly differs from its Latin counterpart at the level of universal Church governance. For example, the Eastern code does not contain canons on the synod of bishops, the college of cardinals, the Roman Curia, or pontifical representatives. See 1983 *CIC* cc. 342-367.

Unique Tribunals of Eastern Patriarchal Churches (*CCEO* canons 1062-1063)[29]

The Eastern revision principle eight called for Eastern Catholics to be able to organize themselves to deal with non-reserved cases in three instances up to a final decision but without prejudice to the exceptional right of recourse (*provocatio)* to the pope (*CCEO* c. 1059). Furthermore, the patriarchal synod was presumably to become the locus of major criminal trials with due regard for possible recourse to the pope. The *coetus* eliminated any reference to the patriarch's judicial power, which was deemed incompatible with his paternal role.

During the revision process, however, the competent authority to judge bishops in criminal matters was changed from the patriarchal synod to the Holy See (*CCEO* c. 1062, §1). However, in principle, every patriarchal church is able to handle cases in all three instances up to final sentence (*CCEO* c. 1063). Therefore, apart from cases reserved to the Holy See (*CCEO* c. 1060, §1), the superior tribunal within the patriarchal territory is the patriarchal synod.

That synod is to elect the moderator of its tribunal and two other bishops, whom the patriarch may replace with the consent of the permanent synod (*CCEO* c. 1062, §2). Such a tribunal may judge contentious cases involving eparchies (dioceses) or bishops (*CCEO* c. 1062, §3).[30] However, outside the patriarchal territory the pope assigns the tribunal to judge bishops and the Holy See adjudicates cases of eparchies (*CCEO* c. 1060, §2). Appeals against patriarchal tribunal decisions are to be made to the full synod without further possibility of appeal. However, exceptionally, recourse (*provocatio*) can still be made to the pope (*CCEO* cc. 1062, §4; 1059).

---

[29] For reflections on the broader decisional prerogatives of patriarchal tribunals by contrast to most of their Latin counterparts, see, for example, Andrews Thazhath, "The Superior and Ordinary Tribunals of a *sui iuris* Eastern Catholic Church," *Studia Canonica* 29 (1995) 375-396.
[30] On areas of exclusive Rotal competency in the Latin church, see *1983 CIC* c. 1405, §3.

Another unique Eastern code feature is the general vigilance role of the general moderator of a patriarchal tribunal comparable to the Signatura; this moderator, for example, rules on objections to judges in the ordinary tribunal of the patriarchate (*CCEO* c. 1062, §5).

Furthermore, an ordinary tribunal of the patriarchal church must be established to deal with cases in three instances;[31] this is distinct both from the aforementioned patriarchal tribunal and from the tribunal of the patriarch's own eparchy (just as a Latin archbishop has his own first instance tribunal). While the patriarch appoints the officials of this patriarchal tribunal with the approval of the permanent synod, they may be removed, however, only with the approval of the full synod (*CCEO* c. 1063, §2).

Common Tribunal of Various *Sui Iuris* Churches

Another uniquely Eastern code feature is the episcopal option of constituting a single tribunal for various *sui iuris* churches in a territory including the Latin church, especially if tribunal personnel are lacking. The bishops involved are to designate one of their own as moderator and formulate pertinent statutes on their own (*CCEO* cc. 1068; 1070). In a Latin context, however, the Signatura would have to approve this development (1983 *CIC* c. 1423, §1).[32] Appeals from decisions of such a tribunal, however, are to be made to a tribunal stably designated by the Holy See.

An Additional Possible Title of Competence

If a judge is otherwise relatively incompetent,[33] he obtains competence if the parties and the authority to which the tribunal is immediately subject approve (*CCEO* 1080); there is no Latin code equivalent of this provision.

[31] For its competency see *CCEO* c. 1063, §4.
[32] For another instance of less notable Signatura involvement in Eastern tribunal activity, see *CCEO* c. 1083 and *1983 CIC* c. 1416 on resolving conflicts of tribunal competence.
[33] See *CCEO* cc. 1073-1079 for the bases of ordinary tribunal competency.

One Clerical Judge Deciding Collegiate Tribunal Cases

Certain cases are reserved by law or by the bishop to a three-judge panel (*CCEO* c. 1084, §1; 1983 *CIC* c. 1425, §1). However, in case of necessity one clerical judge may be authorized to hear the case. The pertinent competent authority differs somewhat in the two codes. The episcopal conference is competent in the Latin code (1983 *CIC* c. 1425, §4) while the Eastern code so empowers the patriarch within the patriarchate, after consulting the permanent synod or the metropolitan living outside the patriarchal territory after consulting the two senior eparchial bishops. The latter provision is also true for the metropolitan of a metropolitan *sui iuris* church; in other cases the Holy See is to be consulted (*CCEO* c. 1084, §3).

Lay Judges

At times a layperson may serve as a judge with two clerics, and the aforementioned authority figures are competent to permit such, i.e., the Latin episcopal conference or patriarchs and certain metropolitans (*CCEO* c. 1087, §2; 1983 *CIC* c. 1421, §2).

Methods of Avoiding a Trial

The Eastern code somewhat more logically situates the canons on ways of avoiding a trial just before those on contentious cases given the preeminent ecclesial concern to resolve conflicts according to Christian precepts without a trial (*CCEO* cc. 1164-1167 on settlements and cc. 1168-1184 on compromises by arbitrators). The Latin code by contrast places the 'conflict resolution' canons after those on the contentious process (1983 *CIC* cc. 1713-1716). The more extensive Eastern treatment of this problematic than that of its Latin counterpart is viewed as more in keeping with the gospel and less dependent on civil law variables.[34]

Contentious Trials
(CCEO *title 25: canons. 1185-1356; CIC canons. 1501-1670)*

At first glance the two codes seem substantially same; this is not surprising given the Eastern code commission effort to ensure as much as possible that all Catholics observe the same procedural laws. In fact, during the revision of the 1982 schema, nearly one half of the original Eastern canons were replaced by their Latin code counterparts. While uniformity between the codes has been largely achieved, some canons are unique to the Latin or Eastern codes; and certain parallel norms differ in some significant respect. However, given limitations of space and the probable concerns of the readers, such differences do not seem to warrant specific mention here[35]

Certain Special Procedures
*(*CCEO *title 26: canons. 1357-1400;*
CIC *canons. 1671-1712; 1740-1752)*[36]

The Eastern title 26 on 'certain special procedures' is subdivided into three chapters: matrimonial procedures, ordination nullity procedures, and the removal and transfer of pastors. By contrast the comparable Latin code provisions on 'certain special processes' (Book VII, part III) are further subdivided into three titles on marriage processes, ordination nullity processes, and methods of avoiding trials (already discussed). The issue of the removal and transfer of pastors is addressed in part V of Book VII at the end of the code. A few observations about these various subdivisions of the two codes should

---

[34] See Abbass, in *Two Codes*, 243-249.
[35] See ibid., 251-278; Pospishil, 720-731.

suffice since not surprisingly there are great similarities between their respective provisions.

Marriage Procedures

This chapter in the Eastern code (*CCEO* cc. 1357-1384; see 1983 *CIC* cc. 1671-1707) is in turn subdivided into four articles: (a) nullity cases (*CCEO* cc. 1357-1377; see 1983 *CIC* cc. 1671-1691), (b) separation cases (*CCEO* cc. 1378-1382; see 1983 *CIC* cc. 1692-1696), (c) presumed death cases (*CCEO* c. 1383; see 1983 *CIC* c. 1707), and (d) non-consummation (see 1983 *CIC* cc. 1697-1706) and favor of the faith cases (*CCEO* c. 1384). A few pertinent observations about this material should suffice for our purposes.

Marriage Nullity Cases

The Eastern canon 1358 on the merely civil effects of marriage alone refers to 'personal statutes' where they may be in force. It also differentiates between such civil effects being adjudicated as the principle case (civil competency) or as an incidental case (possible ecclesiastical competency). The Latin code, however affirms such civil competency in principle in any case while allowing for particular law to permit ecclesiastical competency in incidental cases (1983 *CIC* c. 1672).

In this connection one might note briefly a significant procedural provision on religiously mixed marriages (involving the baptized) contained not in the procedural canons but rather in Eastern marriage law. Besides being subject to divine, canon, and civil law, such marriages are also governed by the distinctive law of the pertinent non-Catholic church or ecclesial community if it has such law; if such is lacking, whatever law binds the non-Catholic is also pertinent (*CCEO* c. 780, §2). This provision, not contained in the Latin code,

---

[36] For a brief overview of such procedures, see Pospishil, 732-744.

pertains not simply to entering marriage but also to adjudicating marriage nullity petitions (*CCEO* c. 781).[37]

The Eastern canon 1359, §3 on the forum of the petitioner differs somewhat from its Latin counterpart (1983 *CIC* c. 1673, 3º) in requiring that the parties live in the same 'nation' rather than the same 'episcopal conference'. Interestingly, the Eastern code uses the same formulation to specify the required approval of the respondent's judicial vicar in such cases and in cases involving the forum of proofs. On the contrary, the Latin code formulations pertaining to the two *fora* differ somewhat (1983 *CIC* c. 1673, §§3, 4).

In the initial canon on the documentary process, the Eastern canon 1372, §2 alone explicitly refers to the fact that the pre-nuptial investigation suffices to prove the freedom to marry of one obliged to follow canonical form but who neglected to do so and attempted marriage before a civil official or non-Catholic minister.

Marriage Separation Cases

Unlike the Eastern code (*CCEO* c. 1379, §1) the Latin code permits the promoter of justice as well as one of the parties to seek the use of the ordinary, not the 'oral',[38] contentious process in such cases (1983 *CIC* c. 1693, §1; see 1983 *CIC* cc. 1656-1670).

Unlike the Latin code which permits the use of the four *fora* of canon 1673 in handling such cases (1983 *CIC* c. 1694), the Eastern code authorizes only the *fora* of the petitioner and respondent (*CCEO* cc. 1380; 1359, §§2, 3).

---

[37] See, for example, James Provost, "Some Practical Issues for Latin Canon Lawyers from the Code of Canons of Eastern Churches," *The Jurist* 51 (1991) 58-59.

[38] The Eastern code speaks of the 'summary' contentious process in this context. See *CCEO* cc. 1343-1356.

Presumed Death Cases

In complex cases the Eastern code alone authorizes recourse to the patriarch within the patriarchal territory while referring to such recourse to the Apostolic See in other cases, as does its Latin counterpart. Only the Eastern code explicitly calls for the involvement of the promoter of justice, not the defender of the bond (*CCEO* 1383, §§ 2, 3; 1983 *CIC* c. 1707 §3.)

Non-Consummation and Favor of the Faith Cases

Unlike the detailed provisions of the Latin code on non-consummation cases (1983 *CIC* cc. 1697-1706), the Eastern code simply calls for the observance of the Apostolic See's norms in these cases and in favor of the faith cases, which are not even mentioned in the Latin code (*CCEO* c. 1384).

Ordination Nullity Procedures
(*CCEO* canons 1385-1387; 1983 *CIC* canons. 1708-1712)

The canons in both codes are quite similar in this area. However, if an ordination case is remanded to a tribunal, the Eastern code explicitly precludes the use of the 'summary' contentious process and insists on the observance of the canons on trials in general and on the contentious trial unless the nature of the matter precludes this (*CCEO* c. 1386, §2). The Latin code does not mention the 'oral' contentious process here but is otherwise formulated similarly although it does call for the observance of the canons in the code (1983 *CIC* c. 1710). It also equates the defender of the bond in such cases to the defender in marriage cases as regards rights and obligations (1983 *CIC* c. 1711).

Removal and Transfer of Pastors

(*CCEO* canons. 1388-1400; *CIC* canons. 1740-1752)

Not surprisingly the canons on removing and transferring pastors are largely the same in both codes. However, given the broader provisions for particular law in the Eastern code,[39] it is noteworthy that, unlike the Latin code, the initial Eastern canon admits possible particular law provisions in this area with the approval of the Apostolic See.

The final Eastern canon on transferring pastors refers not simply to the observance of equity but also to a respect for his acquired rights; however, it does not restate the Latin mention of the good of souls as the supreme law (*CCEO* c. 1400; 1983 *CIC* c. 1752).

Penal Procedures

*(*CCEO *title 28: canons 1468-1487;* CIC *canons. 1717-1731)*

After treating penal sanctions in the Church and dealing with substantive issues such as the notions of delict, penalty, and imputability (*CCEO* title 27: cc. 1401-1467), the Eastern code addresses the procedures for imposing various penalties. One chapter deals with judicial procedure in three articles (*CCEO* title 28: cc. 1468-1485), while a notably shorter chapter treats of the imposition of penalties by extra-judicial decree (administrative procedure) (*CCEO* title 28: cc. 1486-1487).

This organization differs slightly from the Latin code. Book VI (1983 *CIC*), which is divided into two parts, deals with various issues on penal sanctions in general and in particular (1983 *CIC* cc.1311-1363; 1364-1399). Part IV of Book VII (1983 *CIC*) is divided into three chapters addressing basically the same procedural issues as the aforementioned Eastern code articles

[39] See Kuriakose Bharanikulangara, *Particular Law of the Eastern Catholic Churches* (Staten Island, NY: Saint Maron Publications, 1996).

(1983 *CIC* cc. 1717-1731). However, the sole canon 1720 on administrative procedure is not treated separately but rather begins chapter two on the development of the process, which deals almost exclusively with judicial procedure (1983 *CIC* cc. 1720-1728).[40]

Before briefly considering the distinctly procedural canons, we should comment on several general issues of procedural relevance surfacing during the Eastern code penal law revision process.[41] These issues actually seem to be more significant than the specific points to be mentioned in the title on penal procedure.

Canons on Penal Sanctions

First of all, greater emphasis is to be placed on a canonical warning before any penalty is imposed (*CCEO* c. 1407); this reflects a somewhat more noteworthy stress on the medicinal character of all Eastern penalties. The Eastern code does not restate the Latin differentiation between censures, which always require a warning (1983 *CIC* cc. 1331-1335; 1347, §1), and expiatory penalties which do not (1983 *CIC* cc. 1336-1338).

Second, the Eastern code more forcefully expresses a preference for judicial penal procedure to protect better the rights of all concerned[42] than its Latin counterpart. While requiring that perpetual penalties be imposed judicially, the latter states that whenever *just (iustae)* causes preclude a judicial process, a penalty can be 'imposed or declared by extrajudicial decree' (administrative procedure) (1983 *CIC* c. 1342, §§1, 2). By contrast, the Eastern

---

[40] For a brief overview of Eastern penal law, see Pospishil, 745-757. For comparative reflections on Latin and Eastern penal law, see John Faris, "Penal Law in the Catholic Churches: A Comparative Overview," *Folia Canonica* 2 (Budapest, Hungary: Pazmany Peter Catholic University, 1999) 53-93; Green, "Penal Law" (*supra*, note 5).

[41] For a brief overview of that process, see Green, " Penal Law," 411-424.

[42] For example, one might note the right to reputation (*CCEO* c. 23; *1983 CIC* c. 220) and the right not to be punished except in accord with the norm of law (*CCEO* c. 24; *1983 CIC* c. 221, §3). While these rights tend to focus on the accused, one should also be attentive to the rights of the ecclesial community and those of victims of ecclesiastical delicts.

code reprobates contrary customs and in principle requires the imposition[43] of a canonical penalty through a canonical trial. However, if *weighty* (*graves*) reasons preclude a penal trial and proofs of the offense are certain, the competent administrative authority may permit the imposition of a penalty by an extra-judicial decree. Certain Eastern penalties, however, may not be imposed administratively: deprivation of office, title, or insignia, suspension for more than a year, demotion to a lower grade, deposition, or major excommunication (*CCEO* cc. 1402, §§1-3).

Third, only those violating a law or precept deliberately or with seriously culpable negligence or ignorance are subject to a penalty (*CCEO* c. 1414, §1). No Eastern canon is comparable to the final Latin canon 1399 providing exceptionally for possible punishment of an especially serious and scandalous legal violation even if no law penalizes such a violation. Hence the Eastern code affirms the so-called principle of legality, *nulla poena sine lege,* without qualifications.

Fourth, the Eastern code presumes that if a penal law or precept is violated, it is done deliberately unless the contrary can be established with moral certitude (*"nisi contrarium probetur")* (*CCEO* c. 1414, §2); hence there is a somewhat higher burden of proof on the alleged offender than in the Latin canon 1321, §3. This provides that in cases of an external violation of a law or precept, imputability (not *dolus* or criminal intent) is presumed unless it is otherwise apparent (*"nisi aliud appareat"*).

Fifth, the Eastern code is much more streamlined than its Latin counterpart in articulating factors exempting from, mitigating, or aggravating imputability; the former refers generically to 'common practice' and 'canonical doctrine' in clarifying such factors (*CCEO* cc. 1413; 1415-1416) However, the Latin code treats of them in some detail (1983 *CIC* cc. 1322-1327).

[43] The Eastern code speaks solely of the 'imposition' of penalties and not of their 'declaration' because it does not provide for *latae sententiae* penalties.

The two codes largely contain the same basic procedural norms, but we will highlight some key differences between the codes.

As regards factors barring a penal action, the Eastern code alone mentions the death or pardon of the offender; however, the provisions on the prescription of such an action as well as an action to enforce a penalty are basically the same in the two codes (*CCEO* cc. 1152-1153; 1983 *CIC* cc. 1362-1363). The Eastern canons, however, seem somewhat more logically situated in the procedural law chapter on actions and exceptions rather than in penal law at the end of the Latin title on the cessation of penalties.

Furthermore, the Eastern code alone notes explicitly that even if a penal action is technically prescribed, a contentious action for damages is not necessarily precluded (judicial arena); and the hierarch may apply opportune administrative disciplinary remedies to protect the public good (*CCEO* c. 1154; see 1983 *CIC* c. 1348).

Before deciding on a penal procedure (administrative or judicial), the Eastern hierarch must consult the accused and the promoter of justice; he may consult as well with two judges or legal experts. This seems to provide better protection for the rights of the accused (*CCEO* c. 1469, §3). However, while the corresponding Latin canon 1718, §3 also provides for such facultative consultation with judges or legal experts, it does not explicitly require consultation of the accused and the promoter.[44]

In the judicial penal procedure, during the pre-sentence discussion phase, the Eastern code alone requires an oral discussion of the various observations and arguments even if they have already been presented in writing (*CCEO* cc. 1476-1477).

---

[44] One might argue, however, that consultation of the accused is in fact called for. Deciding on a judicial or administrative procedure is an administrative act, and, before issuing such, an administrator is to hear those whose rights can be injured insofar as it is possible (1983 *CIC* c. 50; see *CCEO* c. 1517, §1).

For the validity of administrative penal procedure the Eastern code requires an oral discussion involving the hierarch or his delegate and the accused in the presence of the promoter of justice and a notary. However, unlike the Latin canon 1720, 2°, there is no explicit reference to consultation with two assessors before the hierarch renders a decision (*CCEO* c. 1486). Such consultation is geared to facilitating objective and informed decision-making.

The Latin canon 1720 does not explicitly state that its minimal provisions for administrative procedure are for validity; however, given their foundational character regarding the protection of substantive and procedural rights, it seems that such is the case.

Conclusions

Not unlike numerous other areas of the two codes, their procedural provisions are often quite similar. This is hardly surprising since the same pope promulgated both codes and there are numerous common features in the Eastern and Latin canonical traditions.

However, one will probably note a more significant effort at fostering uniform provisions here than anywhere else in the code although that issue is worth pursuing at greater length. Notwithstanding such similarities, there are some interesting differences between the codes in terms of the organization of their procedural provisions as well as the content of individual canons. Such differences are largely related to the different hierarchical organization of the Eastern churches.

These relatively brief reflections have barely scratched the surface of the complex procedural provisions in the two codes. Just as Lawrence Wrenn has provided extraordinarily valuable procedural and jurisprudential insights for canonists for many years, this author hopes that he and others will explore the procedural similarities and differences of the two codes in an in-depth fashion in the years ahead. Hopefully this brief overview may foster ever more informed collaboration of Latin and Eastern canonists in the service of our respective churches.

PRENUPTIAL AGREEMENTS

JOHN J. JOHNSON

Introduction

When only eighteen year old Adam attempted a civil marriage with Bertha, a non-practicing Catholic. Their common life was happy at first, but Bertha eventually left him and their daughter for another man. Adam next cohabited with Claire for eight years; but she, too, abandoned him. Now in his mid-thirties, Adam discovered his need for a more solid religious foundation. He enrolled in the RCIA process in a nearby church and warmly embraced Roman Catholicism.

Regular practice of his new found faith brought him into contact with Doris, a slightly older Catholic widow. They had many common interests and seemed compatible. After he had obtained the lack of form annulment of his first union, Adam and Doris each hazarded a second marriage.

Even before their wedding there were squall warnings. Adam's daughter was thirteen and she and Doris could not establish an affectionate relationship. These tensions did not disappear after the wedding. Doris's adult son was a more serious problem. She doted on him, and he took advantage of her. This situation worsened shortly after the wedding: he broke up with his live-in girlfriend and, to Adam's chagrin, decided to make his home with the newlyweds. Adam resented Doris's attempts to discipline his daughter, and Doris resented Adam's attempts to get her son to clean up after himself and his not fully housebroken dog. When Adam announced that the young man must leave, Doris moved out. Their cohabitation had lasted less than eight months. Within fourteen months of their wedding they had divorced.

Not wanting to jeopardize his relationship with the Church, Adam approached his parish priest about having the marriage declared invalid. In his preliminary deposition Adam mentioned Doris's resistance to his proposal that they sign a prenuptial agreement. He had been justifiably concerned about the welfare of his daughter, still too young to fend for herself. He had therefore wanted to ensure that his modest assets would provide for her in the event of his death, and he did not want to risk having a divorce settlement diminish them.[1] Doris thought his worries about an early death were morbid. She resented his concern that they might divorce and his fear that she would then turn predatory.

Nevertheless, Adam convinced Doris to sign an agreement two days before their wedding. That agreement began as follows:

> This Agreement is made this __ day of ______, 1995, between Adam and Doris.
> The parties are getting married to each other in the immediate future, and both parties have certain assets of their own. Exhibits attached hereto set forth the major assets owned by Doris and Adam respectively.

In consideration of their marriage and of the mutual agreements made in this document, the parties agree as follows:

> a. In the event that the parties' marriage should terminate by a legal proceeding such as divorce, dissolution or a similar legal process, the parties agree that in any division of their property each of them shall be entitled to receive back those assets, or the replacements of those assets, or their equivalent value, which were owned by them individually prior to the time of the marriage.
>
> b. The parties further agree that in the event of divorce, dissolution, or some similar process, they shall equally divide any liabilities that have been incurred during their marriage.
>
> c. The parties further agree that in the event of divorce or dissolution they shall equally divide any assets that have been acquired during the marriage in their joint names or through their joint efforts; however, those assets that have been acquired from earnings or appreciation of assets owned by them individually prior to the marriage and maintained by them in individual ownership during the marriage

[1] It is noteworthy that two women had left Adam for other men. Experience had taught him painfully that intimate heterosexual relationships do end.

shall remain the property of the individual who originally owned the asset that produced the earnings or was subject to the appreciation.

d. The parties further agree that in the event their marriage should end in divorce, dissolution, or by some similar process, neither Doris nor Adam shall be obligated to pay the other any sum of money for spousal support, either temporary or permanent....[2]

In approaching the tribunal, Adam mentioned this agreement only in passing, in the context of his premarital disagreements with Doris. When the judge instructor requested a copy of the agreement, Adam was puzzled. What possible bearing could this document have on his request for the annulment of his marriage? The judge, on the other hand, speculated that Adam's insistence on Doris's signing a prenuptial agreement might be evidence of an implicit exclusion of the *bonum sacramenti*. The text of the agreement, commencing with four explicit references to the possible dissolution of the marriage, made him even more curious about Adam's precise intentions when he married Doris.

Is this kind of prenuptial or antenuptial agreement[3] evidence of partial simulation? This essay proposes to analyze some elements of a preliminary[4] answer to this question. It will begin with an overview of standard jurisprudence on exclusion of indissolubility. A discussion of the code of Canon Law's treatment of documentary evidence will follow. A concluding section will attempt to bring the canonical principles highlighted in the first two sections to bear on prenuptial agreements.

---

[2] This is not a fictitious agreement. All of the illustrating cases in this essay are based on actual situations, although the names of the parties and some circumstances have been changed to protect the innocent.

[3] The essay will assume that *antenuptial agreement* and *prenuptial agreement* are synonymous.

[4] The author underscores the tentative character of his observations. The question has been discussed too little for anyone to be emphatic. Previous canonical considerations of the question include: James H. Provost, "Canon 1066," in *Roman Replies and CLSA Advisory Opinions 1984*, ed. William Schumacher and Richard Hill (Washington, DC: CLSA, 1984) 54-55; Gregory Ingels, "Canon 1066 Prenuptial Agreements," in *Roman Replies and CLSA Advisory Opinions 1990*, ed. William Schumacher and Lynn Jarrell (Washington, DC: CLSA, 1990) 105-107; and Joseph B. McGrath,"

"Everybody knows," writes one rotal auditor, "that marriage is brought into being by legitimately expressed consent."[5] By means of a mutual act of giving the self and accepting the other,[6] for which no human power can supply a substitute,[7] "a man and a woman establish between themselves a partnership of the whole of life,"[8] a community of life and love. Because every individual is unique, no two marriages are identical; but every marriage has certain essential characteristics.[9] By embracing these essential characteristics with their act of consent, the bride and groom establish with each other a *marriage* rather than some other kind of relationship.[10] If their consent is directed towards something that lacks one or more of these essentials, they do not become married, because only an act of consent embracing those essentials can make them so.[11]

Discovering what makes marriage is a task belonging more properly to the theologian than to the canonist.[12] With varying degrees of success, laws can distill the theological insights of the community into norms of action to guide the community, its ministers, and its judges in understanding what is essential to marriage. Thus Vatican II taught:

The Effect of Pre-Nuptial Agreements on the Validity of Marriage," *The Jurist* 53 (1993) 385-395.

[5] *Coram* Giannecchini, 10 April 1992, *RRDec* 84 (1992) 183.

[6] C. 1057, §2 "...*quo vir et mulier foedere irrevocabili sese mutuo tradunt et accipiunt*... ."

[7] C. 1057, §1 "...*qui nulla humana potestate suppleri valet.*"

[8] C. 1055, §1.

[9] C. 1056 specifies "unity and indissolubility" as the "essential properties" of marriage. C. 1101, §1 indicates that there are additional "essential elements" but does not further specify them. On this question see James H. Provost, "Error as a Ground in Marriage Nullity Cases," *CLSA Proceedings* 57 (Washington, DC: CLSA, 1995) 313.

[10] A superb analysis of how a person reaches out towards another in order to establish marriage is Ladislas Örsy, "Matrimonial Consent in the New Code: *Glossae* on Canons 1057, 1095-1103, 1107," *The Jurist* 43 (1983) 63-66.

[11] Giannecchini puts the matter bluntly: "From the law itself it is already determined what marriage is, how it is contracted, what its essential elements and ordination are: all of these things are so removed from the liberty of the contracting party that a will that presumes out of malice, ignorance or fickleness of spirit to act against what has been established by God turns out to be totally without effect." *Coram* Giannecchini, 23 January 1996, in *Monitor Ecclesiasticus* 123 (1998) 417.

[12] Örsy brilliantly summarizes the relationship of the two disciplines (and the limitations of canon law!) in Ladislas Örsy, "The Theological Task of Canon Law," *CLSA Proceedings* 58 (Washington, DC: CLSA, 1996) 1-23, especially 4-6.

> The intimate partnership of married life and love has been established by the Creator and qualified by His laws. It is rooted in the conjugal covenant of *irrevocable* personal consent. Hence, by that human act whereby spouses mutually bestow and accept each other, a relationship arises which by divine will and in the eyes of society too is a lasting one. For the good of the spouses and their offspring as well as of society, the existence of this sacred bond no longer depends on human decisions alone.[13]

Hence canon 1056 maintains that "The essential properties of marriage are unity and indissolubility, which in Christian marriage obtain a special firmness by reason of the sacrament." "From a valid marriage," adds canon 1134, "there arises between the spouses a bond which by its nature is perpetual and exclusive." "A marriage that is *ratum et consummatum* can be dissolved by no human power and by no cause, except death" (c. 1141). From the point of view of the canons, a person who intends to enter marriage desires to establish with his/her spouse a relationship that is permanent, a relationship that is indissoluble. Because marriage in its essence is indissoluble, the person who desires marriage desires, by definition, an indissoluble relationship.[14]

From the premises that indissolubility is an essential property of marriage and that any party who excludes from the object of his/her marital consent an essential property of marriage does not contract marriage, the conclusion follows that anyone who excludes indissolubility from the object of his/her act of consent does not contract marriage. Such a person may wish to establish with another some kind of intimate relationship; but the resulting relationship would lack one of the essential properties of marriage and therefore could not be *marriage* as the Church understands marriage.[15]

---

[13] Vatican II, decree *Gaudium et Spes*, 48, in *The Documents of Vatican II,* ed. Walter M. Abbott, S.J. (New York, NY: Herder and Herder, 1989) 250.

[14] Cormac Burke puts the matter forcefully: "In the conjugal donation, one either gives oneself permanently, or one does not give one's self at all. Therefore whoever consents to marriage necessarily gives *irrevocable* consent.... Those who see conjugal love as naturally implying a total gift have no difficulty in understanding the intrinsic personalist logic of indissolubility, which is simply the consequence, in time, of totality in the gift." Cormac Burke, "The Object of the Marital Self-Gift as Presented in Canon 1057, §2," *Studia Canonica* 31 (1997) 418-419.

[15] One might exclude indissolubility *consciously* and simulate, or do so *without awareness* and be

Rotal auditors acknowledge that a person might exclude indissolubility either *absolutely* or *hypothetically*.[16] In the case of an absolute exclusion of indissolubility the subject unqualifiedly intends that the marriage be dissoluble. The dissolubility of the marriage does not depend on any other circumstance.[17] John T. Noonan, Jr., provides an interesting example of the absolute exclusion of indissolubility. A Portuguese gentleman named Luis had so frequently visited the home of a young woman named Joanna that her parents feared she had lost her reputation. They importuned him to marry her. He agreed to undergo a ceremony of marriage, but under a peculiar condition. On the day before the wedding he insisted that Joanna sign a document promising that, if he married her, she would immediately enter religious life. When she professed her vows, their unconsummated marriage would be dissolved by the law itself.[18] Luis clearly intended to enter a "marriage" that would be dissolved in short order. He did not want to contract an indissoluble marriage.

One hopes this kind of situation is rare, but it is not unthinkable, even today. For example, American military personnel are sometimes stationed in poor and violence-prone countries. It is not inconceivable that young soldiers might "marry" purely to ease the entry of their spouses into the United States, fully intending to dissolve these unions as soon as it became practicable. There have been rotal cases of marriages solely for the purpose of achieving legal emancipation.[19] In these instances *total* simulation rather than exclusion of indissolubility might be the more appropriate *caput nullitatis*; but the parties

---

acting erroneously. See Lynda A. Robitaille, "Simulation, Error Determining the Will, or Lack of Due Discretion? A Case Study," *Studia Canonica* 29 (1995) 397-432, especially 413. Because acting out of an error which determined the object of one's consent is no less invalidating than simulating, this essay will not distinguish between the two figures, however important the distinction is.

[16] Cf., for example, *coram* Palestro, 15 July 1992, *RRDec* 84 (1992) 409; *coram* Giannecchini, 10 April 1992, *RRDec* 84 (1992) 184. Note also the discussion in Edward G. Pfnausch, "Simulated Consent: A New Way of Looking at an Old Way of Thinking," *The Jurist* 55 (1995) 733-735.

[17] Cf., *coram* Palestro, 15 July 1992, p. 409: *"absoluta est exclusio si pars assertam excludat proprietatem, quin pendeat ista negotio a circumstantia quadam...."*

[18] John T. Noonan, Jr., *Power to Dissolve: Lawyers and Marriages in the Courts of the Roman Curia* (Cambridge, MA: The Belknap Press, 1972) 89-96.

[19] *Coram* Fiore, 17 June 1981, *RRDec* 73 (1981) 326-333; *coram* Serrano, 11 December 1981, *RRDec* 73 (1981) 623-630.

involved would clearly be not intending to establish permanent or indissoluble marriages.

The *hypothetical* exclusion of indissolubility might be more common. In this case what is hypothetical is, not so much the *exclusion* of indissolubility, as the emergence of the situation that would justify the simulator in dissolving the bond. The simulator makes the continuation of the bond dependent upon the presence or the absence of some particular circumstance.[20] Huber observes, "The object of the exclusion of indissolubility" in such a case "is … the reservation to oneself of the right or the faculty of sometime dissolving the entire bond… Whoever in consent by a positive act of the will reserves to himself the right of dissolving the bond in the case of an unhappy outcome of the marriage by that very fact excludes indissolubility from his consent."[21]

An example of the hypothetical exclusion of indissolubility is not hard to imagine. Many parish ministers are familiar with FOCCUS, an instrument designed to assist ministers in preparing couples for marriage. The prospective bride and groom react individually to a series of statements. After collating their responses, the minister meets with them to discuss areas of disagreement and issues about which they have not yet communicated. One item to which the parties respond, "Agree," "Disagree," or "Undecided," reads: "I could not under any condition remain married to my spouse if he/she were ever unfaithful to me." Agreeing with this statement might indicate an intention to make the persistence of the bond dependent on a specific circumstance – the other party's never being unfaithful.[22] If Titius really means that under no circumstances

---

[20] Cf., *coram* Giannecchini, 10 April 1992, *RRDec* 84 (1992) 184; *coram* De Lanversin, 15 April 1992, *RRDec* 84 (1992) 352.

[21] *Coram* Huber, 28 September 1995, *RRDec* 87 (1995) 527-528. One notes again Burke's remark, "In the conjugal donation, one either gives oneself permanently, or one does not give one's self at all." Burke, p. 418.

[22] In his thought-provoking study of the canonical presumption that everyone who marries intends to establish the sort of relationship the Church understands by marriage, Jorgensen cites research showing that some people who claim "that they would not get a divorce in the event they found themselves in unhappy marriages" would nonetheless divorce if their spouses proved unfaithful. He comments on "what almost amounts to a social imperative to divorce in cases of such infidelity." Gerald T. Jorgensen, "Culture and Error *Non Simplex* – Not So Rare," *CLSA Proceedings* 62

would he remain married to Bertha if she were ever unfaithful,[23] he is reserving to himself the right to dissolve the bond if that unwelcome condition should ever be verified.

A hypothetical exclusion of indissolubility is not incompatible with genuine marital affection, with anticipation that the marriage will be happy, or with a willingness to work hard at building a community of life and love.[24] "Even if the contracting party never desires to perpetrate the rupture of the bond and in fact [never] rejects a perpetual bond, by the very fact that he wants to reserve securely to himself the faculty of dissolving the bond he poisons the integrity of his consent."[25] The person who excludes indissolubility absolutely does not want the "marriage" to last. The person who excludes indissolubility hypothetically may eagerly desire a lifelong marriage but has already made provisions for its failure.

The difficulty with cases involving any kind of simulation is proof. Although the expression of marital consent may be external and public, the act of consent itself is internal and not available for judicial inspection. The judge can only infer that simulation has occurred from evidence about the alleged simulator's behavior. There are three traditional sources of evidence: the parties (cc. 1530-1538), their witnesses (cc. 1547-1573), and documents (cc. 1539-1150).[26] There are three elements of proof: an admission of simulation,[27] the proportionate reason for simulating, and circumstances implying that the alleged

---

(Washington, DC: CLSA, 2000) 180.

[23] Not everyone who participates in a process like FOCCUS weighs carefully all of his responses. By marking this statement, "Agree," Titius might mean only: "I do not want Bertha ever to be unfaithful to me"; OR "If Bertha were ever to be unfaithful to me, I would be very upset"; OR "If Bertha were ever to be unfaithful to me, our relationship would change dramatically." None of these meanings would be inconsistent with true marital intent.

[24] For example, *coram* Civili, 22 March 1995, *RRDec* 87 (1995) 212; *coram* Huber, 28 September 1995, p. 528.

[25] *Coram* Giannecchini, 10 April 1992, p. 184.

[26] It is not impossible that the intervention of an expert might be useful in some cases involving allegations of simulation. For example, an anthropologist might enlighten the court about cultural factors predisposing someone to reserve the right to divorce under certain conditions; or a psychologist might demonstrate how someone's emotional development did the same.

[27] Possibly pedantically, this author prefers to avoid the term *confession*. According to canon 1536, a *confession* concerns some fact contrary to one's interests ("*Assertio de aliquo facto ... contra se*

simulator simulated.[28] The judge might discover any of these elements of proof in evidence supplied by any of the three sources. The judge might discover evidence of an admission of simulation in the parties' statements, in the testimony of the witnesses, or in documents. Conversely, a private document might demonstrate an admission of simulation, the existence of the reason for the simulation, or the existence of circumstances implying that simulation occurred. The discussion now turns to what the law prescribes about the use of documents as evidence in ecclesiastical trials.

Documentary Evidence

Book VII of the 1983 *Code of Canon Law* treats documentary evidence in eight canons (cc. 1539-1546),[29] not all of which have a direct bearing on this discussion.[30] The treatment begins by recognizing the admissibility of documents as proof in any kind of ecclesiastical trial (c. 1539). Any party to a trial has the right to offer documentary evidence. Any judge has the corresponding obligation to consider with an open mind the significance of any documents the parties wish to submit in evidence. In the light of canon 1452 the judge might also be obliged, at least in cases involving the public good, to require the parties to produce additional documents pertinent to the resolution of the doubt.[31]

---

peracta"). The admission that one simulated may or may not be contrary to one's interests.

[28] For a more thorough discussion of the elements of proof, see John P. Beal, "The Substance of Things Hoped For: Proving Simulation of Matrimonial Consent," *The Jurist* 55 (1995) 749-775; or, much more briefly, John G. Johnson, "Total Simulation in Recent Rotal Jurisprudence," *Studia Canonica* 24 (1990) 410-415.

[29] The parallel treatment in the *Code of Canons of the Eastern Churches* is found in cc. 1220-1225. With respect to the issues considered in this essay, the differences between the two codes are purely stylistic. Both codes somewhat simplify cc. 1812-1817 in the 1917 *Code of Canon Law*. Because the substance of the law remains unchanged, and because commentaries on the former code tended to be more ample, this essay will rely heavily on the insights of the earlier authors.

[30] For example, cc. 1545 (on the judge's authority to order the production of documents) and 1546 (on the obligation to produce documents). This essay will focus primarily on cc. 1539-1542.

[31] Canon 1452: "§1.... Once a case has been legitimately introduced, however, the judge can and must proceed even *ex officio* in penal cases and other cases which regard the public good of the Church or the salvation of souls. §2. Furthermore, the judge can supply for the negligence of the

Tribunal ministers accustomed to processing marriage cases are well acquainted with documentary evidence. The acts of a typical marriage case would include some record of the marriage and a copy of the divorce decree. If the marriage was celebrated in the Catholic Church, the acts might also include a copy of the prenuptial investigation file or at least an official abstract of the information contained in it. In a case involving allegations of psychological incapacity, records of hospitalization or counseling might be critical proof. Moreover, canons 1686 through 1688 describe the procedures to be followed in cases in which a single *documentum* "*quod nulli contradictioni vel exceptioni sit obnoxium*" clearly establishes the existence of a diriment impediment or some deficiency in canonical form. The provisions of canon 1539 therefore constitute no surprise to the judge, defender of the bond, or notary familiar with marriage cases.[32]

The code does not define *document*. Convinced that definitions do not belong in the law, the drafters of this section of the code chose not to include one.[33] The *coetus* likewise rejected the suggestion that, in order to cover tape recordings and other similar kinds of evidence, canon 1539 employ the expression *per instrumenta* rather than *per documenta*.[34] The significance of this decision is unclear. One consultor had objected that "instruments" often lack such things as signatures which make a document more reliable, but the published materials do not demonstrate that the entire *coetus* concurred with his judgment.[35] At least one contemporary commentator insists, "In canonical

---

parties in furnishing proofs or in lodging exceptions whenever the judge considers it necessary in order to avoid a gravely unjust judgment, without prejudice to the prescripts of can. 1600."

[32] Many American tribunals gather testimony from witnesses by sending them questionnaires through the mail. The *affidavits* they return can also be categorized as documents (see Lawrence G. Wrenn, *Procedures* [Washington, DC:CLSA, 1987] 44-45) in which event the bulk of the evidence in a typical marriage case consists of documents.

[33] *Communicationes* 11 (Città del Vaticano: Libreria Editrice Vaticana, 1979) 105. Classical commentaries on the 1917 code agree that the canons concern "Something written by means of which a fact can be established." See, for example, A. Vermeersch and J. Creusen, *Epitome Iuris Canonici, Tomus III* (Rome: H. Dessain, 1946) 89; P. Francisco Xav. Wernz and P. Petrus Vidal, *Ius Canonicum, Tomus VI, De Processibus* (Rome: Gregorian, 1927) 449

[34] *Communicationes* 11 (1979) 105.

[35] Wrenn understands the matter differently: "This chapter heading has been rather pointedly

procedural law, the terms *documentum* ... and *instrumentum* ... are synonymous."[36] Even if tape recordings, videos, and other electronic media are not *documenta* in the strict sense of the term, the canon does not appear to prevent a judge from considering them as them as evidence.[37]

Although eschewing a definition of *documents*, the code does categorize them. Documents may be either private or public, and the latter may be either civil or ecclesiastical. A *public ecclesiastical document* is drawn up by an ecclesiastical office holder, exercising his/her office, in accordance with the formalities of law (c. 1540, §1). A dinner invitation the bishop of Tarsus sends to his parents would not be a public ecclesiastical document because, although it was drafted by an ecclesiastical office holder; it would not involve the exercise of his office and its preparation would not involve any legal solemnities.[38] By contrast, unless it had been improperly prepared, the letter whereby the same ordinary appointed a priest as pastor of one of the parishes in his diocese would be a public ecclesiastical document.

The code recognizes as *public civil documents* whatever the operative civil law classifies as such (c. 1540, §2). An underlying assumption appears to

---

changed from 'instruments' in the 1917 code to 'documents' in the 1983 code in order to exclude tape recordings and the like whose authenticity cannot be certified." Lawrence G. Wrenn, "Book VII Processes [cc. 1400-1752]," in James A. Coriden, Thomas J. Green, and Donald E. Heintschel, eds., *The Code of Canon Law, A Text and Commentary* (New York, NY: Paulist Press, 1985) 979. But a decision not to change the text of a proposed canon in order to include a kind of evidence is not identical with a decision to change the text in order to exclude it.

[36] Joaquin Calvo, "Chapter II – Documentary Proof," in *Code of Canon Law Annotated*, E. Caparros, M. Theriault, and J. Thorn, eds. (Montréal: Wilson & Lafleur Limitée, 1993) 957. Certainly the usage of classical commentators suggests that the terms are synonymous; but if the *coetus* understood the terms as synonymous (and therefore presumably interchangeable) it is difficult to understand why no consultor said so in response to the proposed revision.

[37] So Robert Bourgon, "Chapter II Documentary Proof," in *The Canon Law, Letter & Spirit, A Practical Guide to the Code of Canon Law*, Gerard Sheehey, Ralph Brown, Donal Kelly, and Aidan McGrath, eds. (Collegeville, MN: The Liturgical Press, 1995) 878. Similarly Craig A Cox, "Part II: The Contentious Trial [cc. 1501-1670]," in *New Commentary on the Code of Canon Law*, John P. Beal, James A. Coriden, and Thomas J. Green, eds. (New York and Mahwah, N.J.: Paulist Press, 2000) 1674. One might note as well the provisions of c. 1540, §2: "Public civil documents are those which the laws of each place consider to be such." If civil law recognized the video tape of a civil court hearing as a public document, this canon would appear to oblige a church court to do likewise.

[38] So Wernz-Vidal, p. 449: "A private [document] is a composition by a private person ... or by a public person, but not by reason of [her] public office, or not prepared in accordance with the solemnities of law."

be that the authority of some civil official would stand behind any document civil law would recognize as *public*.

Any document that does not belong in either of these categories is private (c. 1540, §3). For example, personal letters are private documents. Diaries and journals are private documents. Medical records, bills, and cancelled checks are also private documents.

The code distinguishes between *private* and *public* documents because it accords different evidentiary weight to them. Because "a public person has drawn up the [public] document in the discharge of an office, observing the required formalities," the law accepts the truth of what the document reports:[39] "Unless contrary and evident arguments prove otherwise, public documents are to be trusted (*fidem faciunt*) concerning everything which they directly and principally affirm" (c. 1541).[40] No one needs to prove further what a public document directly and principally affirms unless there is strong evidence controverting it.

Canon 1573 can help the reader grasp the reasoning behind this canon. Canon 1573 prescribes that, as a general rule, the testimony of a single witness "*plenam fidem facere non potest*" – cannot constitute full proof. It then acknowledges an important exception: if a *testis qualificatus* gives evidence about something connected with the discharge of her official responsibilities, her testimony can constitute full proof. What is a *testis qualificatus*? Coronata writes that the term is predicated of "any public official with respect to the matters pertaining to her office."[41] In Wernz-Vidal one discovers an explanation for the exceptional deference the law pays to the testimony of a "qualified" witness: "in such a person specially chosen to give public certainty in matters pertaining to

---

[39] Calvo, "Chapter II," p. 959.

[40] The CLSA translation seems weaker than the Latin would allow: *fidem faciunt* means *they make faith* – i.e., they generate belief, they breed conviction. In c. 1573 *plenam fidem facere non potest* could be rendered "cannot constitute full proof" or "cannot fully prove." One might therefore translate c. 1541 as follows: "...public documents *prove* whatever they directly and principally assert."

[41] P. Matthaeus Conte a Coronata, *Institutiones Iuris Canonici*, Vol. III, *De Processibus* (Rome: Marietti, 1948) 229.

his office and often bound by a special oath there is present a presumption that he discharges his office correctly and does not alter the truth in criminal fashion."[42] When the community chooses a person to certify specific kinds of activity, it thereby expresses a willingness to accept the accuracy of that person's testimony about those activities. The canon merely makes this willingness explicit.

Similar presuppositions underlie the code's attitude toward public documents. Behind a public document stands "a public person designated to express the truth in documents and in many cases bound by an oath to faithfully fulfill a public office."[43] The document expresses in written form what the official could testify about orally. For example, if a deacon officially witnesses a marriage, he could testify as *testis qualificatus* that on a given date in a certain place he had witnessed John's and Mary's exchange of consent. After he had properly recorded that information in the appropriate parish marriage register, the certificate of marriage prepared on the basis of that register would reproduce in writing what the deacon could verify *viva voce.*

This analysis makes clear why canon 1541 specifies limits to the evidentiary value of public documents: they constitute proof of "everything which they directly and principally affirm." Coronata sagely comments, "As a general rule a public document can give full proof only about those matters which occurred in the presence of the person who prepared it."[44] The law presumes the accuracy of a notary's testimony about matters she actually witnessed, not about matters she discovered only indirectly. Indeed, the canon's limitation is even stricter: the law recognizes the probative force of only the

[42] Wernz-Vidal, VI, 423.

[43] Ibid., pp. 455-456.

[44] Coronata, III, 252. An example might clarify this observation. A police report is a public document. If a police officer reports what he actually witnessed as an officer, the substance of his report would constitute solid proof of what he witnessed. By contrast, if the officer reports that a suspect confessed to a certain kind of misconduct, the contents of the confession would not have the same weight. The report would prove only that the suspect in question made the admissions to the officer at the specified time. The admissions might, of course, constitute a non-judicial confession; but they would be evaluated as such and not as the direct and principal assertions of a public document.

information the document *directly and principally* asserts. A notary's seal would prove that two parties signed a given contract in her presence. It would not prove that both parties had the mindset normally reflected in that sort of contract.[45] A fairly common formulary for notarized documents claims that the signatory is acting with sound mind, but the notary's seal does not demonstrate anybody's mental health.[46] Unless the notary were also a clinical psychologist, and therefore capable of offering an expert opinion, her prudential judgment on such a point would have no exceptional value as evidence.

From this it follows that a public document does not *directly and principally* affirm all of the information it contains. For example, a typical baptismal register includes the full name of the baptized person, the date and (at least by implication) the place of the baptism, the names of the parents, the names of the sponsors, and the name of the minister of the sacrament. It may also contain notes about confirmation, religious profession, ordination, and marriage. A baptismal certificate prepared on the basis of an entry in a baptismal register will reflect this information, but it will not *directly and principally* assert all of it. Only some of this information will derive from what the pastor knew of his own knowledge when he performed the baptism. The pastor could testify about *this* information as a *testis qualificatus*, and his testimony on these points would constitute full proof of them. He would know that on the specified date in the specified place he baptized the person bearing a certain name. As a private individual he might know of his own knowledge the date and place of the baptized person's birth, but he would not enjoy this knowledge precisely as the minister of the sacrament.[47] Most of the time the pastor will know the date and place of an infant's birth only because the parents have reported the information. The pastor will know the infant's parents only because they present

[45] So Vermeersch-Creusen, III, 91-92. The authors use the example of a contract of buying and selling. The notary can demonstrate that the parties said they were making such a contract. The notary cannot prove that the one party did, in fact, sell and that the other bought.
[46] So Wernz-Vidal, VI, 456.
[47] It is of course possible that the pastor will have performed the baptism immediately after the child's birth, but the circumstances of most baptisms do not allow the pastor to witness the birth.

themselves to him as such. The information recorded in the baptismal register cannot have greater weight as evidence than would the contemporary testimony of the person responsible for the entry. Hence, the baptismal certificate can fully prove the fact of the baptism. It cannot fully prove paternity, age,[48] or the like. Nor would the certificate directly and principally affirm that the individual in question received the sacrament of confirmation (although it might constitute strong evidence that whoever maintained the parish archives had received official notice that the individual in question had done so).

Public *civil* records can require equally sophisticated interpretation.[49] They often contain more information than they *directly and principally assert*. For example, some counties provide especially useful records of marriage. At the top of the page will be the information the couple provided when they applied for their marriage license. At the bottom will appear some record of the notice the courthouse received from the official witness of the marriage. The information contained in the application for the marriage license can assist the judge investigating an annulment case – it can show, for example, that one of the parties was previously married. Although the certificate containing this information is a *public* civil document (especially if the court house clerk authenticated it), the document is not directly and principally asserting that the party in question had been previously validly married. It is asserting at most that on the date on which the couple applied for their license he/she admitted a prior marriage. On the basis of that information the judge instructor may be able to locate documents that do directly and principally assert the fact of the prior marriage. Even without such documents, the judge may be able to discover

[48] Of course, from the fact that a person was baptized on a given date, the conclusion necessarily follows that he was born prior to that date. The certificate thus indirectly affirms the *terminus ante quem* of a person's birth; and at least some governmental agencies accept it as proof of age.

[49] Beal points out that (at least with one category of document) one must sometimes be careful of accepting even what a public civil document directly and principally asserts: "If the [civil] divorce was granted 'for cause,' the transcript of the master's hearing for the divorce court may contain useful information bearing on the issues in a subsequent ecclesiastical process.... However, care must be taken in evaluating these masters' reports. When most divorces in the United States were granted only 'for cause,' there was a strong incentive for parties to collude and to dissimulate in order to obtain the divorce." Beal, p. 760.

sufficient evidence to justify annulling the second "marriage" on grounds of *ligamen.* By itself, however, the civil record of the second marriage would not sufficiently prove the existence of the prior bond.

If there are limits to what a document produced by a civil official in the discharge of her duties can prove, it is not surprising that there are similar limits to the evidentiary value of documents only witnessed by a civil official. "For instance," writes Doheny, "an affidavit might affirm that a certain person appeared before a notary public on a certain day in the presence of certain witnesses and attested to certain facts. The mere affidavit would not, of itself, establish the truth of the facts asserted...."[50] The affidavit would be a public document in form. Its contents, however, would not enjoy the status of full proof. It seems logical to assume that an agreement drafted by two parties (or their attorneys) might enjoy the status of a public document, if signed before a notary public, but that the contents of the agreement might not possess the evidentiary value of the direct and principal statements of public documents.

A decision *coram* Huber provides some guidance:

> If in the presence of a notary someone makes some declaration against the perpetuity of the bond, the record of this historical fact prepared by the notary is public. 'But this mark of being public by no means extends to the declarations contained in the document, which are not known by the notary' (*coram* Sabattani, 26 April 1963, *SRR Dec.* 55, p. 283, n. 4a). Nevertheless no law prohibits the presentation of civil documents to an ecclesiastical tribunal as if they were private documents. They have the same force of evidence as does the 'extra judicial confession' (c. 1542), which the judge must evaluate 'taking into account all the circumstances'... (c. 1537).[51]

The auditor here is analyzing an affidavit a young man made immediately before a marriage he was unwilling to contract. In form the affidavit was a public civil document; but the direct and principal assertions of the document as public were limited to the facts of date and place and the identity of the affiant. The young

[50] William J. Doheny, *Canonical Procedures in Matrimonial Cases,* vol. I, *Formal Judicial Procedure* (Milwaukee, WI: Bruce, 1948) 406.
[51] *Coram* Huber, 28 September 1995, *RRDec* 87 (1995) 528.

man's assertions, which comprised the contents of the document, were not the document's principal and direct assertions. The judge accordingly could not accept those assertions as full proof of the young man's allegations. He could nonetheless admit them into evidence as if they were the substance of a private document.

The code is somewhat circumspect regarding the evidentiary value of private documents. A *private* document has no evidentiary value unless the party who prepared it has acknowledged it or the judge has admitted it into evidence (c. 1542). Because it is a private act, its weight is considerably lighter than that enjoyed by a public document. Its weight is further determined by the way in which it functions as proof. Against the person who signed the document it functions like an extrajudicial confession.[52] The document rather than a witness verifies the fact of the confession. One might imagine a case involving an allegation of *dolus*. Titius marries Bertha because she tells him that she is carrying his child. After the collapse of their common life, Titius alleges that Bertha knew herself to be pregnant by Gaius when she first had sex with him. She therefore willfully deceived him into marrying her. An authentic letter from Bertha to Gaius, postmarked before the wedding and mentioning that she is carrying his child, would be a private document tantamount to an extrajudicial confession that, at the time she was inducing Titius to marry her, she knew (or at least believed) Gaius to be the father of her unborn child. Conversely, an entry in Titius' diary shortly before the wedding indicating his doubts about the paternity of the child and his intention to marry Bertha whoever the father was would be tantamount to an extrajudicial confession that he had not been inveigled into the marriage by a successful fraud.

Obviously a private document should constitute weaker evidence against the persons who did not prepare it. Canon 1542 prescribes that private

[52] The phrasing of the canon implies that the information contained in a private document will adversely affect the interests of its signatories: "*Documentum privatum ... eandem probandi vim habet adversus auctorem vel subscriptorem ... ac confessio extra iudicium facta ...*" (c. 1542). Occasionally, however, a party will present a private document because it supports his/her

documents have against such persons the same evidentiary weight as non-confessional declarations of the parties. In other words, the judge, in the context of his evaluation of all of the circumstances of the case, is to determine what (if any) probative force those documents should have (c. 1536, §2).

Some Attempts at Application

The seventh edition of *Black's Law Dictionary* defines *prenuptial agreement* as follows:

> An agreement made before marriage usu[ally] to resolve issues of support and property division if the marriage ends in divorce or by the death of a spouse. Also termed *antenuptial agreement; antenuptial contract; premarital agreement; premarital contract; marital settlement.*[53]

Anyone who has read *The Lady in White*[54] realizes that marriage settlements traditionally provided for the division of property, not in the event of a divorce, but in the event of the death of one of the spouses. The existence of that sort of antenuptial agreement would not enlighten a judge about the spouses' attitude towards the permanence of their marriage. Even today it is not inconceivable that a couple might make a prenuptial agreement solely to avoid future squabbles over their individual estates. One might hypothesize the case of George and Martha. Both are in their late sixties. Both are widowed. Both have children and grandchildren. Both are financially independent. Neither has the slightest interest in the other's property. In order to allow both to leave their estates to their children and grandchildren, they might enter a premarital agreement whereby each acknowledges the other's right to bequeath his/her property to anyone he/she wishes and each freely renounces all claims to the

---

contentions.

[53] Relying on this definition, this essay uses these presumably synonymous terms interchangeably. The author apologizes if he thereby overlooks subtle differences among them.

[54] Denise Domning, *The Lady in White* (New York, NY: Signet, 1999)

estate of the other.[55] The fact that they made such a prenuptial agreement would not suggest to a tribunal that either of them had intended to exclude permanence from their marriage.

This example shows that the court must carefully consider what a prenuptial agreement says before drawing any conclusions about its value as evidence of exclusion of indissolubility. The existence of the document would always prove that the couple made some kind of agreement before they entered marriage. The contents of the document might or might not illuminate the mindset with which the parties approached their marriage. If a prenuptial agreement contained no references to divorce, it might constitute evidence *against* rather than in favor of allegations of partial simulation. On the other hand, if a prenuptial agreement made explicit provisions for the possible civil dissolution of their marriage, the court might conclude that the couple (or at least one party) consciously entertained the hypothesis that their marriage might be dissolved.

However, the mere fact that the text of the agreement contains references to divorce might not demonstrate that either party was excluding permanence from the forthcoming marriage.[56] One might hypothesize the case of Benedick and Beatrice.[57] Benedick is the eldest son from a family with a successful and very profitable restaurant. The children all own shares of the business, and the family vigorously defends their interests against "outsiders."

---

[55] This author has seen a presumably valid "Prenuptial Agreement" including the following language: "N understands that she may not be a legatee or devisee under M's will and testament which could leave all of M's probate estate to his heirs… M understands that he may not be a legatee or devisee under N's last will and testament which could leave all of N's probate estate to her heirs…. N and M agree to waive and disclaim any and all rights or claims to dower, inheritance, and a distributive share in and to any of the real and personal property of the other."

[56] Ingels, "Canon 1066 Prenuptial Agreements," 106 opines, "…a prenuptial agreement can be viewed as a civilly acceptable means by which the parties and their families are accorded necessary protection in civil law which they deem necessary." McGrath (394) counters that this argument "cannot withstand canonical scrutiny… when in the name of protecting the legal rights of the parties, the prenuptial agreement anticipates and sorts out all of the legal ramifications for the two parties which would flow from a future separation in divorce." He characterizes such a detailed agreement as coming "close to being an advance divorce settlement." On the other hand, the amount of detail contained in the antenuptial agreement might be determined solely by the nature and number of the parties' assets, liabilities, and responsibilities.

Beatrice has two daughters from a previous civil marriage. Benedick's parents are willing to welcome Beatrice into the business *as Benedick's wife*; but they do not want to benefit her daughters, and they fear that a woman who divorced her first husband might divorce her second. To safeguard the business they insist that Benedick and Beatrice make a prenuptial agreement whereby Beatrice renounces any claims to the restaurant in the event of a divorce. It is not inconceivable that Benedick and Beatrice might sign such an agreement to placate the parents and without any personal intentions against the permanence of their contemplated marriage. It is possible that Benedick would have no intention of ever divorcing Beatrice. At most he might have some concern that she might someday divorce him. It is possible that Beatrice has no intention of ever divorcing Benedick but is merely allaying the fears of her future in-laws. In such an event, a judge could not honestly interpret their signatures on the agreement as constituting any kind of confession of simulative intent.

In two hypothetical situations – when the antenuptial agreement deals only with the division of assets in the event of the death of one of the spouses, and when the parties sign the agreement for reasons that have nothing to do with their own attitudes towards the permanence of their marriage – the existence of a prenuptial agreement will not inspire in the judge any conjectures about either party's exclusion of indissolubility. But when at least one of the parties insists on the preparation of a prenuptial agreement, and when he/she further insists that the agreement make specific provisions for the possible civil dissolution of the marriage, it is difficult to avoid the conclusion that he/she entertained the conviction that his/her contemplated marriage (and not just marriage in general) was dissoluble.[58] Whether the judge might further conclude that the party was

---

[57] See William Shakespeare, *Much Ado About Nothing*.

[58] Provost, "Error as a Ground in Marriage Nullity Cases," 309 distinguishes "simple" from invalidating error by describing the former as "one which does not make any difference in one's actions. It is an abstract idea which does not influence the person's will." Believing that marriage in general is dissoluble is an example of "simple" error. The conviction that the marriage one is proposing to enter is dissoluble would not be so simple.

confessing an intention to establish a dissoluble union would depend on the wording of the document and the circumstances under which it was prepared.

Even if the wording of the document did not impress the judge as constituting an admission of simulative intent, the existence of the document might be a premarital circumstance supporting the conclusion that the party was preparing to simulate. In itself the document might be ambiguous. In the context of other circumstances suggesting a favorable attitude towards divorce, it might become clear and convincing evidence. One might imagine the case of Susan whose parents are divorced and remarried (her mother, three times). Two of Susan's three siblings are also divorced. Susan retained her maiden name during the marriage. She kept her own assets in her own name. At her suggestion, she and her former husband deposited their salaries into separate checking accounts and negotiated the payment of their common expenses. She insisted on signing an antenuptial agreement, two thirds of which concerned a possible divorce. These circumstances weave together into a strong argument that Susan did not intend to bind herself in marriage for life.

Perhaps the only certain conclusion this essay can reach is that the canonical significance of antenuptial agreements is in need of further study and more widespread discussion. Speculating imaginatively about situations involving prenuptial agreements may be of academic interest, but it is no substitute for experiencing actual situations in which couples have used them or for studying the mindsets those couples brought to bear on the agreements and their subsequent marriages. If it does no more than to provoke tribunal practitioners to share this experience, this essay may have had some use.

FROM PROOFS TO JUDGEMENT: THE ARDUOUS TASK OF THE JUDGE

AIDAN MCGRATH, O.F.M.

A Useful Premise

At the very beginning of Book II of the 1983 code, entitled "The People of God", a number of canons identify some of the basic rights and obligations shared by all of Christ's faithful. This list of rights and obligations constitutes a major innovation in the 1983 code. Rights and obligations which at one time had been deduced from other parts of the law are now spelled out explicitly. Canon 221 states:

> §1. The Christian faithful can legitimately vindicate and defend the rights which they possess in the Church in the competent ecclesiastical forum according to the norm of law.
>
> §2. If they are summoned to a trial by a competent authority, the Christian faithful also have the right to be judged according to the prescripts of the law applied with equity.

It is very clear that, whenever the rights of a member of the Christian faithful – lay or cleric, religious or secular – become the object of controversy, the person in question has the further right to have the matter resolved in accordance with the provisions of the law. Individuals, thus, are entitled to vindicate their right to marriage by seeking an investigation of the nullity of a previous union; this investigation must be carried out in accordance with the norms of the code.

Those persons who bring a case are to be treated with respect; such people are doing nothing more than what the law entitles them to do.[1] The personal opinions of the personnel of the Tribunal about the issue at stake or about the personalities of the parties are irrelevant. All involved in the process, and especially the judge, must exercise their duties according to the norm of law.

The Object of the Process

According to canon 1400, §1, 1°, the object of an ecclesiastical trial is, among others, "the pursuit or vindication of the rights of physical or juridic persons, or the declaration of juridic facts." The object for each trial is usually identified very clearly in the petition submitted (cf., c. 1504, 1°-2°). The terms of the controversy are settled more accurately at the joinder of the issue (cf., c. 1513). In cases of marriage nullity, "the formula of the doubt not only is to ask whether the nullity of the marriage is established in the case but also must determine on what ground or grounds the validity of the marriage is to be challenged" (c. 1677, §3). The doubt formulated in this way becomes the focus for the investigation; it is the question to be answered at the end of the process, i.e., "has the nullity of this marriage been proved on the ground or grounds of . ....?" This is the question which must be addressed at length and answered by the judge in the sentence or judgement.[2]

By means of the sentence, the object of the trial is achieved and the formulated doubt is resolved. While it cannot be referred to as the ultimate goal of the process, the sentence may be understood as its end product or final act; it is the means by which the object of the trial is definitively determined. While

---

[1] Speaking to the Roman Rota in 1996, Pope John Paul II touched on precisely this point: "it must be remembered that the spouses, who in any case have the right to allege the nullity of their marriage, do not however have either the right to its nullity or the right to its validity. In fact, it is not a question of conducting a process to be definitively resolved in a constitutive sentence, but rather of the juridical ability to submit the question of the nullity of one's marriage to the competent Church authority and to request a decision in the matter" (Pope John Paul II, Address to the Roman Rota, 22nd January 1996, *L'Osservatore Romano*, Weekly Edition in English, n. 5, 31st January 1996, 5).

[2] Canon 1607 states: "When a case has been handled in a judicial manner, if it is the principal case,

the sentence is the final act of the ecclesiastical process, it is also the end product of a process which is internal to the judge. Having gathered all the evidence and finished the investigation, a judge cannot simply decide the case on his or her own whim. The judge must at all times act in accordance with the law and with complete impartiality.[3] The final decision must also be connected to the rest of the process. In coming to a decision, the judge must not only be able to make the connection between the facts of the case and a conclusion concerning the validity or invalidity of a marriage, but also must be able to articulate that connection in a written sentence.[4]

Reaching a decision

Moral certainty

Canon 1608 contains some useful information about how a judge arrives at the sentence or judgement: first and foremost, "for the pronouncement of any sentence, the judge must have moral certitude about the matter to be decided by the sentence" (c. 1608, §1). This concept of "moral certitude" is, perhaps, one of the most important principles in canon law, at least for those canonists working in a tribunal. It is essential that each person working on a particular case appreciates what moral certainty is and what it is not. The classical text for referring to moral certainty is the address of Pope Pius XII to the Roman Rota in 1942.[5] The Pope "places moral certainty between the two extremes of absolute certainty and quasi-certainty or probability."[6] For him, moral certainty ... is

---

the judge decides it through the definitive sentence."

[3] A. Stankiewicz, "I doveri del giudice," in *Il processo matrimoniale canonico: Nuova edizione riveduta e ampliata, a cura di P. A. Bonnet e C. Gullo,* (Città del Vaticano: Libreria Editrice Vaticana, 1994) 308-321.

[4] In her article, L. Robitaille gives some examples of poorly reasoned sentences, e.g., where all the evidence is recapitulated in the sentence and is followed by a decision in favour of nullity without any argumentation of any kind, or where a decision is given after all the evidence has been accepted uncritically, without any evaluation. See L. Robitaille, "Evaluating Proofs: Is It Becoming A Lost Art?," *The Jurist* 57 (1997) 541-542.

[5] Pope Pius XII, Address to the Roman Rota, 1st October 1942, *CLD,* 3: 605-611.

[6] M. Ryan, Title VII, "The Pronouncements of the Judge," in ed. G. Sheehy et al., *The Canon Law: Letter & Spirit,* (Collegeville, MN: Liturgical Press, 1995) n. 3164.

characterised *on the positive side* by the exclusion of well-founded or reasonable doubt, and in this respect it is essentially distinguished from the quasi-certainty which has been mentioned; *on the negative side*, it does admit the absolute possibility of the contrary, and in this it differs from absolute certainty. The certainty of which we are now speaking is necessary and sufficient for the rendering of a judgement ... Only thus is it possible to have a regular and orderly administration of justice, going forward without useless delays and without laying of excessive burdens on the tribunal as well as on the parties.[7]

In dealing with human affairs, it must be remembered that only very rarely will it be possible to be absolutely certain about anything; when dealing with questions of the invalidity of marriage, such certainty is even rarer. Yet the validity of something so sacred as marriage cannot be decided upon something which is seriously open to doubt. The Pope wisely traces the *via media*, and indicates where moral certainty differs from both the absolute certainty of the physical sciences and simple probability. While clearly the certainty required for a decision must be a conviction on the part of the judge, it must have an objective foundation. Thus, according to Pius XII, moral certainty "is understood to be objective, that is, based on objective motives; it is not a purely subjective certitude, founded on sentiment or on this or that merely subjective opinion."[8] It is not instinct or prejudice or personal opinion or suspicion. It must have a basis in what the judge is convinced is true, a conviction which excludes all prudent doubt.

The Source of Moral Certitude

According to canon 1608, §2, "the judge must derive this certitude from the acts and the proofs." From all the evidence gathered in the case, the judge must determine the facts and consider the meaning of those facts; from all the information available in this way, the judge may conclude that the nullity of the marriage has been established beyond reasonable doubt. Such a decision can

[7] Pope Pius XII, *op. cit.*, 607-608.

only be given, however, on the basis of what is contained in the *acta* of the case. Information which the judge may possess from other sources cannot be used in the quest for moral certainty. Canon 1604, §1 states: "it is absolutely forbidden for information given to the judge by the parties, advocates, or even other persons to remain outside the *acta* of the case." All the relevant information should be placed in the *acta*.

Perhaps the clearest commentary on this paragraph is provided by Pope John Paul II in his address to the Roman Rota in 1980:

> Each (judge) must arrive, if possible, at moral certainty concerning the truth or existence of the fact, since this certainty is an indispensable requisite in order that the judge may pass judgement: first of all, so to speak, in his heart, and then voting in the gathering of the judicial college.

The judge must draw this certainty *"ex actis et probatis."* First and foremost *ex actis* since it must be presumed that the *acta* are the source of truth. Therefore, the judge, following then norm of Innocent III, "must examine everything," that is, he must examine the documents carefully, letting nothing escape his attention. Then *ex probatis*, because the judge cannot limit himself to giving credence to affirmations alone; on the contrary, he must keep in mind the possibility that, during the instruction, the objective truth may have been obscured by shadows brought about by different causes, such as the forgetting of some facts, their subjective interpretation, carelessness and sometimes malice and fraud. The judge must act with a critical sense. A difficult task, because there may be many errors, while truth, on the contrary, is only one. It is necessary, therefore, to look in the documents for proofs of the alleged facts, and then proceed to a criticism of these proofs… .[9]

---

[8] Pope Pius XII, ibid., 608.

[9] Pope John Paul II, Address to the Roman Rota, 4th February 1980, *Papal Addresses to the Roman Rota 1939-1994*, ed. W. Woestman, (Ottawa: Faculty of Canon Law, St. Paul University, 1994) 161-162.

"The judge, however, must appraise the proofs according to the judge's own conscience, without prejudice to the prescripts of law concerning the efficacy of certain proofs" (c. 1608, §3). The weighing of evidence is thus a matter of conscience: the judge must be aware of the facts of the case as presented in the evidence and as submitted by the advocate in the form of arguments for nullity; the judge must be equally aware of the Church's teaching on the indissolubility of marriage, its requirements for a valid marriage and the essential elements of Christian anthropology.[10] Having obtained all the information possible or necessary, the judge must weigh up what he or she has received and consider it in the light of the doctrinal and canonical requirements of the Church. All sessions of the tribunal take place after the invocation of the name of God (c. 1609, §3). So the weighing of evidence in one's conscience is a sacred duty.[11] The judge cannot abdicate this responsibility and permit someone else to influence his or her decision. The evidence must be considered, according to the canon, with due regard for the provisions of law concerning the efficacy of certain proofs. This is a further indication of the objective roots and foundation of the process by which a decision is made. It is not left to the whim or mood of the judge. Clear guidelines are already given in the code by which evidence of different kinds is to be weighed. These are to be followed carefully.

---

[10] Useful summaries of this teaching are to be found in various addresses by Pope John Paul II to the Roman Rota, e.g., that of 1986 (in Woestman, op.cit., 187-190); of 1987 (ibid., 191-196); of 1991 (ibid., 214-218); of 2001 (in *L'Osservatore Romano*, Weekly Edition in English, n. 6, 7 February 2001, 3; 11).

[11] "Since the abstract law finds its application in individual, concrete instances, it is a task of great responsibility to evaluate the specific cases in their various aspects in order to determine whether and in what way they are governed by what the law envisages. It is precisely at this stage that the judge's prudence carries out the role most its own; here he truly *"dicit ius,"* by fulfilling the law and its purpose beyond pre-conceived mental categories, which are perhaps valid in a given culture and a particular historical period, but which cannot be applied a priori always and everywhere and in each individual case." (Pope John Paul II, Address to the Roman Rota, 22nd January 1996, *loc. cit.*, 5).

The Provisions of Law Concerning Proofs

In General

The fundamental principles concerning proofs in canon law are contained in canons 1526-1529. It is clear that a simple affirmation or allegation does not constitute proof of anything. Therefore, the person submitting a petition for nullity has the obligation of providing sufficient information and proof to overturn the presumption of law in favour of the marriage (c. 1060). Some things are recognised by the law as not requiring proof. Among these are "facts alleged by one of the contending parties and admitted by the other unless the law or the judge nevertheless requires proof" (c. 1526, §2, 2°). In cases of marriage nullity, it is not uncommon to find both parties agreeing on certain facts. Yet this in itself does not provide proof of the nullity of the marriage. The agreement of the parties about certain facts may well provide a firm foundation upon which the proof of nullity might ultimately rest. Nevertheless, since both are interested parties, their agreement in and of itself does not constitute proof of the point at issue. Nullity of marriage is precisely one of those cases mentioned in the canon where proof is still needed over and above what the parties might affirm.

In marriage nullity cases, as in other cases, any useful type of proof which is lawful can be introduced (c. 1527, §1). The judge may reject certain proofs, e.g., an excessive number of witnesses; the parties may insist that this proof be obtained, but it rests with the judge whether or not to accede to the request (c. 1527, §2). The parties do not have an absolute right to have all the evidence collected which they deem to be relevant. The judgement about the usefulness and relevance of proofs rests ultimately with the judge. Generally, people are to give evidence before the judge. However, the law recognises that this might not always be possible. If that is the case, the judge must make whatever alternative arrangements he considers most suitable (c. 1528).

Sources of evidence

The code lists five major sources of evidence:

Declarations of the Parties (canons 1530-1538)

In all cases of marriage nullity, the primary source of information concerning the consent of the parties at the time of marriage must be the parties themselves. The law gives the judge the faculty of interviewing the parties to elicit the truth; this becomes an obligation if one of the parties requests it, or "to prove a fact which the public interest requires to be placed beyond doubt" (c. 1530). When lawfully questioned, the parties are obliged to respond and to tell the whole truth; if one or both should refuse to respond, the judge must make a judgement concerning the significance of the refusal in connection with the facts to be established (c. 1531). As a rule, in cases where the public good is at stake (these include nullity of marriage), the parties are obliged to take an oath either to tell the truth or to confirm that what they have said is the truth (c. 1532). Knowledge that the evidence was given or confirmed under oath can be a useful indication to the judge who is seeking to discover the full truth in a particular case. Refusal to take an oath is not of itself an indication that the truth has not been told; but the auditor ought to give some idea of the reason for the refusal so that the judge might take that into consideration.

Of great importance in any process is a declaration by one of the parties which is a "judicial confession." According to canon 1535, this is "the written or oral assertion of some fact against oneself before a competent judge by any party concerning the matter of the trial, whether made spontaneously or while being questioned by the judge." The precise importance of this confession is given in the following canon: "the judicial confession of one party relieves the other parties from the burden of proof if it concerns some private matter and the public good is not at stake" (c. 1536, §1).[12] The significance of this in a dispute between two parties over some private matter, e.g., ownership of some object or right, is that the onus of proof has been removed from the other parties. This, in the view of some recent commentators, does not constitute full proof.[13] The judge must still ascertain by whatever means he considers best whether the alleged confession is genuine, since it will entail the party renouncing his or her rights. The judge must also determine whether or not the confession was made on the basis of an error of fact or as a result of force or grave fear (c. 1538).

A separate provision of law deals with cases involving the public good; these include all cases of nullity of marriage. Canon 1536, §2 states:

> In cases which regard the public good, however, a judicial confession and declarations by the parties which are not confession, can have a probative force which the judge must evaluate together with the other circumstances of the case; the force of full proof cannot be attributed to them, however, unless other elements are present which thoroughly corroborate them.

From this it is clear that, in cases of nullity of marriage, the declarations of the parties, whether they are judicial confessions or not, do have a probative value. They cannot be considered as amounting to full proof, but neither can they be dismissed as having no value. In weighing up what the parties have to say it is important to see whether or not both parties agree, whether or not the witnesses agree with the parties, or at the least do not contradict them, whether or not the circumstances of the case are in some way consistent with what is affirmed by the party or parties. In short, these statements of parties must be weighed up in conjunction with other items of evidence and other aspects of the case.

---

[12] This canon is clearly based on canon 1751 of the 1917 code: "*Si agatur de negotio aliquo privato et in causa non sit bonum publicum, confessio iudicialis unius partis, dummodo libere et considerate facta, relevat alteram ab onere probandi.*"

[13] Cf., L. Chiappetta, *Il Codice di Diritto Canonico: Commento giuridico-pastorale, Vol. II, Napoli: Edizioni Dehoniane*, 1988, n. 5421; T. G. Doran, at canon 1536 in *Comentario Exegetico al Codigo de Derecho Canonico*, Vol. IV/2, Pamplona: Ediciones Universidad de Navarra (EUNSA) 1997, 1299-1300; R. Bourgon, "Title IV: The Canon Law: Letter & Spirit," n. 3054.

In some cases of nullity, the judicial confession of a party can be of immense probative value, e.g., the only person who can really know whether or not a party simulated consent, is the party in question; similarly, the evidence of parties is paramount in a case of nullity based on deceit or condition or grave fear.[14] It is vital that the real meaning of "confession" is understood: it is one thing to say during the course of an interview, "I simulated my consent," and something else to say "Because of my career, I made it quite clear before the wedding that I never wanted to have children." The first statement has little or no probative value; the second is a genuine confession which may well be supported by other elements in the case; indeed, such a statement can be very helpful to the judges in understanding what was going on in a case.[15]

It is also vitally important to note that a "judicial confession" is "an assertion of fact against oneself." It is not an opinion or a conclusion, no matter how sincerely and vehemently held it might be. Thus, for example, in cases of nullity where the grounds are located in canon 1095, one might encounter statements like the following: "I was immature at the time of the wedding"; "I just was not fit for the obligations of marriage"; "I was too young and did not realise what I was doing or taking on." Each of these may well be true; each may well be an honest admission by the party concerned who feels some responsibility for the breakdown of the marriage. But none of them is a confession in the canonical sense.

On the other hand, some statements which might be accepted as confessions are the following: "For six years before the marriage, I was a daily drug abuser, taking heroin or cocaine, and robbing people to pay for my habit"; "Every time I look at a woman, I want to go to bed with her; that is how I have always been,

---

[14] R. L. Burke, "La confessio iudicialis e le dichiarazioni giudiziali delle parti," *I mezzi di prova nelle cause matrimoniali secondo la giurisprudenza rotale, Studi Giuridici,* vol. 38 (Città del Vaticano: Libreria Editrice Vaticana, 1995) 23-29.

[15] According to R. L. Burke, the actual distinction between a judicial confession in the strict sense and other judicial statements of the parties loses a little of its force in cases of nullity of marriage, since the principal focus of the investigation is the truth of the marriage and all involved are obliged to speak the truth (*art. cit.*, 18).

even during the courtship; I went out and slept with several women while I was going with my wife"; "Two years before we were married, I spent six months in a psychiatric hospital and I was diagnosed as suffering from paranoid schizophrenia. I have been hospitalised six times since. The doctors told me that I must take my medicine daily. But when I feel fine, I do not take the medicine and I have a relapse." These really are statements or assertions of fact; they have the essential features of a judicial confession. What they mean in terms of the case under investigation is another matter entirely. Of themselves, they do not constitute proof that the marriage of that person was invalid. Yet, the facts established as a result of such a confession might well be the foundation of proof.

In the past, the declaration of a party in a case where he or she had an interest, e.g., nullity of marriage, was regarded as being of little or no probative value.[16] However, during the course of the revision of the 1917 code, interventions by jurists such as Cardinal Felici[17] began to change this gradually. The fruits of their arguments are seen in the current canon: it is for the judge to weigh up what the parties have said and then see what probative value it might have. The evaluation of the evidence must be done according to some kind of objective criteria and it must be done in conjunction with the rest of the evidence and all the circumstances of the case. A judge cannot simply dismiss what one or both parties affirm in a declaration because of a suspicion that he or she is not credible.[18]

---

[16] While canon 1751 of the 1917 code gave a judicial confession the weight of full proof in cases involving private matters, the Instruction *Provida Mater* made it clear that this did not apply to marriage cases: "The judicial deposition of the parties is not sufficient to constitute proof against the validity of the marriage" Sacred Congregation of the Sacraments, Instruction *Provida Mater*, 15th August 1936, *Acta Apostolicae Sedis* 28 (1936) 337, art. 117; *CLD 2:* 500.

[17] P. Felici, "Formalitates iuridicae et aestimatio probationum," *Communicationes* 9 (Città del Vaticano: Libreria Editrice Vaticana, 1977) 175-184.

[18] Indeed, the Pope has urged judges to pay special attention to the value of these judicial statements by parties: "I would like to call your attention to a procedural issue: it concerns the discipline in force regarding the criteria for evaluating declarations made in a trial by the parties. Undoubtedly, the chief demands of true justice, which are certainty of the law and the attainment of the truth, must be reflected in procedural norms that provide protection from the arbitrariness and carelessness which cannot be allowed in any juridical system, much less in canonical legislation. However, the

Similar care must also be taken when considering what the code describes as an 'extra-judicial confession', i.e., a statement made by a party to someone outside of the ecclesiastical process. Again, such a statement can only be a statement of fact, not simply an opinion. In weighing the significance of such a confession, the judge must take into account factors such as the circumstances in which the confession was made, its connection with other features of the case, when it was made, etc. If the extra-judicial confession was made at a time before the process began, it is described as having occurred *tempore non suspecto.* Since there was no vested interest for either party at this stage, the statement can have considerable weight. On the other hand, if the confession was made to someone after the process had begun, it might be an indication that one of the parties was seeking to construct a case rather than permit the truth to be uncovered. In any case, no conclusion may be made unless the judge takes account of the other circumstances.

Canon 1679 holds special importance when considering the declarations of parties in a case of nullity of marriage. Canon 1679 states: "Unless there are full proofs from elsewhere, in order to evaluate the depositions of the parties according to the norm of can. 1536, the judge, if possible, is to use witnesses to the credibility of those parties in addition to other indications and supporting factors." Ordinarily, the judge will weigh the evidence given by the parties in conjunction with what has emerged from the witnesses. However, the law makes it clear that the judge can use supplementary sources of evidence in order to arrive at a decision: this includes evidence of the credibility of the parties, usually in the form of letters of credibility issued by the parties' parish priest, other clergy, or someone in the community who is above suspicion. What the parties have said must then be weighed in the wider perspective of other indications and supportive elements. It must be stressed here that what is at stake

---

fact that Church law places the ultimate criterion and the decisive element of the judgement itself precisely in the judge's conscience, and thus in his free conviction, albeit derived from the acts and proofs, demonstrates that a useless and unjustified formalism should never prevail to the point of suppressing the clear dictates of the natural law." (Pope John Paul II, Address to the Rota, 15th

is the parties' affirmation of certain facts which the judge must then interpret. Such a canon will be useful in those cases where the ground of nullity is based on the more classical grounds (e.g., simulation, condition, impediments, etc.). As will be made clear later, the interpretation of facts in cases based on canon 1095 normally requires also the assistance of experts; nevertheless, even in those cases, the rule of canon 1679 may be important in determining the facts of a case. This canon is tantamount to a reproduction in the 1983 code of the traditional "moral argument" used in the consideration of cases of dispensation *super matrimonio rato et non consummato.*[19]

Documents (canons 1539-1546)

The canons distinguish between two types of documents which might be used as evidence in a marriage case: public documents and private documents.

- Public documents – These may contain some information about a fact or facts which are relevant to the case. These might be ecclesiastical in nature, e.g., the pre-marriage enquiry might contain a note from the priest charged with the preparation of the couple for marriage; or they might be civil, e.g., a civil marriage certificate, or a police report.

- Private documents – those of a medical nature and other private documents:
  Documents of a medical nature may be clinical records of a doctor who cared for one of the parties during a hospitalisation or period of treatment before marriage, or soon afterwards. Such records, for example, might help establish the existence of a serious psychological disorder at the time of the marriage. Of course, it will be necessary to have the prior permission of the party before such documents can be released. They should be interpreted in the same way as reports from experts introduced by the tribunal;

February 1995, in *L'Osservatore Romano*, Weekly Edition in English, n. 7, 15th February 1995, 2).

[19] Cf., Sacred Congregation of the Sacraments, Instruction *Catholica Doctrina*, 7th May 1923, *Acta Apostolicae Sedis* 15 (1923) 404, art. 60, §1; *CLD* 1:781. I. Gordon sees canon 1679 as extending this principle to all nullity cases; cf. *Novus processus nullitatis matrimonii: iter cum annotationibus* (Romae: Pontificia Universitas Gregoriana, 1983) 33, n. 143.

> Other private documents may be a diary, correspondence which one or other of the parties has kept. These too may prove to be a key to understanding the mind of the parties at the time of marriage.

Before making an assessment of the contents of any document, the judge must make sure that it is the original document or an authentic copy and has not been tampered with (cf., cc. 1543-1544). Unless it is otherwise obvious, "public documents are to be trusted concerning everything which they directly and principally affirm" (c.1541). Thus, for example, the notes of a priest in the pre-marriage papers might constitute proof that the priest had certain reservations about the proposed marriage; they do not prove the nullity of that marriage. Of course, the existence of an authentic document establishing the fact of an earlier marriage, or demonstrating the nature of the marriage between the parties can indeed prove the invalidity of the marriage in question. Documents of a private nature, on the other hand, may be considered as declarations of the persons who wrote them and are to be evaluated in accordance with canons 1536, §2 and 1537 (cf., c. 1542).

The testimony of witnesses (canons 1547-1573)[20]

The taking of evidence of witnesses is a normal part of the process for investigating claims of nullity of marriage. These witnesses are people who will have known one or both of the parties around the time of the marriage – either beforehand or during the early days and weeks of the married life. The code gives some broad indications concerning who may and may not be witnesses (cf., cc. 1549-1557). Whoever is admitted as a witness, regardless of their relationship to the parties, must tell the truth to the judge who questions them (c. 1548, §1). When dealing with witnesses in a case, it is vitally important to bear

[20] The evaluation of all the proofs properly belongs to the judge in the decision-making phase of the process. However, as is clear from the canons, a certain amount of evaluation or weighing of the evidence must also be done by those who actually receive the testimony of witnesses. Of course, it will be for the judge to determine the ultimate value of the evidence obtained, a decision based *inter alia* on a consideration of the testimony itself, the methods used to gather it, of the evaluation of the auditors.

in mind how they are to be questioned (cf., cc. 1558-1571). If these norms are followed carefully, it is likely that the evidence obtained will be of assistance to the judge in determining the truth of the case.

Some of the norms merit a closer look:

- *As a rule, "each witness must be examined separately"* (c. 1560, §1). This is the best practice, especially when dealing with family members in a case. If the evidence can only be taken in the home of the witnesses, there is the temptation to hear them all at once. However, individual examination allows the revelation of some material which the witness might not wish to disclose in front of other members of the family. There is also the risk that a witness might testify under the influence of someone else if he or she was not interviewed individually and alone, something which was raised explicitly in the course of the revision of the code.[21] Of course, it is possible that the witnesses might insist on giving evidence together, e.g., in the case of elderly parents of one of the parties. In such circumstances, the judge must exercise his or her discretion and make a prudential judgement.[22] It will be for the judge to determine later what probative value such testimony might have.
- *"[T]he judge, the judge's delegate, or an auditor examines the witness"* (c. 1561). The questioning is not to be done by the defender of the bond, or the advocates for the parties, even though they may be present (c. 1678, §1). If they have questions which they wish the witness to answer, "they are to propose them not to the witness but to the judge or the one who takes the place of the judge, who is to ask the questions" (c. 1561). At no stage may the parties be present for the interrogation of witnesses (c. 1678, §2). By adhering to this norm, the evidence obtained from the witnesses should be objective in nature and not coloured by any particular interest in the case. Of course, when family members are involved, it is not unusual to find a certain bias for or against one of the parties. The judge must take this factor into account when considering the *acta* as a whole.
- *Before the interview begins, the judge is required "to call to the attention of the witness the grave obligation to speak the whole truth and only the truth"* (c. 1562, §1). A further indication of the

---

[21] During the revision of the code, at the meeting of 22nd November 1978, the possibility was discussed of giving the judge the possibility of examining more than one witness at a time. This was rejected and the consultors explained: "*...nisi enim testes seorsim singuli examinentur, probabilius sub influxu depositionis aliorum suam depositionem facient*" (*Communicationes* 11 [Città del Vaticano: Libreria Editrice Vaticana, 1979] 114-115 at canon 204).

[22] Cf., R. Bourgon, "Proofs," n. 3088, note 3.

value of the testimony of witnesses is the fact that it ought to be given under oath; however, if a witness refuses to give the oath, he or she is to be heard without taking the oath (c. 1562, §2). The judge ought to make some note of the reason for the refusal, e.g., a conscience problem, lack of faith, etc., and give some indication of its likely implications for the value of the evidence (cf., c. 1568).

- *Of great practical assistance to the judge who must weigh up the case are the provisions of canon 1563 concerning the questioning of the witness: "the judge is first of all to establish the identity of the witness, then ask what relationship the witness has with the parties, and, when addressing specific questions to the witness concerning the case, also inquire about the sources of his or her knowledge and the precise time when the witness learned what he or she asserts."* Before considering anyone's evidence, it is essential that the judge is satisfied that the one being interviewed is, in fact, the witness nominated and not an impostor. Then it is vital to know just how well the witness knew the party or parties of whom he or she is speaking: a family member or very close friend will be expected to know quite a lot about one of the parties, but not necessarily of the other; a neighbour may have lived next door to the parties for years but may be aware of little or nothing of relevance to the investigation. It is also essential to discover the precise source of the witness's information: did he or she actually see what is being asserted? Did he or she hear it in person, or was it conveyed by hearsay? Is it first hand knowledge or merely common gossip which no one has bothered to verify? Was it learned at the time, or was it told to the witness only within the past few weeks? If the judge is to have a solid basis for deliberation, he must be satisfied that he is in possession of facts and not just hearsay, gossip or opinion.
- *The manner in which the interview takes place is also important to consider when weighing evidence.* According to canon 1564, "the questions are to be brief, accommodated to the mental capacity of the person being questioned, not comprised of several points at the same time, not deceitful or deceptive or suggestive of a response, free from any kind of offence, and pertinent to the case being tried." Sometimes, when reading the evidence of witnesses, it might appear that they have information which they did not claim to have. Closer inspection of the *acta* reveals that they are simply responding "yes" or "no" to long, leading questions. The purpose of the interview is to find out what the witness knows; it is not to create corroboration for the other parties; nor is it to record what the judge thinks the witness ought to have known.

A skilled interviewer will know how to engage the witness in conversation and will find out exactly what he or she does remember – no matter what implications this might have for the overall case. Canons 1565-1567 make clear the method to be used in gathering evidence: the questions are not to be made known in advance; the answers are to be given orally, and are to be written down. Exceptions to these norms are also indicated and these should be noted if they have occurred in a particular case. All of these will have an impact on the role of the judge in coming to a conclusion.

The Weighing of the Evidence of Witnesses

If satisfied that the testimony of the witnesses has been obtained in accordance with the norm of law and that it appears to be complete or at least sufficient, the judge is now faced with the task of weighing it up to determine what probative value, if any, it has. Canon 1572 gives a series of criteria for weighing the evidence; some of these are internal to the evidence itself, some are intrinsic to the case, and some are extrinsic:

> In evaluating testimony, the judge, after having requested testimonial letters if necessary, is to consider the following:
>
> 1° what the condition or reputation of the person is;
> 2° whether the testimony derives from personal knowledge, especially from what has been seen or heard personally, or whether from opinion, rumour, or hearsay;
> 3° whether the witness is reliable and firmly consistent or inconsistent, uncertain or vacillating;
> 4° whether the witness has co-witnesses to the testimony or is supported or not by other elements of proof.

First and foremost, the judge must consider the condition of the person, i.e., marital and social status, religious practice, relationship to the parties, possible biases or hostilities, etc. This information is usually available to the judge from the *acta*. In addition, the judge must also consider the honesty and truthfulness of the witness, which should also be evident from the *acta*. If there is any doubt or misgiving in the mind of the judge, or if this information is lacking in the *acta*, the judge can request testimonial letters, i.e., character references, for the witnesses.

Secondly, the judge must consider the source of the information received: clearly, if it was something seen or heard personally by the witness, it will have much more value than a rumour or something which was reported second hand or third hand. Again, the judge must be careful to ascertain that the witness was recounting facts, not just opinions or gossip. For example, a useful witness might say: "I was with him regularly before marriage; every evening we went to the pub; he would drink at least ten pints before he left; I never saw him go home sober after work"; a less than helpful witness might say: "I know he was an alcoholic; everyone knew he was drinking; it was often said that he had a problem." Without further probing, the latter statement does not shed any light on the facts. Of course, the fault with the statement might be that the evidence was not well taken. However, the judge cannot presume that; the judge can only make a decision on the basis of the actual evidence before him. If the judge believes that the manner of taking evidence was deficient, the witness can be recalled for further questioning (cf., c. 1570). But any lacuna might well be filled when the original testimony is read in the light of the remainder of the *acta*.

Thirdly, the judge must take into account the manner in which the witness testifies: does he or she always say the same thing? Is he or she consistent and coherent in the narration of events? Or are there times when the witness is unsure of what was happening? Does the witness change his or her mind during the interview? What is the reason for this? Was the witness perhaps nervous at the beginning of the interview? Did a later question trigger a memory of some incident which gives more or less weight to what is being said? Was the witness scrupulous, not wishing to state as fact something which he or she had only heard, albeit from a reputable source? The judge must weigh up all these factors carefully before taking account of any particular witness's testimony.

Finally, the evidence of each of the witnesses and of the witnesses as a whole must be considered in conjunction with the rest of the evidence. Is the testimony corroborated by the other evidence? Is it consistent with it? Is it actually contradicted by it? Obviously, the testimony of witnesses which is corroborated by other sources of evidence is more valuable in the quest for the truth than testimony which is at odds with what others have said or alleged. If the testimony of witnesses is contradicted by the parties or other witnesses or items of evidence, then the judge has a serious dilemma to resolve since he or she can only pronounce judgement based on the truth.

The Juridical Value of One Witness

In marriage cases, it is not uncommon to find that the number of witnesses is very small. Occasionally, only one witness may testify. Such a situation does not mean that the evidence of that witness is of no value. Canon 1573 states: "the testimony of one witness cannot produce full proof unless it concerns a qualified witness making a deposition concerning matters done *ex officio*, or unless the circumstances of things and persons suggest otherwise." The evidence of one witness alone, following the ancient axiom *testis unus testis nullus*, does not amount to full proof of any case. Yet the law makes it clear that there are exceptions: if the witness in question was a 'qualified witness', or if circumstances persuade otherwise. The concept of a qualified witness is worthy of note. It refers to someone who testifies in a case, not on a personal basis, but on the basis of some official involvement, e.g., the priest who officiated at the wedding, a doctor to whom the party confided, a policeman who was called to the house during a domestic quarrel. If the information given by such a witness is directly relevant to the case, then the judge may conclude that he has the truth before him and proceed to judgement.

Even if the sole witness is not qualified, that testimony may amount to full proof when considered in the context of other pertinent circumstances.[23] This was made very clear in two responses of the Apostolic Signatura which are listed as sources for this canon.[24] These responses showed that moral certainty could be obtained where the parties agreed in their declarations, where there was no suspicion or doubt of collusion, where there was at least one witness above suspicion, and where there were present the other elements of evidence, such as presumptions, indications and *adminicula*.

Experts (canons 1574-1578; 1680)

According to canon 1680, "in cases of impotence or defect of consent because of mental illness, the judge is to use the services of one or more experts unless it is clear from the circumstances that it would be useless to do so." The norm of law is quite unambiguous. The intervention of experts in cases of nullity being considered under canons 1084 and 1095 is mandatory, not optional. This was made even clearer in a more recent intervention by the Apostolic Signatura.[25] While the norm admits of an exception, that exception must not become an alternative rule. Without the intervention of a properly qualified expert, there is a very large danger of the confusion of roles. The judge's role is to judge, after hearing all the evidence, the merits of the case before him. It is not to make clinical judgements upon which a further decision will be made. It is vitally important that the judge remains aware of the distinction and separation of the roles.

The fundamental role of the expert is to be found in canon 1574: "the assistance of experts must be used whenever the prescript of a law or of the

[23] C. A. Cox, "The Ordinary Contentious Trial," in *New Commentary on the Code of Canon Law*, ed. J.P. Beal, J. A. Coriden, T. J. Green, (New York/Mahwah: Paulist Press, 2000) 1691-1692.
[24] Supreme Tribunal of the Apostolic Signatura, rescripts 10 November 1970 and 2 January 1971, in X. Ochoa, *Leges Ecclesiae*, vol. IV (Rome: Commentarium pro Religiosis, 1974) cols. 5917, 5963.
[25] Supreme Tribunal of the Apostolic Signatura, Prot. N. 28252/97 VT: Question regarding the use of experts in marriage nullity cases, in *Forum* 9 (1998) 1, 35-38.

judge requires their examination and opinion based on the precepts of art or science in order to establish some fact or to discern the true nature of some matter." They are thus to assist the judge in arriving at an understanding of the truth. They are appointed or admitted by the judge (c. 1575) who may also exclude them or object to them (c. 1576). They do not replace the judge. Experts always remain subordinate to the judge in a case. According to canon 1577, §1, "the judge is to determine in a decree the individual items upon which the services of the expert must focus"; in addition, it is the judge who supplies to the expert whatever information he or she might need to complete the task, and who determines the time frame for the preparation and submission of the report (cf., cc. 1577, §§2-3). The law also gives guidelines to the expert concerning the writing of the report: "experts must indicate clearly by what arguments or other suitable means they gained certainty of the identity of the persons, things, or places, by what manner and method they proceeded in fulfilling the functions entrusted to them, and above all on which arguments they based their conclusions" (c. 1578, §2). Experts are not to be treated as infallible or as gods. Like all those who participate in a process, they are subject to the law. They must explain themselves in terms which others can understand. They are not to draw up a report of a few lines giving their conclusions only; rather they are to explain carefully the method and means by which they came to their conclusions. If the report does not fit the requirements of law, "the judge can summon the expert to supply explanations which later seem necessary" (c. 1578, §3).

Yet, even when satisfied with the report, the judge is still not to consider himself replaced by the expert. Canon 1579 states:

> §1. The judge is to weigh carefully, not only the conclusions of the experts, even if they are in agreement, but also the other circumstances of the case.
>
> §2. When giving reasons for the decision, the judge must express what considerations prompted him or her to accept or reject the conclusions of the experts.

It is the judge who must give a final determination of the case. Although it may be very important, the report of the expert remains only one source of evidence in a case. The judge must weigh up that report in the light of all the other information that has been uncovered and presented. It is the judge who must decide whether the report is consistent with the rest of the evidence, whether it corroborates it, or whether it contradicts it; and it is the judge who must decide on the significance of this.

For example, it is not unknown for witnesses from the family of a party in a marriage case to speak well of their loved one, glossing over certain traits of his or her personality which might be relevant to the plea for nullity: "she was a lovely person; she was always very well adjusted; she had no problems growing up; she was lively and liked to be with friends"; but when a report is received from a psychiatrist who has interviewed this same woman and reviewed her medical records, we might find remarks that are rather different: "she is very manipulative; she is very secretive; she drank excessively, frequently ordering doubles when out in company; she is very promiscuous and had several sexual partners even during the courtship; she has no sense of guilt or personal responsibility for the hurt she may cause others."

The judge must decide whether he will accept the "positive" and bland image of the party conveyed by the family, or the "negative" and more colourful image presented by the expert. Whatever the judge decides, he or she must be able to explain it in the context of the rest of the *Acta*. If the marriage in question lasted thirty years and broke down after the woman suffered some kind of trauma, perhaps the family's evidence is accurate after all; if the marriage lasted only a couple of years which were marked by frequent absences of the woman from the home, infidelity and drunkenness, then perhaps the expert's report might well the more accurate representation of what happened.

Some Guidelines for a Dialogue with Experts

When dealing with experts, it will be necessary for the judges to read their reports carefully. From the jurisprudence of the Rota and canonical literature, it is possible to identify in a broad manner some useful guidelines for use in the dialogue between judges and experts:

- Judges should seek to have reasonably clear notions about the area of psychology involved in a particular case. This information is readily available in standard textbooks of psychology or psychiatry.
- Judges ought to study all the *acta* before reading the report of the expert. In this way they may be better able to weigh the expert's report and relate it to all the other circumstances of the case.
- Judges must be sure of the honesty of the expert, and his or her moral standing.
- Judges must consider the competence and technical skill of the expert; they should examine the method used to ascertain whether or not it was truly scientific. It would be a serious error on the part of the judge to accept a conclusion which was not well founded.
- Judges must make sure that the expert has verified the sources on which the report was based, i.e., was there an examination of the party or parties, or was there an examination of the *acta* alone?
- Judges must ask whether the expert has made use of all the information made available or whether the report is based only on a selective interpretation of some things said by the parties.
- Judges must make certain that the findings of the expert are expressed correctly and professionally, without any personal preferences for the parties.
- Judges must decide if the conclusions of the expert are to be accepted or rejected and must state the reasons in the sentence. Additional experts may be appointed in order to verify the findings of the first expert. The final decision as to the value of all experts' opinions and their bearing on the case is and remains the exclusive province of the judge. The judge must always remain the *peritus peritorum.*
- Judges must bear in mind the different concept of certainty which prevails in the field of psychology and psychiatry. Thus, what an expert indicates as "certain" cannot simply be considered as such in the canonical sense. Conversely, what an expert sometimes expresses in a cautious and qualified manner may well be sufficient in the circumstances for the Judges to reach *moral* certainty.

- Judges must always translate the conclusions of the experts into categories of the juridical order, e.g., it is for the judge to decide from his or her study of all the *acta* whether or not a particular difficulty constituted the impediment of impotence; or whether or not a particular condition constituted a defect of consent which rendered the marriage invalid, i.e., whether it was lack of sufficient use of reason, grave lack of discretion of judgement, or inability to assume the essential obligations of marriage.[26]

Presumptions (canons 1584-1586)

A supplementary source of evidence, and a useful aid in the weighing of other items of evidence is provided by presumptions. What they are and where they might be found is described in the code: "A presumption is a probable conjecture about an uncertain matter" (c. 1584); but "the judge is not to formulate presumptions which are not established by law unless they are directly based on a certain and determined fact connected with the matter in dispute" (c. 1586). The best-known presumption in the code relating to marriage is that of canon 1060 which states that marriage enjoys the favour of the law. Other presumptions include that of canon 1101, §1 about the words or signs used in expressing consent; that of canon 1061, §2 about the presumption of the consummation of the marriage after co-habitation; and that of canon 1096, §2 concerning the minimum knowledge required for consent.

Alongside these legally sanctioned presumptions are others which the judge may use. These are the so-called *praesumptiones hominis*. Many of those used are based on the solid jurisprudence of the Rota, e.g., from the fact that a marriage lasted many years or that several children were born, it can be

---

[26] Cf., A. Jullien, *Juges et avocats des tribunaux de l'Église* (Rome: Catholic Book Agency, 1970) 420-424; E. M. Egan, "The Nullity of Marriage for Reason of Insanity or Lack of Due Discretion of Judgement," *Ephemerides Iuris Canonici* 39 (1983) 41-42; G. Versaldi, *L'oggettività delle prove in campo psichico,* (Brescia: Editrice Morcelliana, 1981) 191-202; Z. Grocholewski, "The Ecclesiastical Judge and the Findings of Psychiatric and Psychological Experts," *The Jurist* 47 (1987) 465-466; T. G. Doran, "Some Thoughts on Experts," ed. J. A. Alesandro, *Marriage Studies: Reflections in Canon Law and Theology*, vol. 4 (Washington DC: CLSA, 1990) 167-168; A. Mendonça, "The Role of Experts In 'Incapacity to Contract' Cases," *Studia Canonica* 25 (1991) 435-436; 440-446; A. McGrath, "At the Service of the Truth: Psychological Sciences and Their Relation to the Canon Law of Nullity of Marriage," *Studia Canonica* 27 (1993) 390-392.

presumed reasonably that both parties were capable of marriage;[27] "a psychosis is presumed to render a person incapable of positing a valid act of marriage consent, at least for lack of due discretion of judgement, when it is proved to have been in an advanced stage both before and after the marriage in question."[28] Within jurisprudence, there is a clear hierarchy of presumptions: a presumption can be described as "light" (*levis*), i.e., the conjecture is possible but unlikely; or "serious" (*gravis*), i.e., the conjecture is very possible, but there is still room for reasonable doubt; or as "vehement" (*vehemens*), i.e., the conjecture is so strong that it cannot easily be refuted.

Presumptions of this kind can be a useful source of subsidiary proof. But they are no substitute for hard facts. In December 1995, the Apostolic Signatura issued a decree formally denouncing the use of a table of presumptions which was in common use in some tribunals.[29] These appear to have reduced the quest for moral certainty to a quasi-mathematical formula: if certain facts were established (i.e., not contested), then the following binding conclusions could be drawn and nullity declared. A cursory glance at the list reveals that they are not presumptions in the sense of canon 1584, but a series of broad generalisations with little or no validity.

Presumptions are not to be dismissed lightly, as the jurisprudence of the Rota shows. On their own, presumptions can prove nothing; taken in conjunction with the evidence of the parties and other established facts, however, they can help the judges to reach moral certainty. If presumptions are not based on certain and determinate facts, they have no probative value at all and they do not constitute a substitute for a properly argued and reasoned sentence.[30]

---

[27] R. Palombi, "Il valore delle *praesumptiones*," in *I mezzi di prova nelle cause matrimoniali, Studi Giuridici, vol. ??* (Città del Vaticano: Libreria Editrice Vaticana, 1995) 101-102.

[28] E. M. Egan, "The nullity of marriage for reason of insanity or lack of due discretion of judgement," 43.

[29] Cf., C. Scicluna, "The Use of 'Lists of Presumptions of Fact' in Marriage Nullity Cases," *Forum* 7 (1996) 1, 45-67; U. Navarrete, "Comentario al decreto della Segnatura Apostolica sulle cosidette presumptions of fact," *Periodica* 85 (1996) 535-548.

[30] "Because presumptions involve hard work and careful reasoning, there can be a tendency to avoid

Conclusion

Having received all the proofs presented in a case and having studied them and evaluated them carefully in accordance with the norm of law, the judge must come to a decision concerning the nullity or validity of the marriage in question. In order to declare the marriage in question invalid, the judge must have attained moral certainty and this must have resulted from a careful weighing and consideration of the evidence presented in the case following the general principles outlined above. According to Pius XII, "the judge must ... decide according to his or her own knowledge and conscience whether the proofs adduced and the investigation undertaken are or are not adequate, that is, sufficient for the required moral certainty regarding the truth and reality of the matter to be decided."[31] In the final analysis, the decision of the judge remains a free act on the part of the judge. It is the result of a interior process by which the judge becomes convinced of the truth of the situation. A recent commentator has remarked: "The weighing of the evidence is both a science and an art. It is, as well, a great challenge. Judges are charged to assess the evidence and reach a decision according to their own consciences. That judgement of conscience is to be guided by the law and jurisprudence concerning the efficacy of various types of proof. But the freedom and responsibility of the judges to weigh the evidence in order to discover the truth is crucial."[32] Yet it is not enough for the judge to declare that he or she is satisfied that the truth has now been revealed. Rather, in conformity with the principles for evaluating each item of evidence, the judge must be able to articulate that process and be able to explain it to the parties in the written sentence.

---

their use. Or, on the other hand, there can be a tendency either to create presumptions rashly or uncritically to accept presumptions made by others. Yet, in the process of conducting the trial and seeking the truth, judges cannot abdicate their responsibility to formulate and apply well-reasoned presumptions." (C. A. Cox, in "The Ordinary Contentious Trial," 1700) See also L. Robitaille, "Evaluating Proofs," 557-558.

[31] Pope Pius XII, Address to the Rota, 1st October 1942, *loc.cit.*, 609.

[32] C. A. Cox, "The Ordinary Contentious Trial," 1716-1717.

At all times, judges must act according to the highest standards. They must act in accordance with the law and not allow themselves to be influenced by any preconceived ideas or prejudices. All personal antipathies and sympathies must be left aside when weighing evidence. The parties in a case, regardless of their "worthiness" or their merits, are entitled by the law of the Church to have their case processed and considered in accordance with the norms of law. Correspondingly, the judges who make decisions have the obligation to respect the parties' rights and to understand and interpret the facts of a case in the light of the teaching of the Church, the constant jurisprudence of the Roman Rota and canonical doctrine. In doing that, they are fulfilling the "arduous task"[33] entrusted to them.

[33] "The arduous task of the judge – that of treating responsibly difficult cases, such as those involving psychic incapacities for marriage, and always taking into consideration human nature, the vocation of humans, and, connected with this, a correct conception of marriage – is certainly a ministry of truth and charity in the Church and for the Church." (Pope John Paul II, Address to the Rota, 5th February 1987, *loc.cit.*, 195).

CANONICAL MINISTRY IN SERVICE TO THE CHURCH

KEVIN E. MCKENNA

Introduction

The Roman Catholic Church for centuries has utilized its own internal rules of law and procedures to guide the lives of the faithful in good order. Pope John Paul II described the importance of the role of law in the ecclesial community when he promulgated the Code of Canon Law in 1983, which he called an act of collegial solicitude. The law provides for the well being of the entire Church, "an indispensable instrument to ensure order both in individual and social life and also in the Church's own activity."[1]

But the law in itself is useless without judicial wisdom, the proper application of law to concrete circumstances and situations by those involved in canonical ministry. The words of Pope Paul VI to the Roman Rota could be applied just as well to others involved in church law: "Your wisdom alerts mankind and strengthens it in its effort to apply reason, justice and law as the noble and only way of achieving a better and more peaceful order in human relations."[2] This article will offer some reflections on canonical work as a ministry of service to the Church, as the praxis continues to unfold in the era following the Second Vatican Council. After reviewing some general observations made by recent popes concerning the role of law in the Church today, it will highlight two specific challenges to the canonical minister: role of theology in identifying the values that must be proclaimed and maintained in the

---

[1] John Paul II, *Sacrae Disciplinae Leges*, in *Code of Canon Law, Latin-English Edition, New English Translation* (Washington, DC: Canon Law Society of America, 1998) xxx.

[2] Paul VI, "The Role of the Judiciary in the Life of the Church", in William Woestman, ed., *Papal Allocutions to the Roman Rota, 1939-1994* (Ottawa: St. Paul University, 1994) 130.

community by the law, and the "ministry of justice." It will conclude by presenting a practical result of these two challenges: the marriage tribunal in service to the Church.

Pope Paul VI and the Role of Canon Law

In 1963 Pope Paul VI used the occasion of his address to the Roman Rota to discuss his vision of the role of the canon lawyer in the modern Church. Pope Paul was convinced that canonical procedures had to be imbued with a spirit of justice. Justice would best be promoted by the fostering of participation of all members of the Church in its life, while promoting a careful and thoughtful emphasis on the proper role of law without any exaggeration of its place in the Church. "It [justice] will appear rather as one facet of ... life – truly an important one – but also one serving the life of the communion as such and leaving to the individual believer the freedom and responsibility ...needed to build up the body of Christ."[3]

Pope Paul also hoped to dispel the myth that the Second Vatican Council had in someway dispensed with the need for any formal legal system in the Church. Legal systems, he believed, would always be needed to assist in the orderly carrying out the of the gospel demands. It would also be important in protecting the true freedom of the individual Church members: "How true it is that a human without law is no longer human! How true it is in practice that a law without an authority to teach, interpret, and enjoin easily becomes obscure, annoys and vanishes."[4]

An important part of justice is subsidiarity, the principle that the higher authority or structure should intervene only when the common good requires it and that suitable discretion should be granted at the appropriate level. There must be a new way of looking at power and authority in the Church. Any hint of

---

[3] Pope Paul VI, "Justice in Service of the Gospel, " in Woestman, 141.
[4] Ibid., 113.

arbitrariness in the legal system must be avoided. Authority must be viewed as service and those who hold office must constantly look to the good of those for whose sake their authority is exercised. The Gospel, far from abolishing authority, institutes and establishes it and places it at the service of others. Jesus wanted his community to be a spiritual and visible reality, but structured and joined in unity with external norms. Therefore, canon law must devote itself to the spirit of love which is its first law.

A basic distinction between the Church's administration of law and that of its secular counterpart is the emphasis of canon law on equity: justice tempered with the sweetness of mercy. "[I]f societal life requires the determination of human law, nevertheless, the norms of this law, inevitably general and abstract, cannot foresee the concrete circumstances in which the laws will be later applied."[5] It was Pope Paul's hope that the spirit of law embodied in such traditional principles as canonical equity would imbue the ecclesiastical judge with moderation and mercy in his/her ministry, taking into account the human person and the demands of a given situation "which may compel the judge to apply the law more severely, but ordinarily they will lead [the judge] to exercise it in a more human and compassionate manner."[6] Such an approach to law as envisioned by PopePaul would infuse the juridical procedures as well: "You want the justice, which you must exercise with canonical equity, to be speedier, more gentle, more even-tempered."[7]

At times the Church has been negatively influenced by the civil law and secular court procedures within which it has found itself and has even taken upon itself some of its more negative features. Again, Pope Paul stated: "It is unfortunately true that the Church, in the exercise of her power, whether judicial (procedural) or coercive (penal) has in the course of the centuries borrowed from

[5] Ibid., 118.
[6] Ibid., 120.
[7] Ibid., 122.

civil legislation certain serious imperfections, even methods which were unjust in the true and proper sense, at least objectively speaking."[8]

Paul VI worked tirelessly for a vision of law which would implement a vision of the Second Vatican Council. In addressing the Rota he said: "The law is not for the law's sake, but both law and judgment are at the service of truth, justice, patience and charity – virtues which constitute today more than ever what should stamp the character of the ecclesiastical judge."[9] The virtues which should characterize the canonical minister are love and humanity. "What shines forth most in your mission is precisely Christian charity, which adds greater dignity and greater fruitfulness to the equity of judgments that was the source of so much honor for Roman law."[10]

Theological Perspective and the Dispensation of Justice

The canonical minister must interiorize the values which the law wishes to dispense. Pope Paul, recognizing that the canonical minister must be imbued with the values which the law holds dear, reminded the Rotal judges of the specific ideals of the canonical minister as the servant of justice:

> You need impartiality ... and that presupposes a profound and unshakeable honesty. You need disinterestedness, because there is a danger that courts can be under pressure from extraneous interests – greed, politics, favoritism, and so on. You need concern, so that you will take the cause of justice to heart because you are aware that it is a lofty service for him who is just and merciful, and righteousness (Ps. 112 [111]: 4), "righteous judge (2 Tim 4:8), "faithful and just" (1 John 1:9).[11]

Paul VI saw new and expanded possibilities for the canonical minister in service to the Church in the aftermath of the Second Vatican Council. Just as the Council would dramatically change the contours of theological speculation,

---

[8] Pope Paul VI, "Judicial Authority in the Contemporary Church," in Woestman, 109.
[9] Ibid., 110.
[10] Pope Paul VI, "Freedom of the Children of God and the Necessity of Law", in Woestman, 98.
[11] Ibid., 99.

so too, a "new way of business" for the canon lawyer would require a wholly new theologically informed legal mentality.

Such a perspective has a long tradition in the Church. In the medieval period, as exemplified by such canonists as Hostiensis, there was a clear appreciation of the role of theology. In such matters, it was thought that the role of canon law should be to formulate in a clear and practical way the Church's dogmatic tradition and that religious principles derived from theology should permeate Christian legislation.[12] Hostiensis frequently supported the law with theological arguments and there is much in his whole approach that is in harmony with this idea of canon law as a practical expression of theology.

Such thinking concerning the relationship between theology and law has once again been restored and accentuated. It is clear that canon law and the canon law specialist can never define completely the Church and its mission which the Second Vatican Council in its constitution Lumen Gentium described as "mystery."[13] The role of law is better clarified and described when its relationship to theology is explored.

Canonists such as Ladislas Örsy have been instrumental in developing the complementary roles of law and theology. Örsy has developed a theory which he calls the "doctrine of horizon." [14] He posits that mental operations are essentially dependent on and limited by their field of vision. During the past, the field of canon law was limited by some of the times and cultures in which it found itself. For example, since the 16th century, the whole body of canon law had been placed into the horizon of the Council of Trent. Ecclesiastical law had

---

[12] Clarence Gallagher, *Canon Law and the Christian Community* (Roma, Università Gregoriana, 1978) 91.

[13] See for example, *Lumen Gentium* 3: "The Church – that is the kingdom of Christ already present in mystery – grows visibly through the power of God in the world" in *Vatican Council II: The Conciliar and Post-Conciliar Documents*, ed. Austin Flannery (Newtown, Australia: E.J. Dwyer, 1992) 351.

[14] Ladislaus Örsy, *Theology and Canon Law: New Horizons and Interpretation* (Collegeville, MN: Liturgical Press, 1992). See especially chapter two, "New Attitudes of Mind: Searching for New Horizons," 18-34.

become very narrowly focused to serve as an instrument of defense against both internal and external enemies.

A new theological horizon which sought to embrace the welfare of the whole human family was a development of the Second Vatican Council. The role of theology is to provide the community with values, an overall vision and self-definition, while canon law is asked to provide norms for action, for the appropriation of those values which are meant to serve the community. "Thus the two worlds meet. If they join and work together in harmony, there is a wholeness, a true integrity of life in the community from which peace follows. If they do not work in harmony, the community is divided 'in its spirit'; there is a split between what it sees and what it does." [15] Each value that the Church promotes must be permeated by its God-given supernatural purpose. Canon 1752 summarizes the spirit of the entire code: "the salvation of souls ... must always be the supreme law." All law must have a redeeming quality; that is, the Church must have a legal system that speaks emphatically of herself as servant, faithful to its servant-leader and founder, Jesus Christ. Law can be a valuable and redeeming tool, helping the community to achieve its common servant ideals and values as these are articulated by theology: the call to canonists to protect individual dignity and respect for each person.

Rights and the Ministry of Justice

One of the key ministries of the canonist is in advocacy, assisting a person who needs legal representation in a variety of fora. One of the many contributions Pope John Paul II has made to the Church is in his outstanding commitment to defending the dignity of the human person and promoting respect for human rights. The Church, the pope believes, has a duty in a world

---

[15] Ladislaus Örsy, "Integrated Interpretation: Or, The Role of Theology in the Interpretation of Canon Law," *Studia Canonica* 22 (1988) 252.

that is frequently characterized by injustice to be a strong defender of the human person:

> As the Church's self awareness has developed, the human – Christian person has found not only the recognition but also, and above all, an explicit, active and balanced defense of personal basic rights in harmony with those of the ecclesiastical community. This, too, is a duty the Church cannot renounce.[16]

The canonist can help the wider community by its own discipline, by an affirmation of those he or she is called to represent as a person endowed with "universal, inviolable and inalienable rights and invested with a transcendent dignity."[17]

Respect for the dignity of the human person is, in John Paul's view, at the core of proper protection of human rights. As he has indicated in many of his writings, particularly the social encyclicals, the Church addresses in its teaching the concrete individual as included in the mystery of redemption. This concern is the principle which inspires the Church's social doctrine, which has developed in a systematic way throughout its history, but especially the last century. This doctrine focuses on the human being as the individual is involved in a complex network of social relationships. But the true identity of each individual is known only through faith. This social doctrine is an instrument of evangelization, proclaiming God and the mystery of salvation in Christ to every human being. Because her activity today meets with particular difficulties and obstacles, the Church devotes herself to new energies and new methods of evangelization to safeguard the transcendence of the human person. "When the Church proclaims God's salvation to man, when she offers and communicates the life of God through the sacraments, when she gives direction to human life through the commandments of love of God and neighbor, she contributes to the enrichment of human dignity."[18]

---

[16] Pope John Paul II, "The Church and Protection of Fundamental Human Rights", in Woestman, 153.
[17] Ibid., 154.
[18] Pope John Paul II, *On the Hundredth Anniversary of Rerum Novarum* [Centesimus Annus]

The place of the person and the dignity that must be accorded to each person was addressed at length by John Paul's encyclical, Evangelium Vitae, (The Gospel of Life). John Paul has described the eclipse within contemporary culture of the sense of God and of the human. When a sense of God is lost in a secularized culture, the sense of the human being is also threatened – the human no longer sees the transcendent character of the human being. In such a context, suffering, a factor of possible personal growth, is always seen as an evil, to be opposed and avoided.

The Gospel of Life is concrete and personal, consisting of the proclamation of the person of Jesus, who said, "I am the way and the truth and the life" (Jn 14:6). Through these words, actions and the person of Jesus, humanity is given the possibility of knowing the complete truth concerning the value of human life. Human reason can also know its essential traits.

The human being has been given a sublime dignity based on the intimate bond which unites each individual to God; in the human being shines forth a reflection of God. All who commit themselves to following Christ are given the fullness of life: the divine image is restored, renewed and brought to perfection in them. Whoever believes in Jesus and enters into communion with him has eternal life because that person hears from Jesus the only words which reveal and communicate to his existence the fullness of life. The dignity of this life is linked not only to its beginning, to the fact that it comes from God, but also to its final end, to its destiny of fellowship with God in knowledge and love of him. "Thus the deepest elements of God's commandment to protect human life are the requirement to show reverence and love for every person and the life of every person."[19] With such a strong articulation by Pope John Paul II concerning the dignity of the human person, it is clear that the mindset of each canonist must be carefully attuned to the promotion of this dignity by protecting the rights which are due the human person.

(Washington DC: United States Catholic Conference, 1991) no. 55, 103.

[19] Pope John Paul II, *The Gospel of Life* [Evangelium Vitae] (Ottawa: Canadian Conference of

The law seeks to provide protection by it use of various administrative procedures and judicial processes that enhance the dignity of the human person. The Church must protect the rights of the individual person, but it must likewise promote and protect the common good, which may even at times require the imposition of penalties, so that the rights of all are protected. Such an orientation fits into John Paul's association of law with a pastoral vision, since they both have the same goal: the salvation of souls. It will be impossible to lead souls toward the kingdom of heaven without the minimum of love and prudence that is found in the commitment to seeing that the law and the rights of all in the Church are observed faithfully.

In the minds of both Paul VI and John Paul II, law continues to have many redeeming roles in the contemporary Church which must be promoted by the canonist. It must help to maintain the communio of all the Christian faithful. It must be vigilant in protecting human rights and making sure that there are available venues for recourse when someone feels aggrieved, that his or her rights have been violated or compromised. The Church in its legal system must mirror justice, showing itself to the world as a society living the values of justice which its founder sought to preach and teach. The Church must also make sure that its officials and administrators work assiduously to promote in their own judicial activity the values of the law. Finally, those who administer justice in the Church should refrain from a rigorous and unbending approach to law when mercy and compassion, which are in fact encouraged by the law, should prevail.

It has been the canonical tradition to see itself within the context of the Church as a visible society as well as the community of the faithful drawn together by the Spirit of God. The stability of the body will, to a great extent, be dependent on the smooth operation of the organization. This smooth operation will be, in turn, dependant on the existence of a recognized body of legal norms ordering and delimiting the various spheres of authority and responsibility and the acceptance of these regulations as binding by the members of the Church.

Catholic Bishops, 1995) no. 41, 72.

One of the welcomed developments of the Second Vatican Council was its emphasis on rights, especially basic human rights. The Catholic Church, by means of its particular theological perspective on humanity and the human person, has provided a distinctive shape and context to the concept of human rights. The basis for the Church's perspective in this area is the dignity of the human person, grounded in the biblical account of the first human's creation in the image of God, as well as the two central doctrines of Christian revelation: the Incarnation and the Redemption. The consultors from the Pontifical Commission for the Revision of the Code of Canon Law gave great emphasis to the role of rights in the revised code. They proposed, and the principle was accepted and confirmed at the Synod of Bishops of 1967,[20] that the essential object of canon law is the determination and safeguarding of the rights and obligations of each member of the Christian faithful. Some effort has been made toward concretizing the work of justice in the code itself. The lives of clerics and religious men and women as well as those of all the Christian faithful should reflect the call to social consciousness and a particular awareness, for example, making sure that ministers and employees are given just remuneration for their services and fulfilling the obligation, imposed especially on clerics and religious, not to tolerate sexism or racism within the Christian community. In addition, pastors are required to be attentive to social justice, since justice is so clearly a part of the gospel they are called to proclaim.[21] The role of canon law in the arena of human rights is a significant one, even while it leaves to theology the task of discerning the particular social teachings that are appropriate and necessary at a particular time.

The Church will be judged concerning human rights by its own practice. Its prophetic defense of human rights and the dignity of the human person can only be credible if the Church itself is perceived by others to be just. Its service to justice and human rights thus pledges the Church to a constant

---

[20] *Communicationes* 2 (Città del Vaticano: Libreria Editrice Vaticana, 1969) 82-83.

[21] See for example, c. 528 which outlines the obligations of the pastor: "...he is to foster works by

examination of conscience and to a continuous purification and renewal of its own life, laws, institutions, and conduct.

Rather than utilize trial procedures to resolve conflicts concerning rights, civil law and recent canonical developments have looked to due process. While the internal judicial procedures for remedies can sometimes be seen as cumbersome and time-consuming, canon law itself encourages parties to turn first to alternative forms of dispute settlement when they are available to resolve differences before considering more formal court procedures. The judge is "not to neglect to encourage the parties to collaborate in working out an equitable solution ... perhaps even employing the services of reputable persons for mediation" (c. 1446, §2) All the Christian faithful "are to avoid lawsuits...as much as possible and resolve them peacefully as soon as possible" (c. 1446, §1).

The recent Year of Jubilee 2000 AD called for new ways to be a Church of justice, perhaps revitalizing diocesan mediation boards gone dormant or even beginning to fashion alternative dispute resolution processes where lacking. In this way secular models used so successfully by many civil jurisdictions, can be transformed, imbuing them with Christian notions of forgiveness, peacemaking and fraternal charity.

Theological Values and the Implementation of Norms: the Marriage Tribunal

The place that has become identified in the minds of most people with the practice of canon law is the diocesan tribunal, used primarily as a marriage court for Catholics (and others) seeking a declaration of nullity.

The Church proclaims through its magisterium the sacredness and sacramentality of the marriage bond in which Christian spouses mirror and give witness to Christ's union with his people. It has, at the same time, taken

---

which the spirit of the gospel, including issues involving social justice, is provided..."

cognizance of the pain and anguish of the many who have not, for one reason or another, been able to live this teaching in its fullness.

The process for the declaration of nullity provided by the Church can be understood only within the broader context of the Church's marriage law. This, in turn, requires a theological understanding of the Church's sacraments as encounters between the Lord Jesus and the Christian believer. Church law attempts to ensure the integrity of those encounters. Marriage law attempts to safeguard the integrity of this relationship, not only for the benefit of the parties themselves, but for the benefit of the Christian community as well.

Although the process is a juridical one in which precise norms and processes are followed, canonists involved in this area like to see themselves as being involved in service to God's people. In fact, many tribunals are actively attempting to serve the pastoral needs of the Church and of the petitioners who seek an examination of the validity of their marriage.

Besides conducting a judicial inquiry, the staff of the average tribunal often spends an enormous part of their time dealing with the raw emotions and fears of petitioners (and respondents) whose lives have in many cases been deeply scarred by their experience of a broken marriage. Many of these people are still hurting deeply and feel alienated from the Church. The shock, denial and anger that accompany divorce can also have devastating impact upon the ecclesiastical proceedings. The importance of a non-judgmental and compassionate listener cannot be overestimated. It may turn out, for instance, that this is not the appropriate time for the party to begin proceedings and the tribunal staff member must help the petitioner make that painful assessment. As one official of a tribunal has commented: "Tribunal personnel need to be aware of the fact that they are often dealing with people who are still hurting deeply, people who at times feel very alienated from the Church, people who are laden with a great deal of guilt."[22]

---

[22] Patrick Power, "Pastoral Role of the Tribunal," in *Catholic Tribunals: Marriage, Annulment and Dissolution,* ed. Hugh F. Doogan (Newtown, Australia: E.J. Dwyer, 1990) 1.

The importance of the Church to the divorced person at this time cannot be overstated. The message of God's faithful love, present throughout one's life, needs to be especially articulated to address the feelings of powerlessness that the experience of divorce can engender. Although this is a legal process, many tribunal staff members find that they might be the only representatives of the Church who are in a position to minister to the petitioner and to provide on occasion something as simple as a listening heart.

It is the judge who must bear the most serious burden in the exercise of a compassionate yet impartial approach in reaching a determination. Lawrence Wrenn has well summarized the role of the canon lawyer as well as the judge:

> The challenge ... is the same for all judges, both rotal and local. They must know their own culture and their own times. They must be able to perceive, and to weigh, and to create suitable, enlightened norms by which justice can be rendered. They must avoid the extremes of being insensitive on the one hand, and pandering on the other. They must be neither too legalistic nor too romantic, neither too demanding nor too excusing. They must, above all, show forth the ability of the Church to treat people as individual persons of the community and not just as cases or stereotypes. Only in this way can jurisprudence continue to be the "ars boni et aequi" for each succeeding generation.[23]

The canonist must attempt to show that good law is an aid to the community of believers. The vitality of the Christian household is promoted and sustained when the law helps it to identify the various gifts of the Spirit that must be properly ordered to be effectively utilized. Canon lawyers, as followers of the Lord and interpreters of church discipline, must always do their work with love and true concern for the people of God and their rights.

---

[23] Lawrence G. Wrenn, *The Invalid Marriage* (Washington, DC: Canon Law Society of America, 1998) 6.

JUSTICE AND EQUITY: AT WHOSE EXPENSE?

AUGUSTINE MENDONÇA

Introduction

S.M. Waddams, a scholar in Canadian civil law, rightly says that justice is an elusive word. According to his explanation, whether one agrees with him or not, the term commonly means "that point of view on a particular issue that I hold myself," as "justice, for the workers," or "let us fight for justice." He maintains that sometimes the word, justice, is deliberately meaningless, as when the clergyman prays for peace with justice in southern Africa, or a just settlement to the transit strike. Because every conflict involves opposing interests, or conflicting values, it is impossible to satisfy every litigant all the time. Therefore, Waddams emphasizes the fact that "if disputes are resolved by fair procedures before an impartial tribunal honestly trying to give rational and consistent reasons for its results, we will not satisfy every litigant all the time, but we will come close as humanly possible to administering justice." It seems then the hallmarks of administration of justice are a fair trial, impartiality, honesty and rational and consistent reasons for the decision rendered. Waddams insists that "the difficult and interesting cases are those that bring the contrasting principles at issue into sharp conflict and compel a choice between them. It is the attempt to make that choice rationally and consistently which we can reasonably call the administration of justice."[1] Is this possible in our systems? Sometimes this might seem like an impossible task!

Equity by definition is justice administered with mercy and compassion. Therefore, because equity is essentially justice, it may be just as elusive as justice itself, and yet it has been regarded as the cornerstone of canonical procedures of which the salvation of souls is the ultimate goal.

The concepts of justice and equity are intrinsically linked to the dignity of the human person as culturally defined. It is also equally linked to the inviolability of the human person and to the rights and obligations inherent in every person. The Second Vatican Council eloquently discoursed on human dignity and rights of persons particularly in the Pastoral Constitution on the Church in the Modern World, *Gaudium et spes,*[2] and in its Declaration on Religious Liberty, *Dignitatis humanae.*[3] The General Assembly of the Synod of Bishops made the issue of rights in the Church its focal point when it published the ten fundamental principles guiding the revision of the code.[4] Again, in his apostolic constitution *Sacrae disciplinae leges,* John Paul II said "that the mutual relationships of the faithful may be regulated according to justice based upon *charity,* with the rights of individuals guaranteed and well-defined."[5]

The spirit of the conciliar teaching is clearly reflected in canons 221 (*CCEO* c. 24) and 223, §1 (*CCEO* c. 26, §1) which lay down the fundamental principles

---

[1] S.M. Waddams, Introduction to the Study of Law, 2nd ed. (Toronto: The Carswell Company Limited, 1983): 5-6.

[2] Second Vatican Council, Pastoral Constitution on the Church in the Modern World, Gaudium et spes, 7 December 1965, in Acta Apostolicae Sedis (=AAS), 58 (1966): 1025-1120; English translation in Austin Flannery (general editor), Vatican Council II, vol. 1, The Conciliar and Post-conciliar Documents (=Flannery I), New Revised Edition (Northport, NY: Costello Publishing Company, Dominican Publications, 1996): 903-1001, especially pp. 913-924. Chapter I is wholly on "The Dignity of the Human Person."

[3] Second Vatican Council, Declaration on Religious Liberty, Dignitatis humanae, 7 December 1965, in AAS 58 (1966): 929-946; English translation in Flannery I, pp. 799-812.

[4] Synodus Episcoporum, "Principia quae Codicis iuris canonici recognitionem dirigant a Synodo Episcoporum probata," 7 October 1967, in Xaverius Ochoa (ed.), *Leges Ecclesiae post Codicem iuris canonici editae, vol. III, Leges annis 1959-1968 editae* (Roma: Commentarium pro Religiosis, 1972) no. 3601, col. 5253-5257, especially principles 5, 6, and 7.

[5] See John Paul II, Apostolic Constitution, Sacrae disciplinae leges, 25 January 1983, in Code of Canon Law, Latin-English Edition, New English Translation, prepared under the auspices of the Canon Law Society of America (Washington, DC: Canon Law Society of America, 1999): xxxi. The English translation of canons used in this study is from this source.

governing the vindication and defence of one's rights according to the norms of law. These principles may be summarised as follows:

First, all Christ's faithful, irrespective of their social or ecclesial status, have certain inalienable rights in virtue of their personhood rooted both in natural law and in ecclesial law by baptism.

Second, nobody has the right to deny or prohibit the exercise of those rights without a *serious* and *just* cause.

Third, even when an action is considered necessary to curtail the exercise of such rights, Christ's faithful have the right to defend and vindicate them before the competent ecclesiastical forum in *accordance with the law.*

Fourth, when judged before a competent court, they have the right to be judged in accord with the provisions of law, *to be applied with equity.* It is in this principle that we find the meeting of *justice* and *equity*; and the Church correctly recognizes this as *a right.*

Fifth, the application of penalties must be done in strict compliance with the norms of law. This implies that the first consideration to be given by the judge in imposing or declaring ecclesiastical penalties is for the well being of the person concerned, without, of course, neglecting the common good.

Sixth, a person's rights are not absolute. They are justiciable only within the context of the common good. Therefore, the law expressly states that, in exercising their rights, Christ's faithful, both individually and in associations, must take into account the common good of the Church, as well as the rights of others and their own duties towards others.

Any person or institution entrusted with the responsibility of making decisions which involve fundamental human dignity and rights of persons in the Church ought to keep in mind these principles when exercising or fulfilling their functions. This is not an easy task because issues of rights are truly complex. Sometimes we may be correctly tempted to ask: How do we mete out justice and equity in complex cases in which opposing rights and obligations militate against each other. Is it really possible to find justice applied with mercy and compassion?

We shall reflect upon the above-mentioned fundamental principles which embody the spirit of justice and equity within the context of three concrete cases of transfer and removal of pastors, suspension, declaration of an impediment to exercise priestly ministry and dismissal of priests. This study will follow a very simple analytical method with a narrative style in reviewing these cases in order to demonstrate how difficult it is to find justice and equity in a given case. After reading each case which will be presented, the reader may be tempted to ask: Where is justice and equity in this case? And, also, ask: "Justice and equity: at whose expense?"

Transfer of Pastors

The bishop of Galloway (Scotland) decreed the transfer of three of his pastors against their will in a diocese-wide reshuffling of priests. The priests involved placed recourse all the way to the Apostolic Signatura against that decision. On 24 June 1995, the Signatura declared such action illegitimate (contrary to procedural law) and provided insights into the practical ways of effecting transfer of pastors. It made two parallel statements concerning the central issues involved in the case.[6] First, the Signatura stated that, as far as the bishop's discernment in the case was concerned, having in mind the needs of the diocese, the needs of the parishes involved in the transfers, the needs of the three priests and the needs of the presbyterate, the actions of the ordinary of the diocese seem to have been just and equitable. Second, as far as procedure was concerned, the Signatura found in favour of the three priests.

As a general observation, the Signatura stated that while the current practice in moving priests is sufficient in cases where all involved agree to the transfer, it

[6] The law section of the Signatura's definitive sentence, with an English translation by Msgr. Charles J. Scicluna, is published in Forum 6 (1995): 2, 117-122. This translation will be used in paraphrasing the Signatura's sentence in the text. It should be noted here that neither the name of the diocese nor the facts and the actual decision of the Signatura as analyzed in this study are to be found in this source.

is not so in cases where a priest was unwilling to transfer. In his sentence, Agustoni, the Prefect of the Signatura at the time and the *Ponens* in this case, highlights the following principles on the matter:

First, the theological principles governing the revised canons on transfer and removal of pastors are derived directly from the ecclesiological themes extensively discussed by the Second Vatican Council and gleaned from its decrees, especially "*Christus Dominus.*"[7] In no. 31, *Christus Dominus* stipulated that each pastor "should enjoy that stability of office in his parish as the good of souls requires."[8] While directing the abrogation of the distinction between *removable* and *irremovable pastors,* the Council ordered that "the procedure for the transfer or removal of a pastor should be re-examined and simplified so that the bishop, while observing the principles of *natural* and *canonical* equity, may more suitably provide for the good of souls."[9]

Second, the intention of the Council and the reason undergirding such directives are clear: On the one hand stability is required in the exercise of the office of pastor since, under the authority of the bishop, the pastors "are given, in a specific section of the diocese, [...] the care of souls as their particular shepherds,"[10] and they "should make their special concern to know their parishioners."[11] The acquisition of such a knowledge on the part of the pastor requires a suitable period of time. However, on the other hand, the good of souls should always be the supreme end so that, where and when necessary, the good of individuals or the good of the pastors themselves, gives way to the good of souls.[12]

---

[7] Second Vatican Council, *Decree on the Pastoral Office of Bishops in the Church, Christus Dominus*, 28 October 1965, in *AAS* 58 (1966): 673-701; English translation in Flannery I, 564-590.

[8] "Parochi vero in sua quisque paroecia ea gaudeant stabilitate in officio, quam animarum bonum requirat" (*AAS* 58 [1966]: 689). English translation adapted from Flannery I, 583.

[9] "*Quare, abrogata distinctione inter parochos amovibiles et inamovibiles, recognoscatur et simplicior reddatur modus procedendi in translatione et amotione parochorum, quo Episcopus, servata quidem naturali et canonica aequitate, aptius necessitatibus boni animarum providere possit*" (ibid.). See Flannery I, p. 583 (emphasis added).

[10] CD, no. 30.

[11] Ibid.

[12] C. Agustoni, 24 June 1995, p. 118, no. 4.

Third, the fundamental principle governing the stability in office of pastors is stated in canon 522 which reads:

> A pastor must possess stability and therefore is to be appointed for an indefinite period of time. The diocesan bishop can appoint him only for a specific period if the conference of bishops has permitted this by a decree.

This canon envisions two distinct modes of promoting and safeguarding stability in office: a pastor may be appointed for an indefinite period of time or a determinate period of time. The second mode is allowed *only* where there is a decree issued by the competent conference of bishops and duly approved by the Apostolic See, which prescribes the number of years for which the appointment of pastor is made.

Therefore, the bishop who intends to proceed with the transfer or removal of a pastor must first consider the juridical condition of his priest since the procedure must suit the same juridical condition: his juridical condition would be different at the lapse of the time period determined by the conference of bishops from other cases.[13]

Fourth, in view of the above general principles, the following points must be taken into consideration when dealing with the transfer of pastors.

- In the case of an appointment of a pastor for a determinate period of time made in accord with the decree of the bishops' conference, his office becomes vacant by reason of the lapse of time from the moment of written advice from the competent authority (cf. c. 186); but the provision for the *de iure* vacancy of the office can be made beforehand according to the norm of canon 153, §2.

- Apart from the specific case mentioned above, there remains in force the fundamental principle declared in canon 153, §1: "The provision of an office which by law [*de iure*] is not vacant is by that very fact invalid and is not validated by

[13] Ibid., 118-119, no. 5.

subsequent vacancy." Therefore, except in the case mentioned in canon 153, §2, a parish cannot be entrusted to a successor until it is vacant.

- According to canon 190, §1, a transfer "can be made only by a person who has the right of providing for the office which is lost as well as for the office which is conferred. This norm implies that one cannot make provision for an office (*ad quod*) unless it is juridically vacant (except in the case of c. 153, §2), nor can he provide for a transfer to such an office. On the other hand, canon 191, §1 contains the principle which refers specifically to the vacancy of the office *a quo*, that is, the office *from which* the person is being transferred, and not to the vacancy of the office *ad quod*, that is, the office to which the person is being transferred.[14]

Fifth, in the absence of a decree of the conference of bishops on this matter, the bishop must consider the following if he still wants to adopt "rotary transfers" of pastors in his diocese:

- If a pastor is agreeable to the transfer, the bishop must first request and accept his resignation according to law (cc. 187-189), and then appoint him to another parish. But in the meantime the same pastor can be appointed administrator of the parish from which he has willingly resigned until he takes possession of the new office.

- On the contrary, a number of difficulties could be raised by pastors who are appointed for an indefinite period of time (or for a definite period of time outside the case of c. 153, §2). It is necessary that the parish *ad quam*, that is, the parish to which the priest is being transferred, is vacant, *before* the procedure for transfer begins. Otherwise such procedure would be illegitimate. This is so, not because of the condition of the office from which the pastor is being transferred [*terminus a quo*], but because of the condition of the office to which the pastor is being transferred [*terminus ad quem*]. This means that in such a situation the transfer would be made to an office which cannot be conferred because it is *de iure* not vacant.

---

[14] Ibid., 119-120, no. 6

Therefore, in order for the diocesan bishop to act not only *legitimately* but also *prudently*, he must ensure the resignation of the pastor of the parish *ad quam* at the start of the procedure for transfer, albeit he may appoint the same priest as administrator until the transfer is completed.[15]

Sixth, according to canon 1748, the just cause for the transfer of a pastor is: "the good of souls or the necessity or advantage of the Church."[16] Canon 1748 also presupposes that the pastor satisfactorily governs the parish *a qua*, that is, the parish from which he is transferred. It would constitute an act of removal rather than of transfer if his ministry in the parish *a qua* were to be harmful or ineffective (cf. c. 1740).[17]

Seventh, a transfer can be made to another *parish* or to another *office*. Canon 2163 of the 1917 code provided for the transfer of a *removable* pastor to another parish which "is not of a very inferior rank" ("*non sit ordinis nimio inferioris*"). This norm is abrogated and, therefore, no longer tenable.[18]

Eighth, the procedure prescribed in canons 1748-1752 should be diligently observed in cases of transfer, except in the case foreseen in canon 153, §2, which does not concern a transfer in the proper sense.

Ninth, the same effect of recourse prescribed in canon 1747 for removal is also applicable to the case of a priest who has been "transferred." This implies that the pastor who is *de facto* transferred, must abstain from exercising the office of pastor, leave the parish house free as soon as possible (unless he is sick – cf. c. 1747, §2) and hand over everything to the person to whom the bishop will have entrusted the parish. However, while the recourse is pending, the bishop cannot appoint the new pastor, that is, he cannot confer the office on another priest, but he is bound in the meantime to provide for the care of the parish through a parochial administrator. In the case of recourse, therefore,

---

[15] Ibid., 120-121, no. 7.
[16] Cf. also *CD*, 31.
[17] *C.* Agustoni, 24 June 1995, p. 121, no. 8.
[18] Ibid.

there is suspension of the decree of transfer "*secundum quid*," which means that as long as the parish is *de iure* not vacant the bishop cannot validly appoint another priest to that office.[19]

Tenth, canon 1752 highlights the spirit which must motivate any action, including that of transfer of a pastor. That spirit is *canonical equity* which urges the bishop to make his decision with kindness and compassion, and the pastor to accept a just and equitable decision with mature obedience and priestly charity. Everything done in the Church must promote the salvation of souls, the supreme purpose of the Church's existence on earth.

In the above case, the bishop of Galloway withdrew the decree of transfer and invited all involved to adopt a spirit of reconciliation and trust in God's healing power. In his statement, the bishop stated:

- the bishop, having taken into account all the present circumstances of the situation, considers that it is right to withdraw the decrees of transfer and therefore does so;
- he invites all concerned to join him in looking to the future in a spirit of reconciliation and with trust in God's healing power;
- he asks for the continued prayers and support of the people of the diocese for himself and all the priests.[20]

It seems that as a result of this new conciliatory approach adopted by the bishop, the three priests involved in the case accepted new transfers.

Although it seems that the bishop of Galloway had no intention of using the mechanism of transfer as an easy way to remove the pastors who had been appointed for an indefinite period of time, the observation made by F. Daneels on the issue of transfer and removal of pastors could be helpful to all diocesan

---

[19] Ibid., pp. 121-122, no. 9.

[20] See Maurice Taylor [Bishop of Galloway], "A Statement by Bishop Taylor Regarding the Transfer of Three Priests to Other Parishes," in *CLSGB & I Newsletter*, no. 104 (December 1995) 22-23, here at p. 23. For a brief commentary on the Signatura's right to involve in disputes concerning transfer of pastors, see Paul Hayward, "The Apostolic Signatura and Disputes Involving the Transfer of Pastors," in ibid., pp. 24-32.

bishops who have the right and the responsibility of making provision for the pastoral care of the faithful according the norms of law. Daneels says:

> As the procedure for a transfer is much easier than the procedure for a removal, there is sometimes the temptation to impose a transfer on a pastor, when the real issue at stake is his removal from office. This would constitute a serious violation of the law both *in procedendo* and *in decernendo.* Indeed the transfer presupposes that the pastor is governing his parish well and that the good of souls or the necessity or the advantage of the Church requires his transfer. If therefore the alleged reason for the transfer would ... be that the ministry of the pastor has become harmful or ineffective, then the decision of the bishop would no doubt violate the law.[21]

The law makes it very clear that reasons for removal and transfer are radically different, and so are the procedures for effecting the two actions. There is no room for arbitrary decisions in these matters. Above all, as Daneels correctly points out, it would constitute a serious violation of the law if the bishop were to use the procedure of transfer outlined in canons 1748-1752 for punishing a pastor instead of the required penal process to impose a penal transfer.[22] The bishops must be aware of the consequences of the actions they might perform contrary to the requirements of law.

Removal of Pastors

Canon 522 declares that a pastor is to be appointed for an indeterminate period of time. The same canon also provides for such an appointment for a specified period of time only if the conference of bishops has allowed it by decree. This stability of office of pastor is directly linked to the spiritual needs of the people entrusted to the pastoral care of the pastor. This stability of office, however, is not to be interpreted as absolute. Like any other ecclesiastical

---

[21] Frans Daneels, "The Removal or Transfer of a Pastor in the Light of the Jurisprudence of the Apostolic Signatura," in *Forum* 8 (1997): 2, 295-301, here at p. 300.
[22] Ibid.

office, it can be lost through different modes established by law. The administr ative removal of a pastor is one such mode through which he can lose his office. It is distinguished from loss of office by the law itself (cf. c. 194), which is more appropriately regarded as a penal remedy,[23] and penal removal (deprivation) from office indicated in canon 196.

The administrative removal of a pastor is governed by strict procedural norms. The general principle governing loss of office stipulates that a person cannot be removed from an office conferred for an indeterminate or determinate period of time except for "grave reasons" and "in accord with the procedure defined by law" (cf. c. 193, §1 and §2). As for removal of a pastor from his office, in canons 1740-1747 the law is very specific both in designating the reasons for and in delineating the procedure to effect it. Because the action of removal of a pastor from his office might incur substantial violation of his natural and/or acquired rights, the law identifies violation of certain elements of the process to be invalidating. Therefore, the bishop who considers the need for removal of a pastor must proceed in accord with the norms of law in issuing the decree of removal. The two definitive decisions of the Apostolic Signatura involving the removal of a pastor discussed below demonstrate the benefit of following the wisdom rooted in ecclesial law.

Facts of the Case[24]

Father Anthony Pastrano was named pastor of the St. Agnes' parish on 23 May 1984. The appointment was not limited by any term. He came into this office with praise for the pastoral ministry he had done in his previous assignments. He took charge of the parish on 17 July 1984. In the parish house into which he came,

---

[23] See Luigi Chiappetta, *Il Codice di diritto canonico: commento giuridico-pastoral,* (Roma: Edizioni Dehoniane, 1996) 1, 282.

[24] Supremum Signaturae Apostolicae Tribunal, c. Palazzini, 17 December 1988, Prot. No. 18190/86 CA (unpublished). All 8 members of this panel were Cardinals: Achilles Card. Silvestrini (Praefectus), Petrus Card. Palazzini (Ponens), Opilius Card. Rossi, Rogerius Card. Etchegaray, Simon D. Card. Lourdusamy, Rosalius Josephus Card. Castillo Lara, Eduardus Card. Gagnon and Alphonsus M. Card. Stickler. This was a plenary panel according to Art. 1, §3 of "Normae speciales."

there lived his predecessor after retirement. Moreover, there was in the parish a woman religious, who functioned as a pastoral associate. Father Pastrano wanted to function independently of these two in his pastoral plans and ministry. This approach of Pastrano led to friction between him and the other two. This, together with other complaints, was reported to the bishop, who, without seeking any information directly from Pastrano, sent letters admonishing him about the problem with a reminder to radically change his behaviour. The complaints which the bishop received about him concerned mainly the following:

- he was too rapid in making changes in the parish;
- he was too strong in criticising parishioners;
- he was tardy in listening to and collaborating with people;
- he had disdain for women;
- he made critical judgments towards co-workers which were destructive.

Because peace did not return to the parish, the bishop sent out another letter on 9 November 1984 and informed Pastrano that he had constituted a group of persons to hear the people of the parish. Moreover, he ordered him to announce this message in the parish bulletin. This was done and on 25 November 1984 the meeting took place.

Since he was not informed of the outcome of that meeting, Pastrano wrote on 1 February 1985 complaining that he had been deserted by his bishop from whom he had expected some support. He also accused his predecessor of leading the opposition against him in the parish, and pleaded with the bishop to have him removed from the parish house. On 5 February 1985, the bishop replied defending himself and reiterating the accusations against Pastrano whom he declared hostile and called for his resignation.

In his letter of 13 February 1985, Pastrano declared that he did not see any legitimate reason for resignation and emphasized the machinations of his predecessor. Moreover, he asked that the proceedings of the 25 November 1984 meeting be made available to him so that he could see the accusations made against him. He also wrote the same to the Apostolic Nunciature and to the Holy See explaining as well the history of his situation in the parish.

Finally, on 25 March 1985, the bishop briefly explained the reasons which suggested resignation, namely:

- a manner of acting which causes grave harm to ecclesiastical communion;
- loss of good name among *upright* and *serious* parishioners and *aversion* toward the pastor which were foreseen as *not quickly coming to an end* (cf. c. 1741, 1° and 3°), and which have reached the point of threats.

In this letter, the bishop advised Pastrano to retain a lawyer.[25]

On 27 March 1985, Pastrano wrote to the bishop saying that he (the bishop) wanted to remove him from office without due process contrary to all canon and civil laws. At this point the bishop in his letter of 2 April 1985 proposed to entrust the entire matter to an arbitrator, a certain priest-psychiatrist. Although Pastrano resisted this arrangement at first, indicating that it was not proper to have a psychiatrist as an arbitrator (because the matter under consideration was of a juridic and not of a psychiatric or psychological nature), he finally agreed and signed the document (without, however, indicating the day, month and year), through which the psychiatrist was appointed as arbitrator in this matter. But he attached certain conditions to this agreement, among which was the

[25] It should be noted that canons dealing specifically with the removal of a pastor do not speak of the services of an advocate. But the general principle stated in c. 1738 governing "Recourse Against Administrative Decrees" (cc. 1732-1739) is applicable to this procedure as well. But the question is at what point in time of the process of removal of a pastor can the priest concerned seek such services? Daneels states the following in regard to this issue: "I note also that canon law acknowledges the right to use the services of an advocate or procurator in the case of hierarchical recourse against the removal of a pastor (c. 1738), but not yet during the procedure for his removal. At this stage of the procedure, therefore, a bishop may refuse to handle the case with the canonical consultant of the pastor and insist on handling the removal directly with the pastor himself. However this does not mean that the bishop could not agree to handle the case with the advocate of the pastor, but only that there is no obligation for the bishop to do so" (Daneels, "The Removal or Transfer of a Pastor," p. 299). Daneels seems to imply here two things: First, there is no provision for the services of an advocate to plead on behalf of the pastor during the removal proceedings until the commencement of the recourse phase of removal, that is, after the decree of removal has been issued by the bishop. Second, even though there is no obligation of the bishop's part to communicate with the advocate, there is no law which would prohibit him from doing so. But in cases of the kind, where the good name of a person might be at stake, it would be appropriate on the

obligation on the arbitrator's part of communicating both to the bishop and to himself the reasons for the decision he would make as arbitrator. Pastrano complained to the arbitrator several times that he was not given an opportunity to read or hear the accusations made against him during the meeting held in the parish on 25 November 1984. The same complaint was reiterated during the meeting held between the bishop, the pastor and the arbitrator. This meeting, held on 28 May 1985, proved futile.

The bishop blamed the pastor for the failure of arbitration because he was not willing to accept the advice and warnings of the arbitrator. By his letter of 21 May 1985 the bishop decreed that the process for removal would go forward and proceeded all the way to the issuance of the decree of removal on 1 July 1985. The pastor placed recourse against that decree before the Congregation for Clergy which, on 4 March 1986, rejected the recourse. However the Congregation recommended to the bishop to confer on the respondent an appropriate office within the diocese taking into consideration his talents and capacity.

The respondent placed recourse against this decision before the Signatura, which by its decree of 9 February 1988 admitted the recourse and on 17 December 1988 pronounced its decision on the way the Congregation for Clergy had rendered its decision.

Legal Principles

In its decree, the Signatura briefly outlines the procedural principles applicable to the case.

First, the removal from office of a pastor must be done according to the special administrative procedure laid down in canons 1740-1747 of the 1983 code. This is not a penal process because the causes for removal may not be

bishop's part to respect the intervention of an advocate whenever it is sought by a pastor so that his natural and ecclesial rights may be properly defended before legitimate ecclesiastical authority.

connected with any serious fault of the pastor in regard to the harmful or at least inefficacious ministry.

Second, the causes for legitimate removal listed in canon 1741 are merely demonstrative and not taxative. That means the bishop can consider other causes for removing a pastor from his office provided that his ministry is rendered harmful or at least inefficacious, for the principal purpose of removal of a pastor is the *good of souls*.[26]

Third, once the bishop has conducted an objective investigation, he must discuss the issue with *two pastors* chosen from among the group stably constituted by the presbyteral council and proposed by the bishop. This discussion is only *consultative* and not *deliberative* in nature. Should the bishop decide that the removal must be done, he must *paternally* invite the priest in writing or orally to resign from office within *fifteen* useful days. For the validity of the removal the decree must give the reason and arguments (c. 1742, §1).

The resignation may be pure and simple or conditional provided that the bishop can legitimately and really accept it (cf. c. 1743). This would avoid the process of leaving the parish without acrimony and in a more favourable condition. To be valid, such a resignation must be done in writing or orally before two witnesses (cf. c. 189, §1), and it lacks all force if it is not accepted within three months (cf. c. 189, §§3-4).

Fourth, should the pastor fail to respond within the predetermined time, the bishop must repeat the invitation, even extending the time period for response (cf. c. 1744, §1). If it is evident to the bishop that the priest has received the second invitation to resign, and has not been impeded in any way from doing so,

---

[26] "*Causae ob quas parochus a sua paroecia legitime ab Episcopo dioecesano amoveri potest, in can. 1741 non numerantur taxative sed demonstrative, quia aliae causae praeter recensitas admittuntur, dummodo iudicio eiusdem episcopi ministerium parochi noxium vel saltem inefficax evadat. Nam agitur de remotione seu amotione parochi a paroecia in bonum animarum [...]*" (c. Palazzini, 17 December 1988, n. 5).

or if the pastor refuses to resign without offering any reasons, the bishop shall decree the removal (cf. c. 1744, §2).[27]

Fifth, if the pastor does not resign, but opposes the cause alleged in the invitation and its reasons and offers motives which do not seem sufficient to the bishop, in order to act *validly* to remove him from office, the bishop must:

- invite the pastor to inspect the acts and to gather contrary arguments in writing, and present even contrary proofs, if any;
- then, after completing the instruction, if necessary, assess the matter together with the same two pastors mentioned in canon 1742, §1, unless others are to be designated due to impossibility on their part;
- decide whether or not the pastor must be removed, and issue the decree immediately about the decision whether affirmative or negative (cf. c. 1745).

Sixth, the bishop should issue this decree in writing. It must express the motives at least in a summary fashion (cf. c. 51), even if the motives are not explained in an analytic manner.[28]

Seventh, if the pastor feels aggrieved by the decision, he can place recourse against the definitive decree before the hierarchic superior of the one who issued the decree, within the peremptory time period prescribed by the canons (cf. cc. 1734, 1735, 1737).

Eighth, the pastor who has been removed, before placing the recourse, should seek from the bishop revocation or amendment of the decree. When such a petition is made, it is understood by that very fact that the suspension of execution of the decree is also requested (cf. c. 1734, §1).

Ninth, if the above-mentioned request has been received by the bishop, the author of the decree, he may within *thirty days,* issue a new decree by which he shall amend the preceding decree or shall reject the petition. In this case, the

---

[27] It seems the jurisprudence of the Signatura regards as an established principle that "the pastor is considered to have received the invitation to resign just the same, if he refuses to accept any communication of the bishop" (Daneels, "The Removal or Transfer of a Pastor," p. 298).

time period for recourse begins to run from the intimation of the new decree. If, however, the bishop does not decree anything on the matter, the time period for recourse begins from the thirtieth day from the time the petition of the pastor has reached the bishop (cf. c. 1735).[29]

Application of the Principles

The Signatura's panel found several serious violations of law in the *procedure* and in the *decision* made by the bishop which was confirmed by the Congregation for Clergy. In their preliminary observations, the judges pointed out that the acts of the case were regrettably incomplete. There was no copy of the report on the parish meeting held on 25 November 1984. Presumably the copy had been destroyed. Before the Congregation for Clergy could decide on the question of rejection or acceptance of the recourse, it usually seeks two opinions, and these were not found in the acts. The bishop's behaviour seemed altogether peculiar and confused throughout the process.[30]

Violation of Law in Procedendo

First, the court considered it necessary to establish the moment when the entire process commenced in view of the complicated succession of events that occurred in this case. The court *rejected* the argument that the process began on 9 November 1984 when a commission was appointed by the bishop to verify the cause for removal of the pastor. The court clearly stated that on that day there began only the preliminary investigation of the cause for removal and not the formal process for removal.[31]

There is no prohibition in law to conduct such an inquiry (cf. c. 1742, §1), but it should be done without detriment to the good reputation or name of the pastor. Even when there is an investigation preceding a penal process, "care is

[28] "*Hoc decretum Episcopus ferre debet scripto expressis motivis, saltem summarie (cf. can. 51), licet motiva non sint analytice enucleata*" (c. Palazzini, 17 December 1988, n. 10).
[29] Ibid.
[30] Ibid., no. 11.
[31] Ibid., no. 13.

to be taken this investigation does not call into question anyone's good name" (c. 1717, §2).

Second, one of the two reasons adduced by the bishop in issuing the decree was: "the loss of the pastor's good name among *upright* and *serious-minded* parishioners." The court argued that the determination of this factor in this case was questionable, because it was not clear whether all those who participated in the meeting of 25 November 1984 had such *upright* and *serious-minded* attributes, particularly in the presence of the retired pastor and the sister. Unfortunately, the proceedings of this meeting were destroyed at the bishop's order, which amounts to destruction of proof.[32]

Third, one cannot deny the fact that the public manner in which the investigation was conducted after being announced in the parish bulletin harmed the good name of the pastor. Furthermore, a second commission "to investigate the health of the pastor" was added to the first one which included first a psychologist and then a priest-psychiatrist. In this way, the investigation must be said to have begun with a prejudicial opinion.[33]

Fourth, when the investigation is complete, the code (c. 1742, §1) admonishes: "If an investigation shows that there exists a reason mentioned in c. 1740, the bishop is to discuss the matter with *two pastors,* chosen from a group stably established for this purpose by the council of priests at the proposal of the bishop." The consultation mentioned in this canon is required for the validity of the process. In this case it was difficult to determine when such a consultation had taken place. The bishop spoke about this matter first with "pastoral vicars" ("*vicariis pastoralibus*") on 24 January 1985 and then with the "pastor-consultors" on the 25th and 29th of the same month. But it is not clear whether these were in fact chosen stably by the presbyteral council from among the group proposed by the bishop.[34]

---

[32] Ibid., no. 14.
[33] Ibid., no. 15.
[34] Ibid., no. 16.

Fifth, if from the consultation it is considered necessary to decree the removal, the bishop should *paternally* invite the pastor, either in writing or orally, to resign within fifteen days, by indicating the reason and the arguments, and this is for the validity of the act (c. 1742, §1). In this case, the bishop neither indicated the time period for resignation (cf. c. 1742) nor the precise cause and arguments suggesting the need for such a resignation.[35]

Further, the judges also found unsatisfactory the discussion held on 13 March 1985 by the bishop in order to weigh the contrary reasons proposed by the pastor and not in conformity with the norm of canon 1745. Moreover, the bishop had not invited the pastor to inspect the acts and to present contrary reasons, if he had any. This is required by canon 1745 for validity of the decision.

It was only in his letter of 25 March 1985 that the bishop explained precisely the reasons for removal, and this was indeed the first juridic act he had placed after the investigation was done. It was in this letter that all the elements required by canon 1742, §2 were included. The pastor was advised through this letter to resign from office within a determined period of time (although more than fifteen days) or to propose contrary reasons.[36]

At this point in time, the process was suspended through the efforts of arbitration which proved unsuccessful. Therefore, the process was reopened on 31 May 1985. The letter reopening the process contained certain contradictions: on the one hand it was stated in it that the contrary reasons offered by the pastor had been discussed with "pastor-consultors" on 12 March, but on the other hand the pastor was advised in the same letter to inspect the acts and to bring forward any contrary reasons. If this was true, the bishop should have recalled the two pastors to weigh the matter after receiving from the pastor contrary reasons or arguments (c. 1745).[37]

---

[35] Ibid., no. 17.
[36] Ibid., no. 18.
[37] Ibid., no. 19.

Therefore, the process itself must be considered incomplete. Moreover, several acts on which the process was based also must be declared invalid. As a result, the decree of removal itself must be said to have been issued illegitimately, since "there was no prior discussion by the bishop with two pastor-consultors stably constituted and selected by the presbyteral council after being proposed by the bishop."[38]

Violation of Law in Decernendo

The decree of the bishop provided two reasons for the removal of the pastor:

- a manner of acting which brings grave detriment or disturbance to ecclesiastical communion;
- loss of a good reputation among *upright and responsible parishioners* or an aversion to the pastor which it appears will not cease in a brief time.

The court, however, said that as far as the first reason was concerned, the decision of the bishop was clearly precipitous because it was made without taking into consideration the difficult situation in which the pastor was placed. The bishop had regarded him as a "fine priest and fine pastor" prior to his appointment, and the pastor sought his bishop's assistance which he did not find in the bishop. The peace which the bishop expected to return to the parish after the removal of the pastor was not realised as in a very short period of time thereafter there followed a succession of administrators.[39]

In regard to the second accusation, the court said that not all who participated in the public meeting could be regarded as *upright and responsible*. Therefore, the decision of the bishop could not be considered to have been made with due consultation. Rather, the manner of proceeding had harmed the good name of the pastor in violation of the norms of canon 1717, §§1-2, which must

[38] Ibid., no. 20.
[39] Ibid., no. 21.

be followed in a penal process; *a fortiori*, those norms must be considered valid also in an administrative process.

Moreover, the use of a psychologist in the commission of investigation and then of a psychiatrist as an arbitrator implied that the fault rested entirely on the pastor, and the insinuation was that his pathological mental state was the root of all evils.[40]

The judges also considered the decree of removal as excessive, because in it the bishop had attached a threat of penalty of suspension against the pastor if he failed to leave the parish within four days. The decree was dated July 1st to be effective on July 5th.

The judges stated: "No one is punished unless the external violation of a law or precept, committed by the person, is gravely imputable by reason of malice or negligence (c. 1321, §1). Nor can one say that the penalty in this case is threatened and subordinated to possible condition of disobedience. Although this manner of proceeding is not *expressly* contrary to the canons, it is at least contrary to the spirit of the law."[41]

The penalty which was threatened was that of suspension; on the contrary it was stated that the penalty would be imposed in accord with the norm of canon 1331, §1, which in fact concerns the penalty of excommunication.

Moreover, the suspension threatened was unlimited which is contrary to the norm of canon 1334, §2. According to this canon, a precept of automatic suspension cannot be imposed without adding determination or limitation.[42]

Therefore, the act of the Congregation for the Clergy was found in violation of the law *in procedendo* as well as *in decernendo*.

---

[40] "*Quodammodo laesiva bonae famae parochi fuit etiam convocatio psychologi in commissione investigativa et, dein, psychiatrae tanquam arbitri: hoc modo inde ab initio insinuebatur causam omnium malorum esse posse anomalum statum mentalem ipsius parochi*" (Ibid., no. 22).
[41] Ibid., no. 23.
[42] See ibid.

Complaint of Nullity and *Restitutio in Integrum*

On 8 May 1989, the Congregation for the Clergy petitioned for *restitutio in integrum* against the above decision of 17 December 1988 in accord with the norm of canon 1645 (*CCEO* c. 1326). An advocate was duly appointed by the Congregation, who lodged on 10 June 1989 a complaint of remediable nullity against the Signatura's decision on grounds of illegitimate number of judges on the judicial panel in contravention of the prescript of canon 1622, 1° (*CCEO* c. 1304, §1, 1°) and, subordinately, *restitutio in integrum.* On 11 November 1989 many more documents from the bishop were produced by the advocate of public administration. These new documents were intended to prove the clear injustice of the Signatura's sentence. The new panel of judges consisted of seven members.[43]

Complaint of Nullity

The law makes it very clear that there is no appeal or recourse against a sentence or decree of the Roman Pontiff (c. 333, §3; cf. *CCEO* c. 45, §3). Furthermore, canon 1405, §2 (*CCEO* c. 1060, §3) stipulates that a judge cannot review an act or instrument confirmed specifically (*in forma specifica*) by the Roman Pontiff without his prior mandate.[44] Canon 1629, 1° (*CCEO* c. 1310, 1°) also reiterates this principle: "[There is no appeal] from a sentence of the Supreme Pontiff or the Apostolic Signatura." The implication of this principle is that when a decision is pronounced by the Supreme Authority of the Church it becomes *res iudicata*. Therefore, it is no longer subject to appeal. That does not preclude, in my opinion, the possibility of *beneficium novae audientiae* by the Supreme Authority if he so decides.

---

[43] The seven members of the panel were (four Cardinals and three Bishops): Bernardinus Card. Gantin, Rosalius Ioseph Card. Castillo Lara, Eduardus Card. Gagnon, Antonius Maria Card. Javierre Ortas, Vincentius Fagiolo (*Ponens*), Philippus Giannini, and Aemilius Eid. Of these members Cardinals Castillo Lara and Gagnon were also members of the previous panel.

[44] See Art. 134 §4 of "Regolamento generale della Curia Romana," 30 April 1999, in *AAS* 91 (1999): 683.

Although the law very clearly states that there can be no "appeal" against a sentence of the Apostolic Signatura, authors have, in my considered view, correctly argued in favor of appeal against such decisions.[45] This would imply that a revision of the code might necessitate legislation allowing appeal against the sentences of the Signatura. But what about complaint of nullity and *restitutio in integrum* against a sentence of the Signatura? Even prior to the promulgation of the Latin Code authors had expressed the view that a complaint of nullity and *restitution in integrum* against the decision of the Signatura were possible as extraordinary remedies [46] and this position is now commonly held by most authors.[47]

Because this was the first case in which the Signatura's sentence was directly challenged with a complaint of nullity and *restitutio in integrum*, the judicial panel sought opinions of three experts on the matter. In accord with the canonical opinions concerning this matter expressed above, all experts agreed that it is possible to present a plaint of nullity and petition for *restitutio in integrum* against definitive sentences of the Signatura except when the court confirms or reverses the decree of rejection in accord with the norm of art. 116 of the *Normae speciales* governing its internal operations. The reasoning undergirding this affirmative view was that neither the 1983 code nor the *Normae speciales* excluded such a possibility. For this reason, the judicial panel proceeded to examine the possibility of either declaring the preceding sentence remediably null or to grant *restitutio in integrum*.

---

[45] See, for example, Joaquín Llobell, "Note sull'impugnabilità delle decisioni della Segnatura Apostolica," in *Ius Ecclesiae* 5 (1993) 675-698; Francesco D'Ostilio, "De appellationis problemate in Sectione Altera Signaturae Apostolicae relate ad causas vigore art. 107 constitutionis 'Regimini Ecclesiae universae' ipsi delatas," in *Periodica* 67 (1978): 698-713.

[46] See, for example, Zenon Grocholewski, "La 'Sectio altera' della Segnatura Apostolica con particolare riferimento all procedura in essa seguita," in *Apollinaris* 54 (1981): 103; G. Lobina, *La competenza del Supremo Tribunale della Segnatura Apostolica con particolare riferimento alla "Sectio altera" e alla problematica rispettiva*, (Roma, 1971): 130.

[47] See, for example, Francesco D'Ostilio, *Il diritto amministrativo della Chiesa*, Studi giuridici XXXVII, (Città del Vaticano: Libreria editrice Vaticana, 1995): 526-527; Francesco Salerno, "Il giudizio presso la '*Sectio altera*' del S.T. della Segnatura Apostolica," in *La Giustizia Amministrativa nella Chiesa*, Studi giuridici XXIV, (Città del Vaticano: Libreria Editrice Vaticana, 1991): 174-175; Joseph R. Punderson, "Hierarchical Recourse to the Holy See: Theory and Practice," in *CLSA Proceedings* 62 (Washington, DC: Canon Law Society of America, 2000): 45.

First, the plaint of remediable nullity proposed by the advocate of the Congregation was based on the assumption that the preceding decision was pronounced by an illegitimate number of judges contrary to the prescript of canon 1622, 1° (*CCEO* c. 1304, §1, 1°). The present panel declared such an assumption to be incorrect because the said decision was in fact pronounced *coram omnibus*, that is, *coram* seven judges in a plenary session. Therefore, there was no lack of legitimate number of judges on the panel which had issued the impugned sentence.[48]

Second, the complaint of nullity could not be admitted because the advocate had presented it without proper mandate from the Congregation. Furthermore, the advocate himself did not pursue the complaint in his final submissions. Therefore, the plaint of nullity was rejected.[49]

Restitutio in Integrum

As an extraordinary remedy, *restitutio in integrum* is allowed by law only in case of manifest injustice. Canon 1645 (*CCEO* c. 1326), which makes provision for *restitutio in integrum* in §1, lists five conditions in §2 under which injustice is clearly verified. Of these five, the following three could be applicable to this case. These three conditions are:

- the sentence is based on proofs which afterwards are discovered to be false in such a way that without those proofs the dispositive part of the sentence is not sustained;
- documents have been revealed afterwards which undoubtedly prove new facts and demand a contrary decision;
- a prescript of the law which is not merely procedural was clearly neglected.

---

[48] *"Imprimis quia querela nullitatis, quam Cl. Patronus Congregationis die 10 iunii 1989 proposuerat ex can. 1622, 1°, utpote lata a non legitimo numero iudicum, dari nequit. Sententia enim lata est coram omnibus, nempe coram octo Em.mis Iudicibus in sessione plenaria; ideoque non defuit numerus legitimus"* (*c.* Fagiolo, 27 February 1993, no. 5). See Secretaria Status, "Normae speciales in Supremo Tribunali Signaturae Apostolicae ad experimentum servandae post Const. Ap. Pauli VI 'Regimini Ecclesiae universae'," in Xaverius Ochoa, (ed.), *Leges Ecclesiae post Codicem iuris canonici editae,* vol. III, *Leges annis 1959-1968 editae* (Roma: Commentarium pro Religiosis, 1972) Art. 1 §1 (total number of judges 12 Cardinals); §2 (ordinarily 5 members for the panel unless the Prefect decides that the full bench must judge a particular case).

[49] Ibid.

The judges ruled as follows on these three conditions as applied to this case:

The first condition stipulates that clear injustice of a sentence is verified when moral certitude necessary for pronouncing a definitive decision was derived from proofs which are later found to be false. In other words, the dispositive part of the sentence which declares the definitive decision was based on false proofs. A sentence based on false proofs is manifestly unjust and must be remedied by *restitutio in integrum*. Was this condition verified in our present case? The judges responded negatively to this question. In other words, they concluded that the proofs on which the preceding sentence was based were not false. Therefore, *restitutio in integrum* could not be granted on this ground.[50]

The second condition implies that after the pronouncement of the sentence new proofs have come to light which were not available to the preceding panel of judges and which demand a contrary decision. Were there any truly new documents which have brought to light new facts relevant to this case? Again the present panel of judges felt that, although several new documents had been presented to the court, there were no new documents which could on their own strength demand a contrary decision. In other words, the documents introduced after the challenged sentence was pronounced were already known to the court.[51]

There remained the third condition to be examined by the panel, that is, whether "a prescript of the law which is not merely procedural was neglected" in the case. It was in the analysis of this condition that the judges found serious flaws in the preceding sentence. The present panel, therefore, examined this condition under four aspects: First, it carefully scrutinized the events of the proceedings in a chronological sequence in order to establish the origin, the manner and the significance of everything that transpired between the pastor and the bishop from the beginning. Second, the judges looked into the specific actions of both parties in order to determine if there were any substantial

[50] Ibid., no. 7.
[51] Ibid.

violations of law *in procedendo*. Third, the panel also attempted to ascertain if there was any violation of law *in decernendo* on the part of the bishop. Fourth, in all these evaluations the judges tried to identify the specific instances where the preceding panel had either misinterpreted or failed to evaluate objectively the evidence contained in the acts, thus leading to the application of the extraordinary remedy of *restitutio in integrum* to the case. We shall closely trace the critical approach adopted by the present panel and its definitive decision on the question of *restitutio in integrum*.

The chronology of events as paraphrased from the sentence is as follows: Father Pastrano was appointed pastor of St. Agnes' parish on 23 May 1984. According to the present panel, prior to his appointment, he was informed of the presence of his predecessor in the parish rectory and of the role of a certain religious sister as collaborator in parochial ministry. He was not only aware of this situation but had also given his full consent to such an arrangement.[52]

The present panel argued that the pastor began his ministry in the parish with great zeal, which was indeed commendable. But the zeal for the house of God is inseparable from the communion with the bishop which is necessary to direct the zeal toward the good of the Church and of souls. This requires tempering of zeal with prudence. In the absence of this balance one cannot carry out pastoral ministry in peace and harmony without arousing disturbance among the faithful. The present panel felt that in this case the pastor seems to have expended his zeal to the detriment of ecclesial communion and of peace among many of the faithful, who immediately reported to the bishop about the imprudent manner of acting of the pastor.[53]

One of the principal points the impugned sentence had stressed was the haste in which the bishop initiated and went ahead with the process of removal of the pastor. But the present panel found evidence to the contrary. Its own findings demonstrated that the bishop acted throughout the process with patience

[52] Ibid., no. 8.
[53] Ibid.

and pastoral solicitude both toward the pastor and toward the good of the parish community. This was evident in his actions as noted in the following chronology of events.[54]

On 13 September 1984, the bishop telephoned the pastor to inform him of the many complaints he had already received concerning the hasty changes he had introduced in the parish, his excessively harsh manner of reprimanding parishioners, his aversion towards women, and a lack of patience and charity towards collaborators in his ministry. According to the present panel, the bishop was very patient and prudent in dealing with the pastor. He did not reprimand the pastor immediately but patiently requested him properly and effectively to attend to the care of souls.

The situation became worse as events began to unfold fast. The religious sister left the parish in September to the surprise of many. Some parishioners complained again to the bishop saying that the actions of the pastor were proving detrimental to the parish and called for a reasonable resolution of the crisis for the sake of good of souls, but they did not call for the pastor's removal.

On 7 November 1984, the bishop personally visited the pastor and listened to him. During this meeting the bishop asked for some sort of reconciliation between the pastor and parishioners in order to heal wounded relationships. At this time the bishop also mentioned to the pastor that he had constituted a commission to investigate properly the problems affecting parish life. The bishop indicated to members of the commission that: the pastor had consented to the commission and the members were duty-bound to observe total secrecy about all matters confided to them. The bishop wanted an announcement made in the parish bulletin about the constitution of the commission so that the faithful of the parish may collaborate in restoring harmony and peace within the parish community.

On 25 November 1984, the commission heard, without any discrimination, several parishioners (about 80) including the pastor. The members of the

---

[54] This chronology of events is paraphrased from nn. 8-18 of the sentence.

commission did not write a collegial report, rather each one of them submitted his/her own report on the results of the hearings. Nevertheless, all reports agreed on one issue, that is, there was confusion, discord and division in the parish, and the principal cause of it all was the pastor himself. The view of the commission as a whole was that the pastor's behavior was not readily changeable for the better. Therefore, it concluded that, if the pastor were allowed to remain in office, dissensions would become more serious.

According to the present judicial panel, the commission intimated to the bishop what he really did not want to do, that is, to remove the pastor. He was really hoping that the pastor would continue in office with a radical change in his pastoral approach. Therefore, the judges were of the opinion that, contrary to the conclusion of the impugned sentence, the commission was not constituted as a first step toward the removal of the pastor. They dismissed as incorrect the impugned sentence's view that the date of 25 November 1984 was the beginning of the process of removal. This observation of the panel was derived from the following facts: After the commission had completed its mandate and submitted its reports, and after he had heard each member of the commission, the bishop took no action against the pastor nor did he indicate his intention to remove the pastor, rather he visited the pastor on **12 December 1984** and, as a good pastor himself, advised him to seek out reconciliation with the parishioners who might have felt hurt by his actions. But when he learned that the pastor was obsessed with the vindication and assertion of his authority in the parish, the bishop pleaded with him to seek expert psychological help. Although such a pastoral way of dealing with the pastor had little effect, it certainly confirmed the fact that the bishop was being just and truly equitable in his treatment of the pastor.

On 24 January 1985, as there was no indication of the possibility of resolving the crisis in peace, after consulting his episcopal vicars (*vicariis episcopalibus consultis*), the bishop came to the decision to substitute the pastor with another priest for the good of the parish community. The present panel considered this date, **24 January 1985**, to be the moment when the process for removal truly began, although from a strictly juridic point of view such a process was really not in place yet. It seems to have begun the very next day, **25 January 1985**, when the bishop discussed the matter with one pastor consultor (*parocho consultore*), and then on 29 January 1985 he did so with another pastor consultor. Both consultors were of the opinion that there could be no peace in the parish so long as the pastor remained in office. In response to this opinion, the bishop met with the pastor to discuss the matter and proposed to him resignation from office allowing him 15 **days** to do so. The pastor rejected the bishop's proposal and on **1 February 1985** wrote to the bishop asking him to remove his predecessor from the parish residence.

On 5 February 1985, the bishop wrote to the pastor explaining how he had supported him all along, but he could no longer do so. Therefore, he suggested to the pastor that for the good of the parish and for his own good he should resign from parochial administration.

On 8 February 1985, the bishop visited the pastor again, but this proved futile. In fact the pastor treated the bishop in a disrespectful manner. The pastor wrote to the bishop on **10 February 1985** demanding access to the reports and tape recordings of the commission's hearings of 25 November 1984.

On 19 February 1985, the bishop invited the pastor in writing in which he gave reasons why he should resign from office. The pastor refused even to receive the letter. The bishop sent a priest on 2 March 1985 to hand-deliver the same letter, but the pastor reported that priest to the police.

On 25 February 1985, the pastor reported his bishop directly to the Supreme Pontiff and sent several documents. He also had the matters published in the local daily newspaper on **1 March 1985** making public even the information that was strictly personal.

On 4 March 1985, the bishop wrote to the pastor extending the time limit for resignation to the 14th of March or to show cause in writing for his refusal to abide by his proposal to resign. These efforts of the bishop were in vain as the pastor wrote two letters, one on the 12th of March and the other on 18th of

March, reiterating his intention not to resign from office and his right to inspect the acts and to have access to the tapes of the commission's hearings of 25 November 1984. He contradicted the bishop saying that the good of the parish did not call for his resignation, indeed the majority of parishioners, he claimed, did not want him to resign.

On 15 March 1985, the end of the extended period of time suggested for resignation of the pastor from office, the bishop, together with two pastor-consultors (*parochis consultoribus*), examined everything the pastor had written. The very same day the bishop wrote to the pastor to invite him to come and inspect the acts on the 20th of March and demanded that he present his reasons and contrary proof, if any, by the 25th of March. The pastor did not accept this invitation, that is, he did not appear to inspect the acts.

On 25 March 1985, hoping to resolve the impasse in a peaceful manner, the bishop wrote again to the pastor asking him to resign from parochial office. The pastor again turned down this request and reiterated his earlier demands. In the meantime, the bishop even proposed a mediator. However, the mediator failed to do anything because of several circumstances.

On 17 April 1985, the bishop reviewed again the entire matter with the two above-mentioned pastor-consultors (*parochis consultoribus*) and found no sufficient reason to withdraw his decision to remove the pastor from office. Furthermore, the consultors did not think that the reasons put forth by the pastor against his removal from office were legitimate and just as required by law. Therefore, on **31 May 1985**, the bishop again invited the pastor to inspect the acts at the vicar general's office and to present his reasons before **17 June 1985**. The pastor rejected this invitation.

On 7 June 1985, the bishop re-evaluated the matter with the same two pastor-consultors (*parochis consultoribus*), who recommended that the pastor be removed from office. The bishop did not issue the decree of removal at this point in time. However, on **21 June 1985**, the pastor placed recourse *ad cautelam* before the Congregation for the Clergy.

It was only on **1 July 1985** that the bishop issued the decree of removal which the pastor refused to receive. The bishop wanted to explain the matter in person so that the pastor might be disposed to accept the decree which was sent through both registered and ordinary mail. The pastor sent two letters dated 3rd and 4th of July in response to the bishop's decree, and on the 5th of July he sent off his recourse against the decree to the Congregation for the Clergy.

This chronological sequencing of events leading up to the issuance of the decree of removal demonstrates, according to the present panel of judges, that the bishop had done everything possible to safeguard the good of the parish as well as that of the pastor. The judges also affirmed that the bishop had gone beyond the demands of justice in trying to assist the pastor during the period of such turmoil in the parish.[55]

One of the issues about which the impugned sentence had complained concerned certain documents missing in the acts. Despite this complaint, the authors of the impugned sentence stated that "the acts were sufficient to reach a decision."[56] The allegation of the preceding panel was true in regard to some documents. The tape recordings of the commission's hearing on 25 November 1984 were certainly missing. But these had little relevance to the challenged decree. Although those tapes were destroyed, there were nevertheless four reports of the commission members on the results of that meeting. The impugned sentence also alleged that the opinions of experts, which the Congregation for the Clergy usually requires before making its decision on any recourse, were missing in the acts. But the present judges felt that those opinions had no relevance to the resolution of the matter under consideration.[57]

The judges who pronounced the impugned sentence stated that the acts presented to them seemed insufficient to sustain the decision of the bishop. Yet,

---

[55] *"Ex his omnibus clare deducitur multa patravisse perficisseque Episcopum in bonum tum paroeciae tum parochi; et dici etiam posse videtur plus egisse Episcopum quod ius exigit. At, omnia quae episcopus fecit non habentur in sententia impugnata; vel pauca in ea deprehenduntur vel considerata"* (ibid., no. 17).

[56] *"Ipsa sententia impugnata dicit documenta deesse in actis, et 'nihilominus asseritur acta sufficientia fuisse ad decisionem capiendam in casu"* (ibid., no. 18).

the same judges failed to explain why their own decision was based exclusively on the documents presented by the pastor without examining the several documents which attested to the manner in which the bishop had acted toward the pastor, a manner which the impugned sentence itself acknowledged as "neither confused nor entirely singular (cf. p. 11)."[58] As noted above, the present judges felt that the bishop had done everything he could to help the pastor, while the pastor on his part pursued his own good rather than that of the faithful entrusted to his care.

Violation of Law in Procedendo

The impugned sentence had identified several procedural violations when the bishop issued the decree of removal of the pastor. The present panel tried to respond to the arguments adduced by the preceding panel concerning these violations.

First, the impugned sentence alleged that the constitution of the commission to investigate the reasons for trouble in the parish tarnished the good name of the pastor. But the present panel did not think that this interpretation was correct. In fact, this panel argued that already prior to the constitution of the commission there were complaints in the parish about the pastor's unsatisfactory manner of acting. Did the inclusion of the psychologist/psychiatrist in the commission call into question the mental health of the pastor as alleged by the impugned sentence? The judges did not think so, because the faithful were more surprised at the manner in which the pastor was carrying out his pastoral ministry and by his uncivil (*inurbane*) way of dealing with people than by the presence of a psychological expert in the commission.[59]

---

[57] Ibid.

[58] "*[...] quin examinata fuerint acta plurima quae modum agendi Episcopi referunt, qui modus neque confusus neque omnino singularis fuit, uti sententia impugnata scribit* (cf. p. 11)" (ibid., no. 18).

[59] Ibid., no. 19.

Second, the first panel of judges of the Signatura had found questionable the participation of certain members of the parish community in the commission's hearings. The impugned sentence had stated that "not all those who participated in the meeting of 25 November [1984] had ... such upright and serious minded attributes."[60] What was insinuated in this statement was the alleged participation of the retired pastor and of the religious sister in the commission's hearings. The second panel regarded this assertion to be a gratuitous because there was nothing in the reports of the commission's members to indicate lack of their own probity and sense of responsibility. The same reports also made no mention of the participation in the hearings of the retired pastor or of the religious sister who had already left the parish in September.[61]

Third, the impugned sentence alleged that the bishop's action was precipitous and was taken with little regard for due process. But the present judges felt that such an allegation was based on the fact that the preceding panel had failed to examine or to evaluate properly all issues, especially all the efforts the bishop had made to restore peace and harmony in the parish and to assist the pastor, as demonstrated by the many initiatives he had undertaken for this purpose. When the process of removal was actually started on 24 January 1985, the canonical reason for removal of the pastor was already clear and this was properly explained to him. In other words, by the time the process had begun the requirement of a cause stipulated in canon 1740 (*CCEO* c. 1389) had already been met and was considered as certain. Likewise, the bishop had proceeded properly when he presented the entire matter to two pastor-consultors (*parochis consultoribus*) as required by (*CIC* c. 1742, §1; *CCEO* c. 1391, §1) and discussed with them the advisability of removing the pastor.[62]

Fourth, the impugned sentence argued, "at least it is not clear that the (pastor-consultors) were from the group established for this purpose in a stable

---

[60] Ibid.
[61] Ibid.
[62] Ibid., no. 20.

manner by the presbyteral council at the proposal of the bishop."[63] The preceding panel raised this issue as proof of violation of procedural law. But the present panel disagreed with such a conclusion. It countered this conclusion saying, if it was not clear or evident, how could it be assumed as a probative argument against the bishop? Rather than assuming, the preceding judges should have proved that the said pastor-consultors (*pastores consultores*) were not the ones identified in the law. The present panel took a broader, but legally correct, interpretation of the requirement of canon 1742, §1 (*CCEO* c. 1391, §1) concerning the identity of the two pastors mentioned in it. The panel argued that, although the said pastor-consultors (*pastores consultores*) were strictly not the ones mentioned in canon 1742, §1 (*CCEO* c. 1391, §1), but because they were pastors and consultors, the demands of the law seem to have been sufficiently met by the bishop. The present judges, therefore, correctly concluded that the substance and spirit of the relevant canonical norm was adequately observed when the bishop reviewed together with two pastor-consultors (*pastores consultores*) the acts and pastor's responses. The bishop had indeed consulted two pastors from among the presbyteral council. Therefore, the difficulty regarded as very serious by the impugned sentence could not be sustained by the facts. The judges concluded that the impugned sentence suffered from a serious defect because there was no evidence that the bishop had perpetrated any substantial violation of law *in procedendo*.[64]

Fifth, the impugned sentence had noted some other procedural irregularities as further proof of violation of law *in procedendo*. But the present panel regarded those irregularities as of minor importance.

The first irregularity concerned the absence of a notary at the meeting that took place on 30 January 1985 between the bishop and the pastor. The panel pointed out that the pastor had indicated his opposition to the presence of the vicar general or episcopal vicar at that meeting. Although no notary was

[63] Ibid.
[64] Ibid.

present, the bishop had written a report on matters discussed during that meeting which he himself had signed together with the vicar general. The panel, therefore, asked: "Shouldn't the bishop be trusted in this matter?"[65]

The second irregularity was related to the two important requirements of canon 1742, §1 (*CCEO* c. 1391, §1): the bishop had not explained properly to the pastor the cause and arguments behind his demand for the pastor's resignation (requisite for validity of the process) and he had failed to give him 15 days' notice for submitting it. But the present panel did not find evidence supporting these irregularities because there was sufficient proof that the bishop had fully complied with the stipulations of canon 1742, §1 (*CCEO* c. 1391, §1).

When the bishop was convinced that the pastor had to be removed, he tried his best to persuade him to resign in fifteen days indicating appropriate reasons and arguments during the meeting they had on 30 January 1985. The impugned sentence completely overlooked this meeting and directed it attention solely to the letter of 5 February 1985 produced by the pastor in which there was no mention of the 15 days for submitting the resignation. From this letter the preceding judges concluded that the requirement of 15 days notice stipulated by canon 1742, §1 (*CCEO* c. 1391, §1) for tendering the letter of resignation from office was not fulfilled by the bishop. In response to this argument, the present panel rightly stated that in a procedure of this kind truth demands that the proofs and documents presented by both parties are carefully evaluated without any partiality. The bishop on his part had requested the pastor to resign because of aversion on the part of many parishioners toward him and because of his manner of governing the parish. The present panel, therefore, found no reasonable foundation for the conclusion of the impugned sentence that the norms of canon 1742, §1 (*CCEO* c. 1391, §1) were not observed by the bishop. Such a conclusion was possible only because the preceding panel had failed to examine

---

[65] Ibid., no. 21.

carefully the letter of 5 February 1985 which the bishop had written to the pastor.[66]

Furthermore, in his letter of 19 February 1985 sent by registered mail, the bishop had again explained to the pastor the reasons for demanding his resignation, and observing the prescript of canon 1744, §1 (*CCEO* c. 1393, §1) had invited the pastor to resign from office and had once again extended the time period for his response. The pastor had received a copy of this letter although he had refused to accept the one sent by registered mail. Finally, the bishop wrote to the pastor on 4 March 1985 informing him that the time limit for his resignation had been extended to 14 March 1985, requesting him at the same time to present within the stated time limit his reasons, if any, for refusal to resign.

The judges concluded from all the arguments presented above that the bishop's manner of proceeding in this case was fully in accord with the prescripts of canon law. The bishop had indeed heard the pastor-consultors again on 15 March 1985 as required by canon 1745, 2° (*CCEO* c. 1394, 2°) before issuing the decree of removal. The present panel found that the impugned sentence had ignored or overlooked many things the bishop had done.[67]

Therefore, the present panel felt that there was only one clear and certain response to the question raised concerning the bishop's action, that is, he had properly followed the prescripts of canons 1742-1745 (*CCEO* cc. 1391-1394) *in procedendo*.[68]

---

[66] Ibid.

[67] Ibid.

[68] *"Bene vero perpensis omnibus ab Episcopo patratis, una clara certa et valida conclusio habetur. Episcopus in procedendo cann. 1742-1745 rite observavit; forsitan nimis observavit, eo nempe sensu quod plurima iterum iterumque fecit, dum sufficerent ea quae Codex praescribit. At non est reprobandus pastor qui zelum et amorem tam egregie explevit erga suum sacerdotem, semper lege et spiritu legis Ecclesiae observatis"* (Ibid.).

Violation of Law in Decernendo

The impugned sentence had argued that there was insufficient evidence in the acts of those reasons required by law for the removal of a pastor. The sentence stated that the bishop's action was "too precipitous" because after only a few months of taking possession of office, he had started to speak of removing the newly appointed pastor.[69] The present panel, as already explained above, did not find this to be true because the bishop really did not want to remove the pastor immediately, rather he advised him several times to mend his approach to parish ministry. In fact, the bishop had personally tried to help the pastor in resolving his problems. He had admonished the pastor several times before issuing the decree of removal.

The impugned sentence argued that the pastor had received no support from his bishop in times of his difficulties. This could be true if one were to believe only the pastor's side of the story. The present panel found the contrary to be true, that is, the bishop had "considered, supported and helped the pastor for several months as his brother and friend." In fact he once told the pastor: "Just as you are a good priest, you can become a good pastor." These were words that came straight from the bishop's heart and were addressed to the pastor himself.[70]

The preceding panel had argued that the inclusion of a psychologist in the commission of inquiry and then the appointment of a psychiatrist as mediator had compromised the good name of the pastor. But the present panel considered this allegation to be untrue because the inclusion of the psychologist in the commission was not intended to evaluate the psychological condition of the pastor but rather to facilitate the inquiry into the problems caused primarily by the pastor's manner of exercising parochial ministry. Although the pastor had tried to shift the blame for all his problems on to others, the judges said that there was sufficient evidence to prove that the behavior of the pastor was the

---

[69] Ibid., no. 22.

[70] *"Episcopus per plures menses habuit, sustinuit, adiuvavit parochum tanquam fratrem, amicum. 'Tanquam bonus sacerdos, tu es et bonus pastor tu potes fieri'; haec sunt verba quae ex corde boni pastoris, uti est Episcopus, fluxerunt et scripta sunt parocho"* (Ibid.).

principal cause underlying his inability to carry out his parochial ministry as a "good pastor." Therefore, the conclusion of the second panel at the Signatura was:

> Therefore, since it appears that all the information contained in the acts had not been examined by the impugned sentence, which is found to have been based more on the documents presented by the pastor than on those produced by the bishop, it is lawful to conclude that *restitutio in integrum* should be granted against the impugned sentence which had become *res iudicata*.[71]

According to canon 1648 (*CCEO* c. 1329), if *restitutio in integrum* is granted, the judge must pronounce on the merits of the case. The judges of this panel decreed that in view of all that has been stated above, "there is no proof of violation of law either *in procedendo* or *in decernendo* in respect to the act of the bishop issued on 1 July 1985 and confirmed by the Congregation for the Clergy on 4 March 1986."[72] In essence, the present panel upheld the legitimacy of the decree of removal of the pastor issued by the bishop.

Any critical reader of our analysis of this case will certainly find substantial differences between, even clear contradictions in, the two Signatura's sentences. Each panel seems to have analyzed the facts and interpreted legal principles quite differently, thus arriving at different conclusions to the same questions. It seems evident that the second panel has tried to provide a more objective evaluation of the facts and a much more integrated approach to the interpretation of legal principles by going beyond the letter of the law. In light of what has happened to this case until this point, can this second sentence be regarded as final? In other words, because of the obvious differences and contradictions in the two sentences, would it be legitimate for someone to ask the question

---

[71] *"Ideo, cum omnia, quae in actis habentur, non videntur examinata fuisse a sententia impugnata, quae innixa deprehenditur potius documentis a parocho exhibitis, quin dicatur de illis ad Episcopo allatis, concludere fas est adversus sententiam impugnatam, quae transiit in rem iudicatam, concedendam esse restitutionem in integrum"* (Ibid., n. 23).

[72] *"In casu, cum de causa principali iam peramplum contradictorium habitum sit, cumque ex supradictis satis appareat quid ad rem censendum sit, statim decernimus non constare de violatione*

whether the second sentence is in fact *res iudicata*, and therefore, not subject to appeal or open to *restitutio in integrum*?

Dismissal from the Clerical State

A cleric may lose his clerical state in three ways: (a) by a judgement of a court or an administrative decree, declaring the ordination invalid; (b) by the penalty of dismissal lawfully imposed; (c) by a rescript of the Apostolic See (c. 290). The case discussed in this section is an example of the second hypothesis.

As an expiatory penalty perpetual in nature, dismissal from the clerical state cannot be laid down by particular law (c. 1317), nor can it be threatened by way of a precept (c. 1319, §1) or imposed or declared by means of a decree (c. 1342, §2). The spirit underlying the Church's penal law clearly implies that the decision made in regard to the imposition or declaration of such a serious penalty must reflect the principles of justice, equity, and evangelical charity. The following case presents to us a concrete scenario in which an interplay of strict justice and equity seems clearly evident in the two decisions pronounced by the Church's courts on the dismissal of a cleric from his clerical state as a penalty for committing the crime mentioned in canon 1395, §2.

Facts of the Case[73]

Father John was ordained in 1978. From July 1978 to 1986 he did his pastoral ministry in a parish. From 1988 to 1990 he was assigned to hospital ministry. It was at this stage that all faculties were withdrawn and he was prohibited from celebrating mass.

Several accusations against Father John were received from the very beginning of his ordination involving serious violation of the prescription of canon 1395, §2. All warnings and penal remedies proved futile. Finally, the ordinary decided to initiate the penal procedure and the action was instituted by

---

legis tum in procedendo tum in decernendo relate ad actum ab Exc.mo Episcopo N. die 1 iulii 1985 latum et a Congregatione pro Clericis die 4 martii 1986 confirmatum" (Ibid., n. 24).

[73] Decision *c.* Colagiovanni, 14 June 1994, in *Monitor Ecclesiasticus* 122 (1997): 90-95.

the promoter of justice. On 18 February 1990, the petition was accepted by the collegiate tribunal which was constituted by the bishop for this case.

On 2 April 1992, the grounds of accusation were determined as follows: Whether John offended against the sixth commandment of the decalogue with minors under the age of sixteen?

If he is found to have committed such an offense or offenses, what penalties, if any, should be applied?

After completing the instruction of the case through the acquisition of several complaints against the respondent concerning sexual crimes against minors below the age of sixteen and after considering both the violations of canon 1395, §2, and the penal and spiritual remedies as well as the psychological treatments he had received, the court responded to the doubts on 26 August 1993 as follows: Affirmative, to the first (there was proof of accusations); John is dismissed from the clerical state – to the second.

On 2 September 1993, the respondent appealed to the Apostolic Signatura which remanded the case to the Roman Rota. On 9 April 1994, the rotal *turnus coram* Colagiovanni determined the terms of the controversy as follows: "Whether the respondent had violated the prescription of canon 1395, §2 and indeed had perpetrated the crime mentioned in the canon with a minor below the age of sixteen, and if the response is affirmative, what penalty should be imposed, that is whether the sentence of first instance should be confirmed or overturned." The sentence of 14 June 1994 by Colagiovanni is quite brief but very precise in its explanation of the legal principles and their application to this particular case.

Legal Principles

In the law section of his sentence, Colagiovanni outlines several important juridical principles concerning three issues, namely:

- The concept and finality of penal law
- Imputability of the crime
- The predisposing factors

The Concept and Finality of Penal Law

First, Colagiovanni admits that in recent years there has been a serious controversy in regard to the concept and finality of penal law in the Church. Three principal goals are being pursued in the application of penalties in the Church:

- reparation of the scandal
- restoration of justice
- conversion of the guilty (c. 1341)

These goals are the principal aim of *medicinal* penalties (cf. c. 1312, §1, 1°; cc. 1331-1333).

While through *expiatory penalties* (cf. cc. 1312, §1, 2°; 1336) the demands of justice and good of the Church are restored through the reparation of scandal, in *medicinal penalties* the reparation of scandal is in some way included in the penitent's will, and therefore, in the willing disposition of the penitent, restitution of justice is also achieved. In *expiatory penalties*, however, the penalty has a significance autonomous from the will of the delinquent. This goal was more explicitly expressed in the 1917 code through more severe expressions under the term: "vindictive penalties." But in all penalties, the ultimate goal to be pursued is "the salvation of souls."

Second, canon 1342, §1 declares the general principle that penalties can be imposed or declared "through an extra-judicial decree." But the second paragraph of the same canon *excludes* perpetual penalties from being imposed or declared by extra-judicial decree. Therefore, in case of canon 1395, §2, only a judicial process is allowed.

Third, recourse to penalties must be made only when *fraternal correction* or other pastoral approaches have proved futile (c. 1341). Moreover, even though the perpetrator of a crime is not to be exempt from a penalty, the penalty described in the law or precept must be diminished, or a penance substituted in its place, if the offence was committed by persons under extenuating personal circumstances (cf. c. 1324, §1). In such circumstances the judges can invoke "equitable pastoral economy" in imposing penalties that are suitable to the condition of the delinquent.[74] This principle is of much importance to the solution suggested by the *turnus coram* Colagiovanni in this case.

Fourth, in order to impose a penalty, the judge must have *moral certitude* derived from the acts and from the proofs concerning the commission of the crime, its gravity and imputability (cf. c. 1608).

Fifth, the judicial confession against oneself from the accused (c. 1535), where the public good is not at stake, relieves the other party of the onus of proof (c. 1536, §1). However, testimonies, documents, expertise, etc., will certainly be useful in determining the objective gravity of the delict and the imputability, that is the extent of freedom exercised in violating the law.[75]

Imputability of the Crime

Colagiovanni explains, citing DSM-III-R,[76] that there is no doubt that pedophilia must be considered one among the more serious deviations or disturbances of personality. According to DSM-III-R, such an attraction of instinct is one of the "Sexual Disorders"[77] which "is recurrent," and in which there are "intense sexual urges and sexually arousing fantasies of at least six months' duration involving sexual activity with a prepubescent child. . . . The age of the child is generally 13 or younger ... same sex, opposite sex or same and opposite."[78]

---

[74] *"At etiam in poenis applicandis ordine juridico servato, illae poenae irrogandae sunt quas sufficere judices tenent quin ad graviores applicandas procedant, in aequa oeconomia partorali continendas, prae oculis habitis circumstantiis ipsam personam attingentibus eiusque libertatem et responsabilitatem imminuentibus recensitis in canone 1324 §1"* (Ibid., 92).

[75] Ibid.

[76] *Diagnostic and Statistical Manual of Mental Disorders* (Third Edition Revised) [*DSM-III-R*] (Washington, DC: American Psychiatric Association, 1987): 279-296. It should be noted that some important changes are introduced into its fourth edition. See *Diagnostic and Statistical Manual of Mental Disorders*, Fourth Edition [*DSM-IV*] (Washington, DC: American Psychiatric Association, 1994): 493-538.

[77] In *DSM-IV*, this group of sexual disorders are under the general diagnostic title: "Sexual and Gender Identity Disorders."

[78] *DSM-III-R*, 284; *DSM-IV*, 527-528.

In this case it was not pure homosexuality, because the accused had committed serious violations against the sixth commandment with boys as well as girls. In fact, his sexual disorder was accompanied with fetishism. Colagiovanni argues that without doubt such "intense sexual urges," because they constitute a true psychic pathology, diminish one's freedom and lessen the responsibility.[79]

Further, it is a progressive disorder: "The course is generally chronic, especially in those attracted to boys. The frequency of pedophilic behavior often fluctuates with psychological stress. The recidivism for people with pedophilia involving a preference for the same sex is roughly twice that of those who prefer the opposite sex."[80]

Predisposing Factors

Many people with this disorder were themselves victims of sexual abuse in childhood.[81] In this case, the respondent states "to have been sexually abused ... between the age of 10 and 12. The abuser used to bring him and other boys to his desk in the classroom and he would feel their genitals."[82]

Whatever might have been the nature of such an abuse, the structural factors and the habit protracted well over ten years, certainly intensified the impulses which, even if they did not destroy his freedom, they certainly diminished it.[83]

Application of the Principles

First and foremost it is important to prove that the alleged crime was in fact committed by the respondent and that it was imputable to him:

---

[79] For a more precise explanation of imputability in cases of this kind, see decision *c.* Davino, 4 May 1996, in *Forum* 7 (1996): 2, 379-383.

[80] *DSM-III-R*, 285; *DSM-IV*, 528.

[81] *DSM-III-R*, p. 285. This information has not been reproduced in *DSM-IV*.

[82] *C.* Colagiovanni, 14 June 1994, 93-94.

[83] Ibid., 94: "*Quidquid sit de tali abusu, certo certius factores structurales et habitus per ultra decennium protractus, auxerunt illas pulsiones quae, si libertatem minime abstulerunt, certo imminuerunt.*"

- There was an admission of the crime. The respondent confessed before the judge that he had violated canon 1395, §2: the crime against the 6th commandment of the decalogue "with a minor under the age of sixteen years."[84] Thus, there is no doubt that the respondent had confessed his sexual crimes with minors.
- Recidivism was evident in this case. His abnormal behaviour was constant: All warnings, admonitions, threats of sanctions were in vain. Also, spiritual and psychological treatments proved futile.[85]
- The penalty to be imposed must take into account his serious psychological infirmity.

Unlike the local court, the rotal *turnus coram* Colagiovanni felt that, in view of the complex *subjective circumstances* of the accused, the penalty of reduction to lay state, a very serious and perpetual penalty, was not to be imposed at this stage of his life. The *turnus* acknowledged that according to the norm of canon 1395, §2, the priest must be punished with a just, serious and long penalty, which, together with prayer, meditation and divine grace, might heal his wounded personality, so that he might be able to regain full freedom, human and priestly dignity with the hope that he would not commit again the same crimes. Should he do so the maximum penalty provided in canon 1395, §2, that is, dismissal from the clerical state, must be imposed.[86]

The *turnus* also noted that there is a possibility for the respondent to seek from the Supreme Pontiff the favour of dispensation from the law of celibacy, which carries with it the reduction to lay state. This is particularly advisable in view of the deviant sexual impulses rooted in his personality long before his ordination to priesthood, and it became manifest both before and after his priestly ordination, namely during his diaconate and immediately thereafter.[87]

---

[84] Ibid.
[85] Ibid.
[86] Ibid., 94-95.
[87] Ibid., 95.

Therefore, the decision of the rotal court was as follows: There was proof of the crime mentioned in canon 1395, §2. However, as far as the penalty was concerned, the court's decision was *iuxta modum*, that is, to say:

- The priest was barred from all ministry for ten years. However, he would be allowed to celebrate Mass during this time in the monastery mentioned in ii);
- The priest must spend the ten years mentioned above in a monastery under the supervision of its superior;
- The ordinary was charged with the task of executing this sentence.

Concluding Reflections

The supreme value which ecclesial law intends to promote is the "salvation of souls" (*salus animarum*). Hence every legal decision made in the Church must reflect this divine mission. In the proclamation of this supreme value, the law also has built-in safeguards for the exercise of one's rights and for the fulfillment of one's obligations. In this way the good of each individual as well as the common good of all Christ's faithful is peacefully realized within the context of ecclesial communion. Unless both these aspects of the supreme goal of ecclesial law are properly understood and appreciated, the decisions ecclesiastical authorities or institutions make are likely do more harm than good both to individual members and to the Church. The cases discussed above attest to some of the problems that arise when laws are implemented in an inappropriate or illegitimate manner. However, and this is most important, these cases illustrate how the procedural laws of the Church can be used remedy faulty decisions and arrive at the truth.

When a decision concerns a transfer or removal of a pastor or suspension or dismissal of a cleric, one must first and foremost keep in mind that the law is only a means to administer justice and equity in a given case. Thus, it is important that the bishop follow the law faithfully both to protect the rights of Christ's faithful as well as to insure that his decisions will be acceptable to the universal Church. A bishop, or any ecclesiastical authority for that matter, should keep in mind that in the law lies his protection. A decision made in accord with the letter and spirit of the law, with fairness, impartiality, honesty and rational and consistent reasons, will always be regarded as just and equitable. This necessarily implies that in making decisions one must know well the law(s) to be applied and takes into consideration while applying it all the extenuating circumstances of the concrete person involved. Equity means just application of the law to a concrete case with mercy and compassion. The spirit of ecclesial law necessarily demands such an application. This is most apropos when decisions involve the imposition or declaration of penalties. In these situations utmost respect is due to the dignity and fundamental rights of persons. A decision that is made in view of the salvation of souls and with deep respect for the dignity and well being of the concrete person will always reflect the spirit of justice and equity.

A Few Reflections on Canon 1060

ELISSA RINERE, CP

Introduction

As the Catholic Church nears the century mark of having codified law, one cannot but be amazed at the constant change and development coming from this form of law, intended at the outset to be stable and unchanging. Certainly the 1917 code was the subject of much attention and study, and now the canonical world constantly delves into the text of our second universal code, still finding new meaning, application and interpretation for what was promulgated in 1983. For instance, still in constant development at this time are the new canons on the obligations and rights of the Christian Faithful (cc. 208-223) and, especially in light of developments in lay ministry, canon 129, §2 on the cooperation of laity in the exercise of the power of governance.

Canonical developments surrounding texts such as these which are new to the law are, in a certain sense, to be expected. However, with an eye to a contrary pattern, this paper will consider a canon which is not new, but which came to the 1983 code substantially unchanged from the 1917 code. The text of the canon has not changed in substance, but the canon itself has indeed undergone very significant development with very significant consequences, especially for tribunal ministry. Our subject is canon 1060:

> C. 1060: Marriage possesses the favor of the law; therefore, in cases of doubt, the validity of the marriage must be upheld until the contrary is proven. [1]

This statement, short, sweet and unassuming as it is, is the foundation stone upon which stands all tribunal procedure concerning the adjudication of claims of nullity of marriage. That is a broad statement, but even a very cursory study of certain aspects of the canon will easily prove the statement to be true.

In this paper, consideration will first be given to the history of the predecessor to canon 1060, canon 1014 in the 1917 code and the ways in which that canon influenced tribunal practice. Then attention will be given to two separate but interrelated forces which acted upon the canon and brought new meaning to it: the unique experience of American tribunals from 1971 to 1983 under the American Procedural Norms, and the revision of the 1917 code. Finally, having tracked our canon through the better part of the 20th century, we will consider some points on what its course of development might be in the 21st century.

History of the Canon

The canonical principle that marriage enjoys the favor of the law arose within the context of *ligamen* situations, when determinations were needed about which of a number of successive marriages for one individual was to be held as the binding union. The choices, of course, would be between a first marriage which had already been terminated, and a subsequent marriage which was "in possession." A marriage "in possession" meant "the parties, in good

---

[1] *Codex Iuris Canonici auctoritate Ioannis Paulii PP.II promulgatus* (Vatican City: Libreria Editrice Vaticana, 1983) C. 1060: "*Matrimonium gaudet favore iuris; quare in dubio standum est pro valore matrimonii, donec contrarium probetur.*" Translation taken from *Code of Canon Law, Latin-English Edition: New English Translation*, (Washington, DC: CLSA, 1999). Hereafter, 1983 code.

faith, considered themselves married and were commonly considered to be married by others in the community."[2]

When faced with such situations, Pope Innocent III (d. 1216) determined that it was "more tolerable" to favor the indissolubility of the first marriage than to recognize the validity of the subsequent union, even though it was in possession.[3] Thus, in *ligamen* situations, the favor of the law was given to first marriages over subsequent marriages in order to protect indissolubility.

A second and variant thread in the history of the favor of the law toward marriage, listed in the 1917 code as a source for canon 1014,[4] was an instruction issued by the Holy Office in 1887.[5] The instruction stated, again within the context of *ligamen* situations, that in the presence of doubt about the validity of the first and broken marriage, it was possible to conclude that the subsequent and existing marriage was valid.

This instruction clearly showed that marriage enjoyed the favor of the law in the 19th century. However, the purpose of the favor was to recognize the validity of a marriage already in possession in good faith and to remove whatever slight doubts there might be.[6]

Before the publication of the 1917 code, both these approaches for *ligamen* situations were argued by canonists, some following the mind of Innocent III and others that of the Holy Office.[7]

Then, the compilers of the 1917 code took the principle of "favor of the law" from its initial context of *ligamen* and established it as a legal presumption

---

[2] John Beal, Title VII, "Marriage" [cc. 1055 – 1165] in *New Commentary on the Code of Canon Law*, ed., John Beal et al. (Mahwah, NJ: Paulist Press, 2000) 1256. Hereafter, *Commentary*.

[3] X.2.20.47; this is referenced in Robert Thrasher, "Canon 1014 and the External Forum and Internal Forum Solutions: An Update," in *Marriage Studies I*, ed. Thomas Doyle (Toledo, OH: CLSA, 1980) 146.

[4] *Codex Iuris Canonici Pii X Pontificis Maximi iussi digestus Benedicti Papae XV auctoritate promulgatus* (Vatican City: Typis Polyglottis Vaticanis, 1917) C. 1014: "*Matrimonium gaudet favore iuris: quare in dubio standum est pro valore matrimonii, donec contrarium probetur, salvo praescripto can. 1127.*"

[5] SCS Off., intr. (*Ad Ep. Nesquallien*) 24 ian. 1877, *Codicis Iuris Canonici Fontes*, ed., Pietro Card. Gasparri (Romae:Typis Polyglottis Vaticanis, 1926) n. 1050, p. 366 ff.

[6] Thrasher, "Canon 1014, 146.

[7] See, for instance, F. Wernz and P. Vidal, *Ius Canonicum* (Romae: Apud Aedes Universitatis Gregorianae, 1928) 5: 53-55.

for all marriages. Since, by common canonical tradition, all juridic acts were and are considered valid until proven otherwise, the canon indicated a stronger presumption for the validity of marriage than ordinarily provided by the law.[8]

Debate continued after the publication of the 1917 code over how the favor of the law applied to *ligamen* cases, but this debate was eventually terminated by decisions from the Commission for the Authentic Interpretation of the 1917 code.[9] However, the newly articulated favor of the law calling for the presumption of validity for all marriages took on a life of its own. Validity of a marriage was to be upheld even in the absence of any evidence that a marriage had been celebrated; the obligations stemming from validity were binding in the internal as well as the external forum, and the presence of doubt, either of fact or of law, had no impact on the presumption.[10]

With reference to procedures, the 1917 code mandated that marriage nullity petitions be heard by a three judge college (c. 1576 §1, 1°); required the involvement of the defender of the bond in every marriage case (c. 1586); obliged defenders of the bond to appeal every affirmative decision (c. 1986) and permitted the defender to appeal a second conforming decision to a higher court (c. 1987). None of these procedural requirements was new to the law, but their "chilling effect" on tribunals in the first half of the 20th century is well documented.[11] A 1968 survey of tribunals in the United States found that of the

---

[8] Francis Wanemacher, *Canonical Evidence in Marriage Cases* (Philadelphia, PA: Dolphin Press, 1935) 240-241: "Finally, a presumption differs from the favor of the law. The latter is wider in its extent. The legal presumption has to do only with the proving of a case while the law's favor extends in marriage to other matters of procedure, whereby, *e.g.* witnesses are heard who would not be admitted in other cases, or are heard a second time even after their testimonies have been published, or a marriage case is reintroduced allowably, even after two conformable decisions have been rendered, etc."

[9] The basic principle was established in a decision of June 26, 1947 which stated that in the presence of positive and insoluble doubt about the validity of a first marriage a second marriage is to be declared invalid, "provided the case is handled according to the ordinary course of law." This principle was then applied in two instances by the Holy Office in 1957 and 1959. See *Canon Law Digest,* vol. 3, ed. T. Lincoln Bouscaren (Milwaukee, WI: Bruce, 1934-1956) 404 and vol. 5, ed. T. Lincoln Bouscaren and James I. O'Connor (Milwaukee: Bruce, 1958-1969) 496-497. Hereafter, *CLD.*

[10] Felix Cappello, *Tractatus Canonico-Moralis: De Sacramentis* (Taurini/Roma: Marietti, 1950) 5:46-47.

[11] Lawrence G. Wrenn, "In Search of a Balanced Procedural Law for Marriage Nullity Cases" *The Jurist* 46 (1986) 602-623. In commenting on developments in procedural law from the time of Pope

116 responding tribunals, only one processed more than 30 cases in a year while 60 tribunals processed none at all.[12]

Although innumerable sociological and theological factors can be cited as influences on this lack of tribunal activity, one undeniable factor was the impact of canon 1014 of the 1917 code. In addition to its influence through the procedural points already cited, the canon overshadowed the more subjective elements of tribunal work: the rigor with which the required procedures were followed and, a related factor, the standards for moral certitude applied by tribunal judges.

Procedures

Because of the law's presumption of validity of a marriage even in the presence of doubt, the tendency was for a judge to collect as many proofs as possible in an effort to remove all doubt about validity. Multiple witnesses were common, as well as exhaustive interviews, medical examinations and reports. In 1936 the instruction *Provida Mater*[13] was issued to supplement the procedural law of the code. In it there was a specific bias against agreeing depositions from petitioner and respondent,[14] and article 117 established the procedural principle

---

Benedict XIV to the promulgation of the 1983 code, the author states: "It seems to us now that the bond of marriage was under protected prior to 1741 and overprotected in the years following 1917. Whether the 1983 code has, in fact, now found the proper balance between these two extremes remains, for many, an arguable point" (604).

[12] Lawrence G. Wrenn, "The American Procedural Norms," *The American Ecclesiastical Review* 165 (November 1971) 178.

[13] Congregation for the Discipline of the Sacraments, instruction *Provida Mater*, August 15, 1936: *AAS* 28 (1936) 313-361. Hereafter, *Provida.* All text and translation taken from William Doheny, *Canonical Procedure in Matrimonial Cases,* volume 1, *Formal Judicial Procedure* (Milwaukee, WI: Bruce Publishing Co., 1948). In the decree accompanying the instruction, a concern for procedures is made clear: "For the Church is often cunningly and boldly attacked by the enemies of Christianity, upon the pretense that she prepares the way for divorce, whereas on the contrary in these cases the sole question at issue is the validity or the invalidity of the marriage. Wherefore, in order better to provide for the prompt and secure trial and decision of these cases. . . this Sacred Congregation has deemed it not only appropriate but necessary to draw up some rules which may serve as an exact guide to diocesan judges in handling these very important matters." Translation taken from *CLD,* 2: 202-203.

[14] *Provida, articulus 113, §2: "Si utraque pars matrimonium accusaverit, aut pars conventa responderit se nihil opponere accusationi, instructor, etiam ex officio, caute inquirat de rationibus ob quas ambae in accusatione concordent aut non dissentiant."*

that these depositions were never sufficient by themselves to prove nullity.[15] Further, article 171 of the instruction was a verbatim restatement of canon 1014, while the article following tried to temper too strict an application of the presumption of validity.

> Article 172: The doubt, whether of fact or law, which favors the validity of the marriage, ought to be prudent and founded on a probable basis so that there may be grounds for presumption for the validity of the marriage.[16]

The commentary on this article indicated that its inclusion in the instruction was "intended as a caution against undue timidity in utilizing the presumptions recognized by law."

> Canon 1014 clearly states that marriage enjoys the favor of the law. This does not mean, however, that the validity of the marriage may never be impugned or that the parties may not introduce their cases before diocesan tribunals. When such cases are being studied, the doubt involved must be a reasonable one. If there is no basis whatsoever for a presumption in favor of the validity of a marriage, there is no justification in upholding the validity in the face of overwhelming evidence and clear facts. Futile and groundless objections are intended to be excluded by the present Article.[17]

Perhaps, without such strong reaction to c. 1014 when it appeared in the 1917 code, there would have been no need for an additional text which sought to restore a missing balance.

Article 113, §2: If both parties have attacked the marriage or if the defendant replied that there is no opposition to place against the accusation, the Instructor, even *ex officio*, shall cautiously examine into the reasons of the agreement between the parties or the reason why they do not disagree."

[15] *Provida, "Articulus 117: Depositio iudicialis coniugum non est apta ad probationem contra valorem matrimonii constituendam."*

"Article 117: "The judicial deposition of the consorts is not admissible as proof against the validity of the marriage."

[16] *Articulus 172: "Dubium sive iuris sive facti, quod faveat matrimonio, debet esse prudens, seu probabili fundamento nixum, ut presumptioni pro matrimonii valore locus sit."*

[17] Doheny, 416.

Associated with rigorous application of procedures was a high standard for moral certitude. *Provida mater*[18] restated the 1917 code on moral certitude[19] and commentators made a direct link between a judge reaching moral certitude and the favor of the law toward marriage.

> The judge must possess moral certitude about the matter to be settled by the decision before he can pronounce any sentence. He must obtain this moral certitude from the acts and proofs of the case. He must evaluate the proofs according to his own conscience. . . The judge who cannot arrive at this certitude after a diligent examination of the case should decide: *Non constare de matrimonii nullitate in casu.*
>
> Canon 1014 states that marriage enjoys the favor of the law. Wherefore, in case of doubt its validity is to be maintained until the contrary is proved . . . Hence, if the judge in a particular matrimonial case cannot arrive at moral certitude, he must decide in favor of the validity of the marriage.[20]

Perhaps as a corrective, in his famous allocution of 1942,[21] Pius XII reminded rotal judges, and all tribunal judges, that moral certitude is found between the extremes of absolute certainty and mere probability. However, he cautioned that to require absolute certainty would be "to demand of the judge and of the parties something which is unreasonable; it would put an intolerable burden on the administration of justice and would very seriously obstruct it."[22] It has been suggested that this allocution was delivered in response to a rotal decision in which the judges dismissed as unreliable the consistent statements of seven medical experts.[23]

Taking these factors into account, it seems reasonable and correct to conclude that the new context for canon 1014 in the 1917 code was one

---

[18] *Articulus 197.*
[19] C. 1869.
[20] Doheny, 475.
[21] Pius XII, allocution to the Rota, October 1, 1942: *AAS* 34 (1942) 338-343. English translation in *CLD* 3: 605-611.
[22] *CLD* 3: 607.

significant factor which had a chilling effect on the work of marriage tribunals in the first half of the 20th century.

Impetus for Change

The impetus for change of canon 1014 arose as Vatican II was ending, notably from within the Canon Law Society of America (CLSA),[24] and resulted in a proposal of alternative tribunal procedures designed to better serve the needs of the people. Formulated by the CLSA, the proposed procedures were studied by the National Conference of Catholic Bishops and from there were sent to the Holy See for approval. In April 1970 the text of the American Procedural Norms (APN) were approved for a three-year trial in the United States, beginning July 1, 1970.[25]

From that time until the implementation of the 1983 *Code of Canon Law*, American tribunals operated under a simplified procedural law which had its roots in pastoral concern, and which sought to respect both the sacredness of marriage and the dignity and rights of Christians.[26]

---

[23] James H. Provost, "Canon 1095: Past, Present, Future," *The Jurist* 54 (1994) 103.

[24] Thomas J. Lynch, "Implementation of Past CLSA Research in the Area of Marriage" *CLSA Proceedings 35* (Toledo, OH: CLSA, 1974) 13-16. The author recounts three areas of activity within the Society: substantive research, beginning with a 1967 symposium on indissolubility of marriage and associated issues; procedural research which led to the proposal for the American Procedural Norms; jurisprudential research which led to the publication, in 1970, of the first edition of *Annulments* authored by L.G. Wrenn. The most recent edition of this now basic text is: Lawrence G Wrenn, *The Invalid Marriage*, (Washington, DC: CLSA, 1998).

[25] Council for Public Affairs of the Church, rescript April 28, 1970. For the complete text of the APN and commentary, see *CLD* 7: 951-966. For more details on the history of the approval of the Norms, see Lawrence G. Wrenn, "The American Procedural Norms" *The American Ecclesiastical Review* 165 (1971) 175-186. On the approval of the norms the author wrote: "It was a happy day for Tribunal people. A friend of mine even passed out cigars that day. The cigars didn't say anything on them like "It's a boy" or "It's a girl" but they were very good cigars. And we had a very good set of procedural norms for use in our marriage courts" (176).

[26] Thomas Green, "The American Procedural Norms – An Assessment," *Studia Canonica* 2 (1978) 317. Also, see Wrenn, "The American Procedural Norms," 180-186 for more explanation of the pastoral goals of the APN. During the years that the United States functioned under the APN, a few conferences of bishops did received indults to apply particular norms in their respective territories. These included the Canadian Procedural Norms of 1971 and 1974, and also norms for Australia, Great Britain and Belgium. See, I. Gordon and Z. Grocholewski (eds.), *Documenta recentiora circa rem matrimonialem et processualem* (Rome, Pontificia Universitas Gregoriana, 1977) vol. 1, 256-260. Tribunals of other countries functioned under *Causas Matrimoniales*, promulgated by Paul VI on June 11, 1971. For a comparison of this document with the APN, see Green, 328-336.

A comparison of the APN and the points of universal procedural law associated with the favor of the law toward marriage focuses on one general approach and some specific norms. The general approach has already been alluded to. Where the favor of the law and the presumption in favor of validity were understood to protect the bond of marriage over the rights of persons, the APN sought a better balance. This was done, specifically, by mandating a greater role for the advocates of both parties in relation to the Defender of the Bond.[27] In contrast, the 1917 code and *Provida Mater*, art. 175, allowed advocates to have access to the acts only at the end of the evidentiary phase of the trial, just before the publication of the acts. The greater access allowed by the APN had the effect of bringing the parties of the marriage into the process as participants rather than excluding them because of suspicion about their honesty or motives.

Concerning other specific procedural points, the APN allowed for marriage cases to be decided by one judge under certain circumstances, rather than by a college.

> A collegiate Tribunal must be constituted for each case. The Episcopal Conference, in accordance with faculties to be sought from the Holy See, may permit the competent ecclesiastical Tribunal to derogate from this norm for a specified period of time so that a case may be handled by a single judge.[28]

The circumstances to be determined by the Ordinary which permitted implementation of this norm were 1) a grave reason for granting the derogation; and 2) no formal opposition expressed prior to the definitive sentence by either the judge, defender, promoter of justice or either of the parties.[29]

And, finally, the APN provided the possibility of a dispensation from mandatory appeal.

> Norm 23 II: In those exceptional cases where in the judgment of the defender of the bond and his Ordinary an appeal against an affirmative decision would clearly be superfluous, the Ordinary may

[27] Green, 325. The author listed norms 8, 11, 13, 15, 17, 18 and 19 as having this goal.
[28] Text is taken from *CLD* 7: 951- 966. Hereafter, *APN Commentary*.
[29] *APN Commentary*; *CLD* 7: 953.

> himself request of the Episcopal Conference that in these individual cases the defender of the bond be dispensed from the obligation to appeal so that the sentence of the first instance may be executed immediately.

Not only did this provision take personnel shortages at the time into consideration, but also it focused the entire nullity process more clearly on the issue of truth rather than on needless process. The commentary on the norms, after noting that the decision concerning the appeal rested primarily with the defender of the bond, stated:

> The judgment of the defender, therefore, should not depend on whether the appeal court is efficient or inefficient, liberal or conservative, but solely on whether or not the truth has already been served in the process of first instance and whether therefore an appeal would be superfluous to the cause of truth.[30]

With respect to moral certitude and the standards customarily applied under the 1917 code and *Provida Mater*, the APN had norm 21:

> The judge will render his decision according to moral certitude generated by the prevailing weight of that evidence having recognized value in law and jurisprudence.[31]

The focus was on the "prevailing weight of evidence," and into that evidence was brought "all the documents, presumptions and oaths" permitted in universal law.[32] The commentary made special mention of the undue and inaccurate emphasis placed by tribunals on the necessity of "clear and decisive corroboratory testimony of two independent witnesses" to the exclusion of other forms of evidence recognized in universal law, and sought to restore proper balance.[33]

On the concept of moral certitude, the Commentary stated:

> Furthermore, that adequate, sufficient proof must not be eroded or contradicted by prevailing proof to the contrary. When that is verified, the judge is considered by this norm to be convinced, i.e., morally certain of nullity. Moral certitude is not something over and

---

[30] *APN Commentary; CLD* 7: 953.
[31] *CLD* 7: 961.
[32] *APN Commentary*; *CLD* 7: 962.
[33] *APN Commentary*; *CLD* 7: 962.

> above adequate, prevailing proof. It is simply the subjective state which adequate prevailing proof produces in the mind of the mature judge.[34]

The APN were used by way of experiment for three years and then were renewed in 1974 for an indefinite period of time to cease with the implementation of the revised code.[35] However, it was clear very early in the experiment, even from the outset, that American tribunals came to life under this new procedural law. In the second year of use, the number of tribunals processing thirty or more cases in a year increased from one to twenty-six. The number processing no cases at all fell from sixty to fourteen. Tribunal personnel reported being encouraged and energized by these simplified procedures, working with new-found "zeal and confidence and a desire to help people," and a new experience of being pastorally effective[36]

Wrenn suggested three causes for this positive response. First, the APN were workable, that is, 23 norms were easier to handle than the 623 canons of the 1917 code plus the 240 articles of *Provida Mater*. Second, the APN were more attuned to the nature of the church as a community, as had recently been articulated in the documents of Vatican II. This meant that the APN properly reflected the common spirit of the community and its commonly held sense of justice, rather than imposing an adversarial relationship on members of the community. Third, the APN showed an appreciation for the bond of marriage and also for the rights of persons. In short, "The new procedural norms have ushered in a whole new spirit."[37]

Revision of the 1917 Code

The more than 20 years spent in revising the 1917 code (1965-1983) coincided in large part with the APN years (1971-1983), and it is clear that each

[34] *APN Commentary*; *CLD* 7: 962.
[35] See Green, 318-321 for the history behind this renewal.
[36] Wrenn, "The American Procedural Norms," 179.
[37] Ibid., 176-182.

phenomenon influenced the other. During the revision process, canon 1014 was criticized on many fronts. Canonist Stephen Kelleher, writing just two years after the conclusion of Vatican II, broadly criticized the entire nullity procedure and advocated a completely new alternate process for nullity petitions. However, he specifically cited canon 1014 as a major obstacle to justice and advocated that the presumption of validity of all marriages in cases of doubt be reduced to favor the rights of the individuals involved in the marriage.[38] Kelleher pointed to mandated suspicion toward the statements of the principals, collegiate tribunals and mandatory appeal, as off shoots of the presumption of validity and called for change.[39] Finally, he put forth the opinion that, although the stated purpose of canon 1014 and its presumption was protection of the common good, there was greater harm to the common good in holding so many individuals to marriages which had already broken down and been abandoned.

In a similar vein, Bernard Häring wrote: "The right of a person to marry . . . should prevail against the doubtful validity of an already broken marriage."[40] A 1977 publication on marriage in Africa also suggested that the revised law should favor the existing marriage over the one which had already broken down.[41]

The CLSA Task Force which critiqued the proposed schema on marriage in 1975 suggested that canon 1014 was insensitive to the rights of persons and would be better placed in a section of the code dealing with second marriage and *ligamen*. This, of course, was the original context for the text of the canon.[42]

The possibility of removing the favor of the law for marriage and the accompanying presumption from the new code was considered by the *coetus* for the revision of marriage law, but the advantages of the canon in bringing

---

[38] Stephen Kelleher, "Canon 1014 and American Culture," *The Jurist* 27 (1967) 9.
[39] Ibid., 5
[40] Bernard Häring, "A Theological Appraisal of Marriage Tribunals," in *Divorce and Remarriage in the Catholic Church,* ed. Lawrence G. Wrenn (New York, NY: Newman Press, 1973) 24.
[41] Benezeri Kisembo, Laurenti Magesa and Aylward Shorter, *African Christian Marriage.* (London: Geoffrey Chapman, 1977), 51-52 as cited in Craig Cox, *Procedural Changes in Formal Marriage Nullity Cases from the 1917 Code to the 1983 Code: Analysis, Critique and Possible Alternatives,* Canon Law Studies 528 (Washington, DC: The Catholic University of America, 1989) 128.

stability to marriage were considered more important than the cited disadvantage of offending against the rights of persons, and the suggestion was rejected. The *coetus* did note that the canon itself was not of divine law, but rather based on a point of divine law concerning the essential properties of marriage.[43]

The final result of all this debate and discussion is that the canon from the 1917 code was not revised in any substantive way. Its successor in the 1983 code, canon 1060 lacks only the reference to the one exception from the favor of the law for marriage, the privilege of the faith. Commentators explain the canon in the same way, referring readers back to the classic commentators on the first code for background and explanation. Nothing new is noted.[44] The same procedural impact of the canon is assumed.

> The favor of the law toward marriage can also be seen in procedural law: a marriage whose validity is challenged is represented by its own attorney, the defender of the bond (c. 1432); marriage nullity cases are normally reserved to panels of at least three judges (c. 1425, §1, 1°); and affirmative decisions in marriage nullity cases must at least be reviewed and confirmed by a second independent tribunal before the parties are free to marry.[45]

However, the realities of tribunal activity in the United States indicate that something is new. Throughout the process of revision of the code, and indeed for sometime before that, the "favor of the law" given to marriage was criticized as a primary problem which caused the lack of activity in tribunals. Now, thirty years later, tribunal are functioning at unheard of levels, but this canon has not changed, nor has interpretation of it been altered in canonical texts. Procedural

---

[42] Cox, 129.

[43] Communicationes 3 (1971) 70: "*Quod attinet ad canonem 1014, de favore quo gaudet matrimonium et de consequenti praesumptione validitatis matrimonii in casu dubii, donec contrarium probetur, . . . etsi opinio, recenter proposita, hanc scilicet praesumptionem esse abolendam cum praesumptiones non instititui, sed personis favere debeant, in coetu fuit considerata, canonem integrum servandum esse visum fuit, non tantum ad praecavendas frequentes incertitudines de statu matrimoniali, sed maxime quia canon non quidem est iuris divini, tamen nititur iure divino circa matrimonii proprietates essentiales.*"

[44] See, for instance, Donal Kelly, "Title VII: Marriage," in *Canon Law: Letter & Spirit*, ed. Gerard Sheehy, et al. (Collegeville, MN: Liturgical Press, 1995) 576; Luigi Chiappetta, *Il Codice di Diritto Canonico: Commento giuridico – pastorale* (Napoli: Edizioni Dehoniane, 1988) 2: 174-175.

[45] Beal in *Commentary*, 1257.

laws have been modified in some ways, but not substantially.[46] And the 1942 papal allocution on moral certitude is still the standard.

But what has brought about the drastic change in tribunal activity?

1983 Code of Canon Law

With the implementation of the revised code in November 1983, American tribunals had to adjust their procedures from the APN back to universal law. Because of developments during the revision process, as mentioned earlier, tribunals retained the possibility of single clerical judges, and the law provided a better balance between the advocates of the parties and the defender of the bond.[47] But on the other hand, the revised code mandated a return to mandatory appeal of every first instance decision, reflected no change in the common understanding of moral certitude and, more importantly, canon 1060 reflected no change in the favor of the law toward marriage and the presumption of validity of a marriage even in the presence of doubt. But despite these points, under the revised code marriage tribunals in the United States continued, and continue, to process nullity petitions in unprecedented numbers.

Currently, this fact is the focus of much heated debate throughout the church. Do these numbers reflect a cavalier attitude toward law and the sacrament of marriage? Or do the numbers reflect a timely and still inadequate response to pastoral need?[48] There does not appear to be a single clear answer for either question at this time in the life of the church. What is clear, however, is

---

[46] The 1983 Code maintains the standard of a three judge college for hearing marriage nullity case, but does allow for the possibility of a single clerical judge (c. 1425, §4); the role of the defender of the bond has been maintained (c. 1432); and the defender is obliged to lodge a mandatory appeal after an affirmative decision in first instance (c. 1682, §1).

[47] For a more complete consideration of procedural changes in the 1983 code which reflect the influence of the APN, see John Beal, "Making Connections: Procedural Law and Substantive Justice," *The Jurist* 54 (1994) 113-182.

[48] Beal in "Making Connections" notes the complexity of the situation and attributes increased tribunal activity to a combination of generous investment of personnel and finances on the part of individual diocese, technological advances which have enhanced efficiency and several "creative adaptation" of procedural law which have occasioned criticism from the Apostolic See. He then treats each of these criticized elements individually.

that tribunal ministry, just as every other element of church life, has undergone a transition. Guided by the APN experience and under the influence of the Vatican II teachings on the church and on marriage, tribunals have shifted the principle now articulated in canon 1060 from a leaning which favored the bond of marriage to one favoring the rights of persons. The balance which Innocent III found "more tolerable" in the 12th century was found not to be so in the 20th century. In this adjustment, the favor of the law toward marriage, which is not itself divine law, has responded in harmony with the whole church to the ecclesiology and theology of Vatican II, which placed such emphasis on the rights and dignity of each individual.

Thus, the canon which has not changed in basic wording has nonetheless evolved significantly. The evolution was certainly not an aberration of any sort, but an appropriate response to the times, and a rather happy commingling of law, pastoral concern and theological insight. As such, the evolution is a fitting response to the broader life of the whole Church which underwent such extraordinary development in the course of the 20th century.

Conclusion: The 21st Century

At the time of their implementation, the APN were heralded as a means of addressing certain severe pastoral problem concerning marriage, divorce and access to the sacraments.[49] However, also from the outset, they were recognized as an inadequate solution to those problems. Even in 1973, a year of such extraordinary activity for the CLSA, canonist Bertram Griffin challenged his colleagues to continue their research into procedures and jurisprudence because he saw so much more that remained to be done.[50]

---

[49] Green, 332: "The CLSA stance and the bishops' decision (to implement to APN) were based on a sense of their pastoral responsibility to people seeking annulments. There seemed to be no doubt that the APN helped greatly in correcting injustices, expediting pastoral service and improving tribunal effectiveness. Furthermore, they were based on sound theological, canonical and pastoral foundations. Otherwise the Holy See would not have approved them in the first place."

[50] Bertram F. Griffin, "Future Challenges in the Area of Marriage Legislation" *CLSA Proceedings 35* (Toledo, OH: CLSA, 1974) 22-32. Even while acknowledging the progress made through the APN,

In 1986, Lawrence Wrenn wrote of specific points in the procedural law of the 1983 code which seemed "ill suited" to the reality of marriage nullity procedures.[51] He provided a broad historical landscape for viewing procedural developments over the course of centuries and brought to light a tradition of procedural flexibility not currently seen or expected in universal law. He cited the APN and *Causas matrimoniales* as manifestations and continuations of that tradition of flexibility.[52]

Clearly, this tradition of procedural flexibility has not had its last or final expression. The very subtle evolution of the favor of the law toward marriage is evidence of its presence and its activity in our own day. Equally present in our day is evidence that this shift to a better balance between the rights of the bond of marriage and the rights of individuals is insufficient to ease the burden which the whole church experiences because of failed marriages. More is required.

These two elements of evolution and continuing insufficiency of response will carry the law forward into new procedural and jurisprudential territory which, at present, we cannot see. For the time being, reflection on canon 1060 and its journey through these two codes can leave us with the following conclusions. First, development will come and cannot be denied to those who seek it. Second, canon law is a vital element of church life; proven by its timely response to pastoral need and theological development. Third, there is great power for good in the exercise of canonical expertise in concert with theology and pastoral concern. May this integration continue through the new century for the benefit of all the people of God.

---

the author saw a critical need for development of a jurisprudence which would take cultural realities into account. He saw special needs for this development with respect to the American culture.

[51] Wrenn, "Balanced Procedural Law for Marriage Nullity Cases," 619.

[52] Ibid., 619: After discussion a number of procedural developments through history, particularly *Saepe Contingit* and *Dispendiosam* issued by Pope Clement V in the 14th century, the author stated: "The *American Procedural Norms* were very much in the spirit of *Saepe Contingit* and *Dispendiosam*. The content, of course, was quite different (it was a different age), but the spirit was very similar. It was a spirit in search of a judicial procedure that could be conducted *'simpliciter et de plano, ac sine strepitu iudicii et figura.'* When Paul VI issued *Causas matrimoniales* in 1971, he, to some extent at least, passed that spirit on to the rest of the world."

PROFILE OF CLIENTS OF A MARRIAGE TRIBUNAL

MYRIAM WIJLENS

Introduction

Many couples annually say in a public ceremony "yes" to each other and do so full of hope and trust. They are willing to share their lives with each other and would like the world to know this and want to be treated as persons with rights and obligations flowing from the marital state. Catholics not only know a wedding as a civil ceremony from which flows effects in civil law. They consider the ecclesial wedding necessary in order to be truly married. Current canon law prescribes that Catholics belonging to the Latin Church *sui iuris* who have not left the Church by a formal act (c. 1117) are bound by the canonical form (cc. 1108 and 1116). Catholics belonging to an Eastern Church *sui iuris* are bound by the prescribed canonical form as well (*CCEO* c. 828). With respect to the Orthodox faithful the Catholic Church has recognized the prescribed form by the Orthodox Church: when they want to be married validly they are to observe the form prescribed by their Church.[1] In order that persons other than Catholic or Orthodox may not live in invalid unions the Catholic Church considers those marriages to be valid which were entered into by way of "some public form of celebration."

[1] C. 1127, §1; CCEO c. 834, §2; Pontificium Consilium ad Christianorum Unitatem Fovendam, "Directoire pour l'application des principes et des normes sur l'œcuménism," *AAS* 85 (1993) 1039-119, English translation: *Directory for the Application of Principles and Norms on Ecumenism*, (London: Catholic Truth Society, 1993) here n. 153.

A marriage that has been entered in accordance with the prescribed form enjoys within the Catholic Church the favor of the law (c. 1060; *CCEO* c. 779). From this valid marriage arises a bond which is perpetual and exclusive (*CIC* c. 1134). Not all marriages, however, last until the partners depart by death; increasingly marriages fail – a fact which the Catholic Church acknowledges in particular when such a separation appears to be definite and irreversible. The couple often obtains a civil divorce and one or both partners get to know a new partner whom they would like to marry. The Catholic Church, however, teaches the indissolubility of those marriages, which were entered into validly, and thus a "new" ecclesial wedding is not possible. At the same time, the Church acknowledges that not every marriage was entered into in agreement and in accordance with the conditions prescribed by the law of the Catholic Church. Hence, the Catholic Church offers to these people, Catholics or not, the possibility to determine whether the marriage entered into fulfills all the criteria established in law for contracting a valid marriage.

The invalidity of a marriage can exist because of a defect in the prescribed form, a deficiency in the consent or the existence of a marriage impediment. Besides a declaration of nullity of a marriage, the Catholic Church also has procedures for the dissolution of the bond when the marriage was not consummated or when the privilege of the faith is possible.

Why do people submit a request for a declaration of nullity of their marriage? Colleagues who regularly give canonical advice to people who consider filing for a declaration of nullity of their marriage report that many of these persons do not consider submitting a petition because they have already a new partner and would like to get married again, but they do it foremost in order to obtain clarity in regard to their own conscience. They are interested in an objective answer to the question whether the marriage they entered into was indeed – in the eyes of the Catholic Church – a valid marriage. Hence, they intend to obtain a clarification of their legal standing in the Church and to learn whether they enjoy the rights and obligations flowing from the marital state or from the single state.[2]

It is from within the context of her own understanding of marriage that the Catholic Church offers assistance to those persons who are in need. Thus, the Church offers the possibility to conduct a judicial investigation for determining the nullity of a marriage and it offers other kinds of procedures that might lead to a dissolution of the bond. Theologians and canonists are continuously investigating the nature of marriage and its (canonical) implications and present their findings in theological and canonical publications. In particular, canonists have focused on the implications in as far as they concern the grounds for declaring the nullity of a marriage. In the context of this *festschrift*, it ought to be mentioned that Lawrence Wrenn himself has contributed to a better understanding of the canonical implications of marriage. He has done so far beyond the boundaries of the archdiocese to which he belongs; his publications have circulated around the world and undoubtedly have served many canonists in their ministry and through them many divorced people who turned to the Church have found assistance in their need. The Church can and should be grateful for his continuous service to the people of God.

---

[2] Even though it might be interesting from a sociological or theological perspective to know whether people petition for a declaration of nullity or for a dissolution of the bond because of their conscience or because they would like to marry a new partner, canon law is in a way not really interested in the motives for submitting such a petition. I believe marriage cases do not have as the predominant object the determination of the nullity of the marriage, but the juridical question behind them has more to do with the legal status of the partners and the corresponding rights and obligations flowing from this status. Hence, the true question raised by the petitioner is: "Do I enjoy the rights and obligations of a single person or of a married person? In order to answer that question a trial is set up to decide on the (in-)validity of the marriage. When the matter is considered from this perspective, one can understand and explain why the respondent enjoys a right to participate in the trial; based on the publicly given consent to marriage he or she might presume that he or she enjoys the rights and obligations of a married person. Should the nullity of the marriage been proven, then this respondent would also enjoy no longer the rights and obligations of a married person, but of a single person. That is the reason why the respondent enjoys such strong rights in a trial and that one can speak about a "right of defense." At the same time, understanding the trial in this way allows for the explanation of why the trial can be conducted without the participation of the respondent: when the respondent declares explicitly or implicitly that he or she has no interest in participating in such a trial, the judge may conclude, that he or she has no interest in a clarification of his or her status, although the status of the respondent is also clarified. In such a case the right of the petitioner to obtain juridical clarity about his or her status prevails.

Whereas Lawrence Wrenn has focused in particular on procedures and on the grounds of nullity of marriage, I would like to focus on the people who are involved in marriage cases, i.e., the petitioners and respondents. Little is known about these people because annual statistics of tribunals reveal usually only the number of cases, the grounds used and the kinds of procedures that were applied. We do know little, however, about these people themselves, about their socio-cultural background, their education, their religious denomination, their age, the number of children that are affected by their separation, etc.[3] Yet, when the Church understands its judicial system ultimately to be a ministry – something which recent Popes especially since Vatican II have often emphasized – and when it states that every person has a right to have his or her status in the Church determined, then the following questions might have to be raised:

- Does the Church adequately provide the necessary information to those who have been separated?
- Does the Church use the appropriate channels through which people might be reached?
- Do the tribunals consider sufficiently the background of their clients and whether these persons can understand the language used in the letters, forms, sentences etc.?

These questions can be answered probably only by drawing a profile of the clients and drawing such a profile is the intent of this study. The results might lead to a reflection on the improvement of the current system.[4]

---

[3] Elissa Rinere published results from research she conducted concerning the way people perceive the tribunal. She took into consideration the answers by both people who had come to the tribunal and those who were divorced but had not come. Her article reveals why people were interested in getting a declaration of nullity of their marriage or why they had no such interest. Furthermore, she asked how the clients felt they had been treated by the tribunal staff and how they had experienced the trial. Those who did not go to the tribunal answered questions such as to whom they would go, when they should have an interest? How long did they estimate a trial would take? How much, did they think, would it cost and what would be the chances to obtain such a declaration of nullity. See Elissa Rinere, "Marriage Tribunals – The Mystery Ministry," in *CLSA Proceedings* 50 (Washington, DC: Canon Law Society of America, 1988) 181-197.

[4] Ultimately an improved ministry to divorced persons might lead to a diminishing number of remarried divorced persons. See in this context also the clear and pronounced tasks outlined for the tribunal of first instance by Paul Wesemann, "Das erstinstanzliche Gericht und seine pastorale

Formulating a Questionnaire

In an attempt to draw a profile of those people who seek contact with the Church to obtain a declaration of nullity or who petition a dissolution of the bond, the first step was to consider how such a profile could and should be made. I decided to set up a questionnaire to be completed by the person could fill out who has the responsibility for collecting the evidence in accordance with canon 1428, §1 and canon 1700. The idea was that this person should be able to do so on the basis of the petition only and that a personal interview with the petitioner would be superfluous.

A further consideration concerned confidentiality. Even after completing the questionnaire there should be no possibility of discovering the identity of the actual persons behind the completed questionnaire. This implied that the questions should be phrased in such a way that no identification of the parties would be possible at any time. The next issue was to obtain the data. This was not easy since the petitions enjoy confidentiality and documents are not accessible to the public. I was able to conduct this research over the years 1998 – 2000 in the diocese of Münster (Germany).[5] I should like to point out that all petitions whether they concerned the request to obtain a declaration of nullity or whether they concerned a petition for a dissolution of the marriage bond were taken into consideration.

Hence, this study presents statistics based on data obtained in the marriage tribunal of Münster, a diocese in the Northern part of Germany which hears marriage cases in first, second and, when the Apostolic Signatura grants

Aufgabe," in *Dilexit Iustitiam, Studia in Honorem Aurelii Card. Sabattani,* Zenon Grocholewski, Vincente Cárcel Ortí (eds.) (Vatican: Libreria Editrice Vaticana, 1984) 91-118.

[5] I am grateful to the judicial vicar of the diocese of Münster, Martin Hülskamp, who saw the need for such a study and gave permission to ask my colleagues at this tribunal to fill out the questionnaires for those cases for which they were responsible as an instructing judge in first instance. To them I am grateful as well, since I could not have performed this investigation without their help.

competence, in third instance.[6] In 1998 I set up a first questionnaire, distributed it to the responsible persons for filling it out and in the beginning of 1999 I received them back. During the next year I, furthermore, asked and obtained feedback from those persons who had completed the questionnaire. As a result, I adapted the questionnaire that was to be completed for the judicial years of 1999 and 2000. Thus, I added questions concerning a possible existing pregnancy at the time of the wedding and concerning the children that were born out of these marriages. Another change concerned the cases for dissolution of the bond. Even though in 1998 the cases adjudicated by way of a documentary process were taken into consideration, the petitions that led to a procedure to dissolve the existing bond had not been taken into consideration. In 1999 and 2000 these marriages were considered as well, because the data collected in 1998 revealed that for drawing a profile of the clients, it is of less relevance to distinguish by way of the kind of procedure that is applied than to discover what kind of persons find their way to the Church to have their marital situation canonically regulated. Hence, it was felt necessary to consider all petitions irrespective of the canonical procedure that was applied.

The experiences with completing the questionnaire in 1998 and studying it, however, also resulted in a limitation: in 1998 all cases for which the tribunal of Münster was responsible in first, second or third instance were considered, but as of 1999 the cases pending in second and third instance were not further considered. The reason was simple: I felt that an imbalance might occur when the cases of second and third instance were also considered since it would not reflect the complete situation of the respective lower instances.[7]

Finally, it should be pointed out that for technical reasons it was impossible to consider one major group of cases, namely those which concerned a "defect of form."

---

[6] The city of Münster has a total population of 4,212,631 out of which there are 2,085,526 Catholics. There are 1075 diocesan and 113 religious priests, 541 lay pastoral workers and 201 permanent deacons.

The statistics below are based on the petitions requesting a declaration of nullity or dissolution of the marriage bond and that were presented to the diocese of Münster as competent forum in the years 1998, 1999 and 2000. With regard to the presentation of the results it should be noted that because of rounding of the percentages, an addition of the percentages does not always lead to exactly 100 percent.

Number of Cases in First Instance

The tribunal of first instance is the competent forum not only for marriage cases but also for other kinds of contentious trials and other procedures. The first question then is: How many cases were there in the years 1998-2000 in first instance?

	1998	**1999**	**2000**	**1998-2000**[8]
Marriage cases	114	86	108	308
Other	2	1		3
Total	**116**	**87**	**108**	**311**

Figure 1

[7] Thus petitions presented at a lower level which would never come to a second or third instance could not be considered.

[8] These are the cumulative results of the years 1998, 1999 and 2000, leading to an average number. This also applies to the statistics under figures 4 and 7.

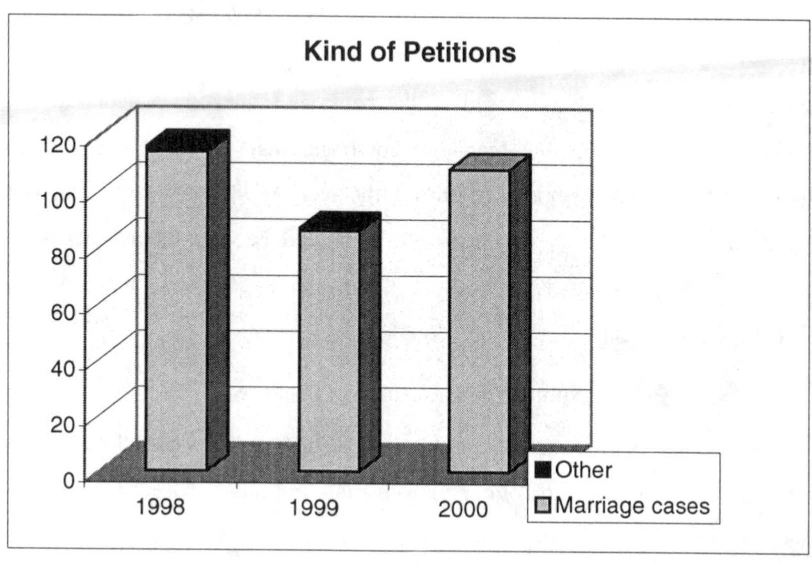

Figure 2

The statistics reveal that the number of cases dropped in 1999. This raises the question whether this is to be seen as a sign that numbers may drop in the coming years or whether the year 1999 was an exception. The statistical report made for the Holy See annually reveals that 1999 appears to be an exception in comparison to the other years. Nevertheless, a reason for this sudden drop could not be found.

The statistics reveal that in the years 1998-2000 a total number of 308 petitions related to marriages was submitted. This implies that the tribunal had to get into contact with 616 persons either as petitioners or as respondents. The petitions presented did not always allow for determining whether these petitioners and respondents had already new partners nor for establishing whether they wanted to marry their new partner. It is for that reason that the number of people who in one way or the other, that is, directly or indirectly, are touched by a marriage case can only be estimated. The maximum number would then be 616 x 2 = 1232 persons. Furthermore, the data revealed that the petitions presented in the years 1999 and 2000 involved 167 children (see section entitled *Children* below).

Considering the fact that every case implies the hearing of at least two witnesses, the total number of witnesses would be minimally 308 x 2 = 616 persons. These numbers taken together display the following picture:

308 cases	616 parties
616 parties	616 new partners (maximum)
1999 & 2000	167 children (minimal, since 1998 findings are excluded)
308 Cases	616 witnesses (minimal)
Total	**2015 persons**

Figure 3

Hence, in a period of just three years the tribunal might have touched the lives of 2015 persons, either directly (as party or as witness) or indirectly (as new partner or as a child).

Male or Female Petitioner?

Now that its clear how many cases were introduced, the next question is: Is there a difference between the number of men and the number of women presenting a petition?

	1998		**1999**		**2000**		**1998-2000**	
Gender	*Absolute*	%	*Absolute*	%	*Absolute*	%	*Absolute*	%
Woman	71	62	58	67	65	60	194	63
Man	43	38	28	33	43	40	114	37
Total	**114**		**86**		**108**		**308**	

Figure 4

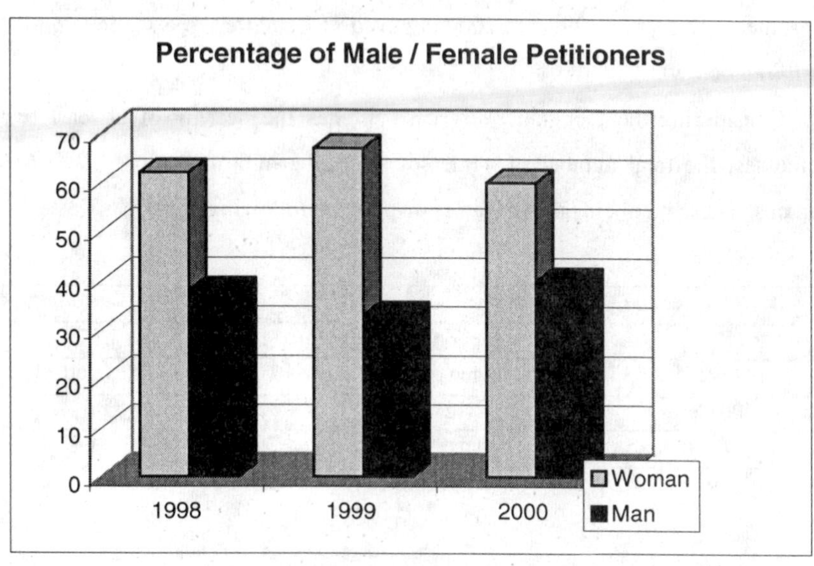

Figure 5

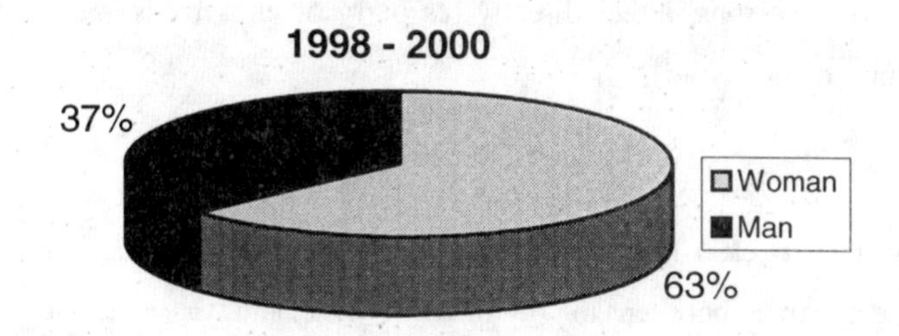

Figure 6

The numbers reveal that men do not present a petition as often as women do. Even though the number of men submitting a petition increased in the year 2000 in comparison to 1998, it appears that a span of only three years is too short a time from which to draw the conclusion that men might increasingly submit petitions in the coming years. This is an issue to be observed attentively in the years to come. It is, however, remarkable that over the period of three years women clearly display a much greater interest (almost two thirds) in presenting a petition than men do.

Should we conclude from this that women more often take the initiative to terminate a marriage? Even though the statistics might point to a positive response to this question, nevertheless, such a quick reply might be hasty, because it would not take into consideration that there might be a difference between what each actually does. One partner may leave the marriage with the felt need to obtain clarity about the legal consequences; the other partner files for a civil divorce or petitions for a clarification of his or her status in the Church. Nevertheless, these statistics point to three questions:

- Why do men submit fewer petitions than do women? Do they have no interest or do they lack knowledge about the possibilities of doing so? This difference between men and women also raises questions about pastoral care: Are men sufficiently informed and is this information presented in a way appropriate to men?
- Considering the fact that women more often file a petition, how does the Church inform them about the possibilities it can offer? The question may also be asked: how and where did these women learn about the possibilities the Church offers? Are they more often in touch with the ministers in their parish? Did they read something in e.g., (women) magazines?
- Whereas the former two questions are in particular of relevance for those in pastoral care of divorced people, the statistics also raise a question to the tribunal staff: Is the marriage tribunal sufficiently prepared to respond adequately to male and female petitioners? For example, studies in medicine reveal that consultations between male or female patients with either a male or female physician differ substantially in nature, length of consultation, and outcome.[9] This raises the question whether this also applies to the (ecclesial) courts, an issue that could be the object of further investigations.

---

[9] L. Meeuwesen, *Spreekuur of Zwijguur. Somatische fixatie en sekse-asymmetrie tijdens het medisch consult.* Nijmegen, 1988. The reference made to medicine should not be understood as an indication that only male staff members could speak with male clients and only female staff members with female clients. On the contrary, a healthy mix of male and female staff members in a tribunal seems to be desirable. Now that with the 1983 *Code of Canon Law* priests, (married) deacons and married or single lay men and lay women can be appointed judges, auditors, or defenders of the bond, the bishop has the possibility to appoint such a mixture of staff members that the needs of the clients can be considered and that the requirements of the law (c. 1421) can be fulfilled.

As far as I am aware, there is no study concerning possible relevant differences in the way trials are conducted and their outcome depending on e.g. whether the auditor is male or female.

Composition of Marriages with Respect to Confession

The *Code of Canon Law* allows every person regardless of confessional affiliation, whether they are Catholic or baptized non-Catholic or non-baptized, to request a clarification of marital status within the Catholic Church. Even though a marriage case concerns Catholics directly as a party or indirectly as the Catholic future spouse, it is nevertheless important to determine how the confessional composition of marriages is investigated. This information in this regard could have implications for judges and defenders of the bond as they become more aware of the problems arising from the socio-cultural environment of the clients which may have been influenced to some degree by the respective denomination or religion of the marriage partners. This in turn could lead to an improvement of the collected evidence as well of the judicial evaluation of the dispositions of the parties and witnesses.

Confession		1998		1999		2000		1998-2000	
		Abs	*%*	*Abs.*	*%*	*Abs.*	*%*	*Abs.*	*%*
Cath.	Cath.	74	64.9	61	70.9	76	70.4	211	68.5
Cath.	Prot.	22	19.3	8	9.3	15	13.9	45	14.6
Cath.	Unbapt.	10	8.8	1	1.2	6	5.5	17	5.3
Prot.	Prot.	3	2.6	7	8.1	4	3.7	14	4.5
Prot.	Unbapt.	3	2.6	3	3.5	2	1.9	8	2.6
Orth.	Cath.			2	2.3			2	0.6
Orth.	Prot.			2	2.3	1	0.9	3	1.0
Angl.	Prot.	2	1.8	2	2.3	4	3.7	8	2.6
Unbapt.	Unbapt.								
Total		**114**		**86**		**108**		**308**	

Figure 7

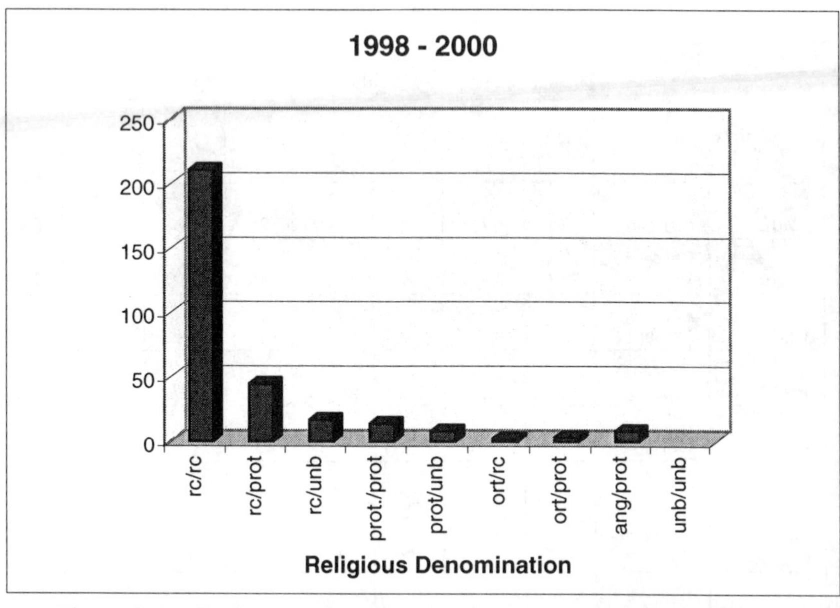

Figure 8: In this figure rc = Roman Catholic; prot = Protestant; unb = unbaptized; ort = Orthodox; ang = Anglican.

The statistics reveal the need to follow attentively in the coming years a possible increase in marriages in which both partners are Catholic. One should notice that it is not so remarkable that in two thirds of the marriages (68.5 %) both partners are Catholic, but that in almost one third of the marriages (32.5 %) at least one partner is not Catholic. This is significant, considering the fact that there is quite a difference between the number of male and female petitioners (see above). There is the further question is to be answered about the possible difference between the gender of the petitioner and confessional composition of the marriage (see next section).

Religious Denomination of the Petitioner 1998-2000

The next question was: What kind of a marriage was entered considered from a confessional or denominational perspective when the woman or when the man is the petitioner? Since the answer did not really differ for each year considered separately, the results presented here reveal the three years together.

Furthermore, the results below can be read in different ways because they respond to different questions such as:

- What is the percentage of the cases in which both partners are Catholic and where the woman or the man acted as petitioner?
- What is the answer to the previous question when the marriage is composed of a Catholic and a non-Catholic partner? Is it then more likely that the Catholic or the baptized non-Catholic partner will act as petitioner?
- Are there any differences which correlate with the man being Protestant or Catholic as compared with the woman being Protestant or Catholic?

Marriage between		**Petitioner: Man**		**Petitioner: Woman**	
Man	**Woman**	*Absolute*	*%*	*Absolute*	*%*
Catholic	Catholic	78	68.4	133	68.6
Catholic	Protestant	12	10.5	3	1.5
Protestant	Catholic	8	7.0	22	11.3
Catholic	Unbaptized	6	5.3	1	0.5
Protestant	Protestant	6	5.3	8	4.1
Unbaptized	Catholic			10	5.2
Unbaptized	Unbaptized	2	1.8	6	3.1
Orthodox	Catholic			2	1.0
Orthodox	Protestant	1	0.9	1	0.5
Anglican	Catholic			1	0.5
Total		**114**		**194**	

Figure 9

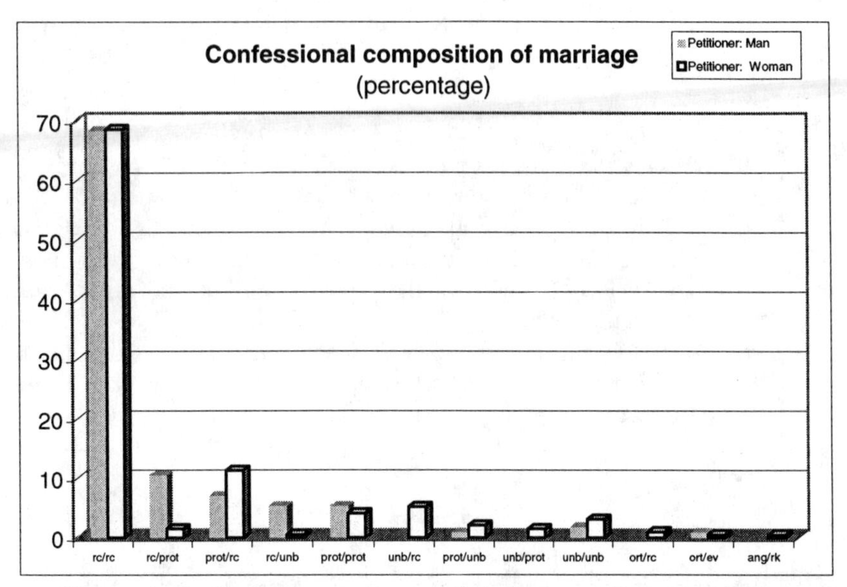

Figure 10: In this figure rc = Roman Catholic; prot = Protestant; unb = unbaptized; ort = Orthodox; ev = Evangelical; rk-Reformed Church.

The statistics reveal:

- The petitions presented mostly concern a marriage of two Catholics, whether the petitioner is male or female.
- When the marriage is between a Catholic partner and a baptized non-Catholic partner, the Catholic partner is most times the petitioner.
- When the marriage was between a Catholic and a Protestant and the man is the petitioner – which occurred in 20 cases, then in 12 out of these 20 cases (= 60 %) the man was a Catholic. In cases were the women acted as petitioner, this was even more significant: out of a total of 25 cases, in 22 cases (=88 %) the female petitioner was Catholic. At the same time, this also implies that in relatively many cases (34 out of 45 = 75.6 %) the respondent is a Protestant. The collected data does not allow for a clarification whether these non-Catholic respondents have participated as often in the marriage cases as Catholics do, or whether the courts declare them more often absent from the trial in agreement with canon 1592, §1.
- All possible combinations of confessional affiliation of the partners occur within the work of the tribunal office of Münster.

The statistics pose the question to tribunals, which might have similar figures, whether the language used in the decrees, the forms and letters take sufficient notice of the diversity in religious affiliation of the parties and in particular of the non-Catholic affiliation of the respondents.

Religious Affiliation of the Petitioner

A further question concerns the confessional or religious affiliation of the petitioner. What follows are the results of the data collected between 1998 and 2000 considered together.

	Woman		**Man**		**Total**	
Confession	*Absolute*	%	*Absolute*	%	*Absolute*	%
Catholic	137	70.6	96	84.2	233	75.7
Baptized Non-Cath.	38	19.6	16	14.0	54	17.5
Unbaptized	19	9.8	2	1.8	21	6.8
Total	194		114		308	

Figure 11

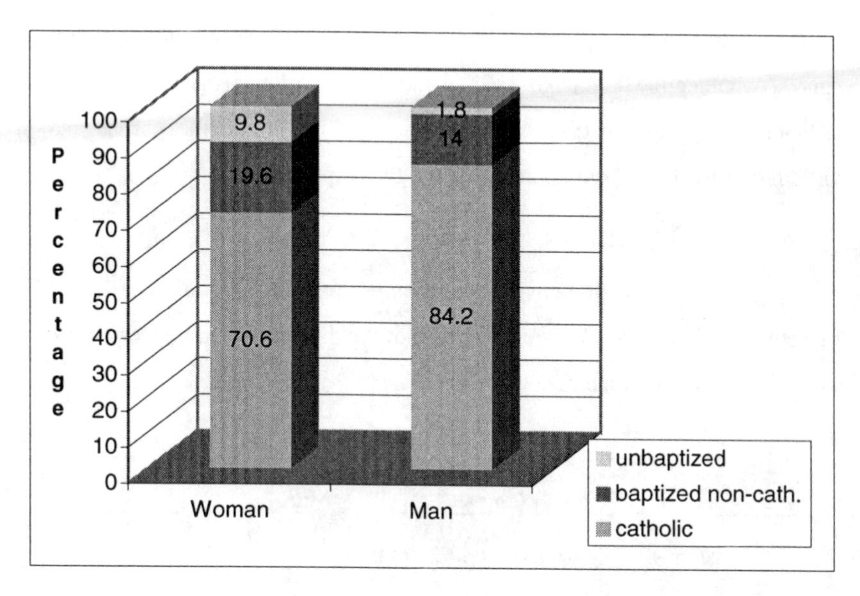

Figure 12

The statistic reveals that about 30 % those who filed a petition were women and about 15 % of the men who presented a petition were non-Catholic (both unbaptized and baptized). This leads to the following questions:

- Why are there fewer non-Catholic men than non-Catholic women who submitted a petition?
- What is the motivation for these non-Catholic petitioners (men and women) to present a petition?
- How did these persons find their way to the tribunal?
- Does the tribunal take sufficient notice of their situation and possible unfamiliarity with the Catholic Church, with its way of thinking and its language as expressed in the forms, decrees and letters that are sent out to these non-Catholic petitioners in the course of a trial?

The Age of the Petitioner

In order to get a profile of the clients of the tribunal a further question concerned the determination of the age of the parties at the time the petition was submitted. Thus the question was raised: In what year were both parties born? The results reveal the total collected data for the years 1998 to 2000.

	Petitioner: Woman		Petitioner: Man	
Year of birth	*Wife*	*Husband*	*Wife*	*Husband*
1927	1			
1931	1			
1932-1934	1	4		
1937-1939	2	2		
1940-1942	1	2	1	4
1943-1945	1	3	2	8
1946-1948	3	3	2	9
1949-1951	1	11	8	13
1952-1954	7	20	16	8
1955-1957	22	22	8	10
1958-1960	24	29	8	13
1961-1963	24	22	13	21
1964-1966	39	35	17	17
1967-1969	31	22	19	9
1970-1972	29	15	12	2
1973-1975	5	1	8	
1976-1978	1	2		
1979	1	1		
Total	**194**	**194**	**114**	**114**

Figure 13

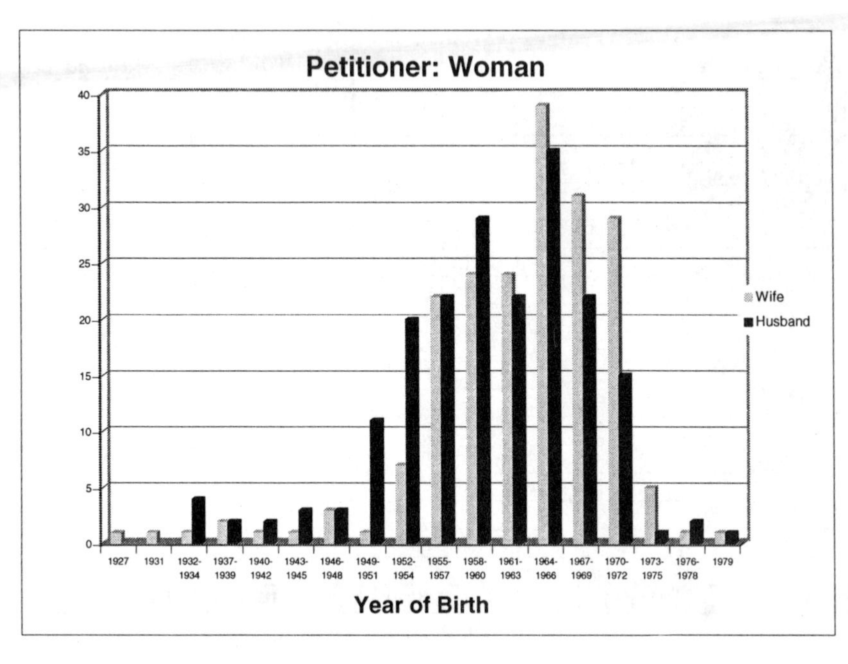

Figure 14

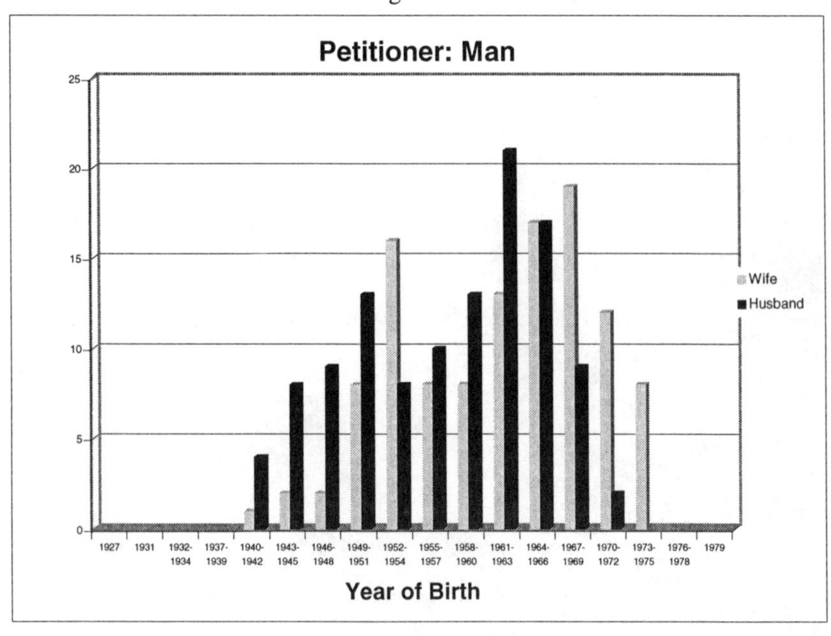

Figure 15

The statistics reveal that the persons whom the tribunal personnel meet as parties can differ considerably in age. The responses on the questionnaires revealed that there was, for example, one petition which concerned a couple both of whom had been born in 1979. They got married civilly and ecclesiastically on the same day in 1997. They separated already after six weeks and were civilly divorced in 1998. They were the youngest couple who approached the tribunal. The marriage of the oldest couple also lasted only six weeks: the woman was born in 1927 and the man in 1934. They got married in 1962 and after six weeks the man disappeared. The civil divorce was in 1966 and only in 1998 did the woman petition for a declaration of nullity. Whereas the youngest couple had married without having successfully completed their education and had been unemployed at the time of the wedding, the situation of the eldest couple was quite different when they got married: the woman had already obtained a Ph.D. and had set up her own firm and the husband had completed an education as a salesperson.

Is there a connection between education and length of marriage, or between the age at which one gets married and the duration of the marriage? Even though one might be tempted to conclude that the statistics reveal that the success or length of the marriage is not necessarily connected to the age at which the partners get married or to their education or employment, nevertheless it might be useful to investigate further such possible connections. It is regrettable that too few questionnaires were completed with regard to education and occupation since this prohibited giving reliable statistics in this matter. The reason the questionnaire could not be completed in this regard lies in the fact that the petitions often do not indicate any connection between education and length of marriage. This fact in itself is remarkable since the question may be raised whether the education someone enjoyed and his/her occupation may have belonged to the identity and personality of a person and, thus, should be of interest to the judges when they have to weigh the evidence and reach at a conclusion. Of course, these details may be obtained during the trial.

These statistics as well as those in the subsequent sub-section reveal how many men and women were between 25 and 35 years old at the time of submitting a petition for a declaration of nullity or for a dissolution of the bond.

This information poses questions to the judges and defenders of the bond: Are they sufficiently aware of and familiar with the "world" in which these persons live, so as to be able to understand the usual forms of interaction, customs, expressions, forms of communication, expectations, etc., in which context these persons gave their consent to marriage? Furthermore, it is important to notice that the witnesses often are of the same age and belong to a similar social-cultural background as the parties do. This implies that court personnel have often to deal with relatively young people. Are they sufficiently prepared for that? How do they keep themselves informed about their world?

The statistics, furthermore, lead to another question: How did these relatively young people find their way into the tribunal office? In meetings and hearings the parties and the witnesses often said – as those who had completed the questionnaire reported orally – that they only seldom attend regularly the celebration of the Eucharist on Sunday. They would, of course, get married in Church, have their children baptized, but they would not further participate in ecclesial life. These persons, as it was reported, would seldom take on a position such as being a member of the parish pastoral council, as lector or Eucharistic minister, as member of a group preparing children for their first Holy Communion or Confirmation. It is interesting to note that despite this often low or reduced participation in the life of the Church, these persons find it important to regularize their life in agreement with the canonical norms of the Church. Thus, the question may be raised whether these persons indeed did find their way into the tribunal by way of ministers in a parish or through some other source of information. This again raises a question concerning the proper and effective distribution of information about the possibilities the Church can offer to the divorced. Are the right channels being used for it?

Petitioners who are between 25 and 35 years old

The results of the previous section, *The Age of the Petitioner,* led to the following question: What was the percentage of those petitioners who at the time of presenting their petition were between 25 and 35 years old? For the years 1998, 1999 and 2000 this question can be answered as follows:

Petitioner	1998	1999	2000	1998-2000
Man	30 %	39 %	58 %	43 %
Woman	54 %	50 %	52 %	52 %

Figure 16

The great difference in particular in regard to the men for the mentioned years is quite remarkable, yet it might be premature to draw any conclusion from this, since the time span of three years could well be too short for determining whether the data changes so dramatically from one year to the other or whether these differences are mere accidental.

Another factor to be noted is that at the age between 25 and 35 years people are at a point in life where they might consider being open to having children. The law prescribes that judges and courts ought to see to a speedy conclusion such that cases of first instance should be finished within one year and cases of second instance within six months (c. 1453). The judges of the courts must take seriously this moral obligation expressed by the law especially when they consider the relative young age and thus the so-called "biological clock" of many couples.

Children

In the years 1999 and 2000 194 petitions were submitted (1999: 86 and 2000: 108). Out of these 194 marriages 167 children were born (1999: 81 and 2000: 86 children).

	Petitioner: Woman		**Petitioner: Man**		**Total**	
	Absolute	*%*	*Absolute*		*Absolute*	*%*
Marriages with Children	64	52	32	45	96	49
Marriages with No Children	56	46	39	55	95	49
Unknown	3	2			3	2
Total	**123**		**71**		**194**	

Figure 17

The data reveals as well that when the woman was the petitioner 107 children were involved and when the man was the petitioner 60 children were involved.

Pregnancy at the Time of the Wedding and Further Children

In relation to children the questionnaire not only contained a question whether children were born at all, but also whether a child was born within nine months after the wedding and whether more children were born subsequently.

The following statistics are based on the 96 marriages out of which one or more children were born. The following questions were raised:

- In how many of the 96 marriages was the woman pregnant at the time of the wedding?
- In how many marriages were there further children after the first one was born?
- In how many marriages was there no other child after the first one was born?

	Petitioner: Woman		Petitioner: Man	
Pregnant at wedding	25 (absolute)		17 (absolute)	
Additional child	14	56 %	7	41 %
No additional child	11	44 %	10	59 %

Figure 18

There are 96 marriages out of which children are born: in 42 of them (= 44%) there was already a pregnancy at the time of the wedding (male petitioner: 17 marriages; female petitioner: 25 marriages). The questionnaire did not foresee a question concerning the causality between the pregnancy and the planning of the wedding.

Considering the relatively high number of pregnancies at the time of the wedding, it certainly would be interesting to ask questions such as these:

- Was the discovery of the pregnancy decisive in planning the time of the wedding?
- Was there no concern about a premarital pregnancy because the wedding had already been planned?

The answer to these questions would certainly be interesting considering the fact that there is such a remarkable high number of marriages in which no further children were born after the woman had been pregnant at the time of the marriage ceremony (22 out of 42 marriages = 52 %). This again could lead to questions concerning the reasons for this situation.

Age at the Time of the Wedding

The data collected also allowed for an investigation of the age of the men and women at the time of the wedding. This question was raised in relation to the children.

The petitions of *female petitioners* revealed the following:

Petition by woman	Age of the woman (in years)		Age of the man (in years)	
	1999 [10]	*2000*	*1999*	*2000*
Pregnant at wedding	20.8	20.6	23.5	24.1
Pregnant after wedding	22.6	23.5	25.5	26.0
No child	24.7	26.2	28.1	29.5

Figure 19

The petitions of *male petitioners* revealed the following:

Petition by man	Age of woman (in years)		Age of man (in years)	
	1999	*2000*	*1999*	*2000*
Pregnant at wedding	23.6	23.0	23.5	26.5
Pregnant after wedding	23.8	22.0	22.8	24.4
No child	24.9	24.6	26.6	28.1

Figure 20

These results are not very clear and self evident yet. One can neither say that there is a tendency to marry at a later age, independent from a pregnancy, nor can one say that there is a development or consistency in the relationship between the age and a pregnancy. It is only possible to say that in those marriages where there are no children at all, the partners, both the man and the woman, marry at a later age than those who do have children. Yet, any conclusion in this regard is premature because the collected data spans only two years. Nevertheless, it is an issue that might need further attention in particular because statistics about age of contracting civil marriage reveal that the Western Europeans tend increasingly to marry at a later age. A further issue would be to

[10] For 1999 one marriage was not taken into consideration since in that marriage both partners were 55 years old when they got married.

relate the age and the children to the ground "exclusion of children" as a ground for the declaration of nullity (c. 1101, §2). How often is that question answered in the affirmative? If it is decided in the affirmative then the subsequent question is: is it affirmative on the side of the woman or of the man?

Conclusion

The introduction to this study set forth the reasons for drawing a profile of the clients of a tribunal. They are deeply connected with the mission of the Church itself which is to minister and be of service to people. Thus, it is the responsibility of the ministers of the Church to see to it that those who are in need are indeed served. The results of this study reveals a certain kind of a profile of the clients of a specific tribunal, but even more so they point to further questions that need to be addressed by the ecclesiastical courts and by those working for and with the divorced in pastoral offices. The most important question seems to be, whether and how the relatively young, not ecclesially connected and non-Catholic people, can be informed about the juridical canonical possibilities that the Catholic Church has to offer as a response to their broken marriages.

It may be necessary to achieve much more publicity, for example, in the secular press, in magazines and on the internet. Maybe ways and means should be sought which are not only parish based. The leaders of the Church should not only be concerned, about how many marriages end in separation, about how many declarations of nullity are issued or how many marriages are dissolved. An important question seems to be why so few people, whose marriage broke up, find their way to the ecclesiastical courts? Why is it that relatively few people show an interest to live their life in agreement with the canonical norms and regulations?

The statistics, furthermore, indicate the need to refine and enlarge the scope of the inquiry: further questions could address issues such as the length of the marriages up to separation, the length of the courtship and whether there is a connection between these factors. A further point of interest would be to consider in more detail the grounds for the declaration of nullity or the basis on which a dissolution was asked and granted. It could also be investigated whether certain grounds are mentioned more often for men than for women or vice versa. All of this could in turn have an impact on the courses preparing couples for marriage.

The statistics presented here are based on data collected in the tribunal of the diocese of Münster. It is virtually impossible to determine whether the data collected is representative of the situation of other tribunals. It is certainly possible that other tribunals in other regions of the world could present other results because of differences existing between one diocese and another. Thus, for example, the socio-cultural background of the people as well as the denominational affiliation might differ substantially. A further factor of influence might be whether the tribunal is within an area that is predominantly rural or mostly urban. This might influence the number of persons interested in seeing to it that they live their life in agreement with the norms of the Catholic Church. The results presented in this study originate from only one diocese in Germany, yet this study might and hopefully will provoke other dioceses and tribunals to reflect on the clients whom they are to serve and on the way they perform their ministry in relation to the needs of these clients.

BIOGRAPHICAL INFORMATION ABOUT THE AUTHORS

JOHN P. BEAL was born in Titusville, Pa and was ordained a priest for the Diocese of Erie, PA in 1974.

He studied canon law at The Catholic University of America and was awarded the doctorate. He is presently an Associate Professor in Canon Law at the same university, a position he has held since 1998. He was previously the Chair of the Department of Canon Law in the School of Religious Studies there.

John Beal is well known from his writings. He has written articles which have appeared in *The Jurist* and other canonical publications.

JAMES A. CORIDEN was ordained a priest for the Diocese of Gary, Indiana in 1957. He is professor of church law and dean emeritus at the Washington Theological Union. He earned his doctorate in canon law in 1961 at the Pontifical Gregorian University in Rome and a JD from the Columbus School of Law at The Catholic University of America.

Since 1975 he has taught canon law at Washington Theological Union where he is presently Professor of Church Law and Dean Emeritus.

He wrote *An Introduction to Canon Law,* New York, NY/Mahwah, NJ: Paulist Press, 1991 and *The Parish in Catholic Tradition*, New York, NY/Mahwah, NJ: Paulist Press, 1996. He was one of the editors of and authors in the *New Commentary on the Code of Canon Law,* New York, NY/Mahwah, NJ: Paulist Press, 2000. His most recent book, *Canon Law as Ministry: Freedom and Good Order for the Church*, New York, NY/Mahwah, NJ: Paulist Press, 2000.

RICHARD G. CUNNINGHAM received a doctorate in canon law at the Pontifical Lateran University in Rome in 1972. He is presently Professor of Canon Law, St. John's Seminary, Brighton, MA and Blessed Pope John XXIII Seminary,

Weston, MA. He was formally the adjunct vicar judicial of the Metropolitan Tribunal of the Archdiocese of Boston. He has taught canon law for almost thirty years, has published various articles and lectured in many dioceses on the revised *Code of Canon Law*.

LUGI DE LUCA is a professor emeritus of the University of Rome (*La Sapienza*). He entered the Italian university system in 1946 as an assistant professor at the University of Cagliari in Sardinia. Hew as first named ordinary professor at the university Catania in Sicily. Thereafter, he served the University of Pisa, the University of Milan before coming to the *Sapienza* in Rome in 1970 where he held the chair of ecclesiastical and Comparative Law in the Faculty of Political Science and then he held the Chair of Ecclesiastical Law in the Faculty of Jurisprudence until his retirement. He has been a rotal advocate since the 1930's and has published extensively.

FREDERICK C. EASTON was born in Bloomington, Indiana, and was ordained to the priesthood for service in the Archdiocese of Indianapolis on May 1, 1966. He received a licentiate in canon law from the Pontifical Lateran University in Rome in 1969.

He has served as notary and Vice Officialis and since May 5, 1980 he has served as Vicar Judicial. His Holiness, Pope John Paul II, named him Prelate of Honor on August 26, 1997.

He served the Canon Law Society of America as Secretary, Vice President and President. He has served on the Program for "Para-Professionals in Canon Law" at The Catholic University of America.

He wrote the article, "The Diocesan Finance Officer" in the *Church Finance Handbook*, K. McKenna, L. DiNardo and J. Pokusa (eds.) Washington, DC: CLSA, 125-134. He has also given a seminar at the 1997 CLSA Convention, "The Defender of the Bond: Then and Now," *CLSA Proceedings* 59 (1997) 136-203.

THOMAS J. GREEN was ordained a priest for the Diocese of Bridgeport, Connecticut in 1963. He is a professor of canon law at The Catholic University of America. He earned his doctorate in canon law in 1968 at the Pontifical Gregorian University in Rome.

After working in the chancery and tribunal of his own diocese of Bridgeport, Thomas Green began teaching canon law at the Department of Canon Law at The Catholic University of America, where he subsequently served a Chairperson of the Department for three years and, since September 1992, occupies the Stephan Kuttner Distinguished Professor of Canon Law Chair

He has published articles in various canonical journals and has served in varying capacities in the Canon Law Society of America. He was one of the editors of and authors in the *New Commentary on the Code of Canon Law,* New York, NY/Mahwah, NJ: Paulist Press, 2000.

JOHN G. JOHNSON was born in Waukegan, Illinois, and was ordained a priest for service in the Diocese of Columbus, Ohio on June 1, 1974

After receiving a B.A. in philosophy and American Studies and a M.A. in theology Pontifical College Josephinum in Columbus, Ohio, he was awarded a doctorate in canon law at The Catholic University of America.

He has been Adjutant Judicial Vicar of the Diocese of Columbus, since 1992 and pastor of St. Peter Parish, Columbus, Ohio, since July of 1993. He had been Vicar Judicial as well as an instructor of Canon Law at the Pontifical College Josephinum.

He has written two articles, "Chapter II: Synod of Bishops" (cc. 342-348) and "Title II: Groupings of Particular Churches" (cc. 431-459) in *New Commentary on the Code of Canon Law: A Text and Commentary,* ed. John Beal et. al., New York/Mahwah: Paulist Press, 2000, 454-463; 566-609. In addition he has contributed articles on various procedural and jurisprudential topics in *Studia canonica* and *The Jurist*.

AIDAN MCGRATH, OFM was born in Banbridge, Northern Ireland. He was ordained a priest on June 29, 1980. At the Pontifical Gregorian University, Rome he was awarded the Diploma in Ecclesiastical Jurisprudence in 1982 and the Doctorate in Canon Law in 1985. His thesis was published in 1988.

He has held and still holds many positions: vice-officialis at the Dublin Regional Marriage Tribunal; from 1995-2001, President of the Canon Law Society of Great Britain and Ireland; Professor *invitatus* in the Faculty of Canon Law at Pontifical Gregorian University, Rome; Provincial Definitor of the Franciscan Province of Ireland. He has been and continues to be a consultant on various canonical matters to a number of congregations of religious.

Aidan McGrath was co-author and co-editor of *The Canon Law: Letter and Spirit*, a commentary on the *Code of Canon Law,* published by the Canon Law Society of Great Britain and Ireland in 1995. His writings are published in a number of canonical publications.

KEVIN E. MCKENNA was born in Rochester, New York, and was ordained on March 4, 1977 for service in Diocese of Rochester

He has earned several academic degrees and among them are: J.C.L. (Gregorian University, Rome, Italy) 1984; J.C.D. (St. Paul's University, Ottawa, 1990) and, Ph.D. Church Law, (University of Ottawa, Canada, 1990).

He has served as the chancellor of his diocese (1992-2001), as judge in the diocesan tribunal (1990 to the present), and as diocesan director legal services (1991-2001). He is presently the pastor of St. Cecilia Parish in Rochester, NY. He is also President, Canon Law Society of America, (Oct., 2001 – Oct. 2002).

He has written a number of articles which have appeared in *The Priest, America Magazine* and *Studia Canonica*. He has also written or edited several books: *The Ministry of Law in the Church Today*, (Notre Dame, Indiana:

University of Notre Dame Press, 1998); *Church Finance Handbook*, (chief editor) (Washington, DC: CLSA, 1999); *A Concise Guide to Canon Law: A Practical Handbook for Pastoral Ministers* (Notre Dame, IN: Ave Maria Press, April 2000); *A Concise Guide to Catholic Social Teaching* (Notre Dame, IN: Ave Maria Press, August 2002).

AUGUSTINE MENDONCA was born in Mangalore, India, and was ordained a priest in 1966. He is presently incardinated in the diocese of Montego Bay, Jamaica, WI. He has earned a number of academic degrees and among them are: MA in Clinical Psychology at the University of Ottawa in 1976; MA in Religion and Medical Care at George Washington University, Washington, DC in 1977; MA (Th) at the Angelicum, Rome in 2000) and STL at the Angelicum, Rome in 2001; Ph.D. in Church Law at the University of Ottawa in 1982); JCD at Saint Paul University, Ottawa in 1982.

He is now a full professor in the Faculty of Canon Law, Saint Paul University but previously was the vice dean of the same faculty.

He has written many articles which have appeared in *Studia Canonica, The Jurist, Monitor Ecclesiasticus, Forum, Philippiniana Sacra*, but especially noteworthy is *Rotal Anthology – An Annotated Index of Rotal Decisions from 1971-1988* (Washington, DC: CLSA 1992).

ELISSA A. RINERE, CP is a member of the Sisters of the Cross and Passion. She received her doctorate in canon law from The Catholic University of America. Since 1999, she has been an assistant professor of canon law at The Catholic University of America. previously, she served as judge and defender of the bond at the Metropolitan Tribunal of the Archdiocese of Hartford, CT from 1981 to 1993 and in the same positions at the Metropolitan Tribunal of the Archdiocese of Los Angeles, CA from 1994 to 1999.

Her many publications have addressed such canonical topics as tribunal ministry, annulments, marriage law, lay ministry and liturgy.

MYRIAM WIJLENS was born in Losser, The Netherlands. In 1986 she earned a STL at the Katholieke Universiteit in Nijmegen, The Netherlands and then in 1990 she was awarded the doctorate in canon law at Saint Paul University in Ottawa, Canada.

Since 1991 until the present Dr. Wijlens first served as defender of the bond and then later as judge at the diocesan tribunal of the Diocese of Münster. She continues to lecture in canon law in the JCL program in Münster, and at the Department of Canon law at The Catholic University of America, Washington DC. Since 1999 she is an assistant professor of canon law at the Theological Faculty of the University of Tilburg, The Netherlands.

Myriam Wijlens serves or has served as a member of several commissions of the episcopal conference of The Netherlands and as canonical advisor to the Conference of Major Superiors in the Netherlands.

Among her significant writings are two books: *Theology and Canon Law: The Theories of Klaus Mörsdorf and Eugenio Corecco*, Lanham: University Press of America, 1992 and *Sharing the Eucharist, A Theological Evaluation of the Post Conciliar Legislator,* Lanham: University Press of America, 2000. She has written two articles, "Title VII: Juridic Acts" (cc. 124-128) and "Power of Governance" (cc. 129-144) in *New Commentary on the Code of Canon Law: A Text and Commentary,* ed. John Beal et. al., New York/Mahwah: Paulist Press, 2000, 177-194. She has also written more than twenty articles in theological and canonical periodicals on ecclesiological, ecumenical-canonical subjects.

TABULA GRATULATORIA

The Canon Law Society of America expresses its profound gratitude to the individuals named below for their financial contributions to support this *festschrift* in honor of Lawrence G. Wrenn.

Cardinals

His Eminence Francis Cardinal GEORGE, OMI, Archbishop, Archdiocese of Chicago, IL (USA)

His Eminence William Cardinal KEELER, Archbishop, Archdiocese of Baltimore, MD (USA)

His Eminence Adam Cardinal MAIDA, Archbishop, Archdiocese of Detroit, MI (USA)

Archbishops

Most Rev. Timothy BROGLIO, Archbishop Apostolic Nuncio, Santo Domingo (DOMINICAN REPUBLIC)

Most Rev. Daniel M. BUECHLEIN, OSB, Archbishop, Archdiocese of Indianapolis, IN (USA)

Most Rev. Thomas KELLY, OP, Archbishop and People of the Archdiocese of Louisville, KY (USA)

Most Rev. Edwin F. O'BRIEN, Archbishop, Archdiocese for the Military Services USA, Washington, DC (USA)

Most Rev. Walter PASKA, Metropolitan Archdiocese of Philadelphia Ukranian, Philadelphia, PA (USA)

Bishops

Most Rev. Gerald R. BARNES, Bishop, Diocese of San Bernardino, CA (USA)

Most Rev. J. Kevin BOLAND, Bishop, Diocese of Savannah, GA (USA)

Most Rev. Raymond J. BOLAND, DD, Bishop, Diocese of Kansas City-St. Joseph, MO (USA)

Most Rev. Raymond L. BURKE, Bishop, Diocese of La Crosse, WI (USA)

Most Rev. Daniel N. DI NARDO, Bishop, Diocese of Sioux City, IA (USA)

Most Rev. Thomas G. DORAN, Bishop, Diocese of Rockford, IL (USA)

Most Rev. Thomas L. DUPRE, Bishop, Diocese of Springfield, MA (USA)

Most Rev. David E. FELLHAUER, Bishop, Diocese of Victoria, TX (USA)

Most Rev. Raymond E. GOEDERT, Vicar General, Archdiocese of Chicago, IL (USA)

Most Rev. Bernard J. HARRINGTON, Bishop, Diocese of Winona, MN (USA)

Most Rev. Daniel A. HART, Bishop of Norwich, Diocese of Norwich, CT (USA)

Most Rev. James R. HOFFMAN, Bishop, Diocese of Toledo, OH (USA)

Most Rev. William R. HOUCK, Bishop, Diocese of Jackson, MS (USA)

Most Rev. Patrick J. MCGRATH, Bishop, Diocese of San Jose, CA (USA)

Most Rev. Joseph PEPE, Bishop, Diocese of Las Vegas, NV (USA)

Most Rev. Daniel L. RYAN, Bishop Emeritus, Diocese of Springfield, IL (USA)

Professors of Canon Law

Rev. John P. BEAL, Associate Professor, The Catholic University of America, Washington, DC (USA)

Rev. Ronald J. BOWERS, Professor of Canon Law, St. Paul Seminary, Archdiocese.of St. Paul and Minneapolis, MN (USA)

Rev. Msgr. Richard G. CUNNINGHAM, Professor of Canon Law, St. John's Seminary Brighton, MA (USA)

Rev. John V. DOLCIAMORE, Associate Professor Canon Law, Mundelein Seminary, Archdiocese of Chicago, IL (USA)

Rev. Msgr. Thomas J. GREEN, Professor of Canon Law, The Catholic University of America, Washington, DC (USA)

Rev. John HUELS, OSM, Professor of Canon Law, St. Paul University, Ottawa (CANADA)

Rev. Emmanuel JADA, Professor, Collegio S. Pietro Apostolo, Rome (ITALY)

Rev. Robert J. KASLYN, SJ, Assistant Professor of Canon Law, The Catholic University of America, Washington, DC (USA)

Rev. Robert T. KENNEDY, Associate Professor of Canon Law, The Catholic University of America, Washington, DC (USA)

Sr. Rose MCDERMOTT, SSJ, Associate Professor, The Catholic University of America, Washington, DC (USA)

Rev. Francis G. MORRISEY, OMI, Faculty of Canon Law, Saint Paul University, Ottawa (CANADA)

Rev. Ladislas ORSY, SJ, Professor, Law Center, Georgetown University, Washington, DC (USA)

Rev. Msgr. Roch PAGE, Dean of the Faculty of Canon Law, Saint Paul University, Ottawa (CANADA)

Rev. Nathaniel REEVES, OSB, Professor of Canon Law (deceased at time of publication), St. Meinrad School of Theology, IN (USA)

Sr. Elissa A. RINERE, CP, Assistant Professor of Canon Law, The Catholic University of America, Washington, DC (USA)

Rev. Nicholas SCHOECH, OFM, Dean of the Faculty of Canon Law, Pontifical Athenaeum "Antonianum," Rome (ITALY)

CANONISTS AND CANONICAL PRACTITIONERS:

Rev. Robert J. AHLIN, Judicial Vicar, Diocese of Pittsburgh, PA (USA)

Sr. Mary Ann ANDREWS, CSA, Tribunal Judge, Diocese of Cleveland, OH (USA)

Rev. Joseph T. ANGINOLI, Adjunct Judicial Vicar, Diocese of Paterson, NJ (USA)

Rev. Thomas C. ANSLOW, CM, Judicial Vicar, Archdiocese of Los Angeles, CA (USA)

Rev. Msgr. Henry ARCHAMBAULT, Judicial Vicar, Suffragan of Hartford, (UNITED KINGDOM)

Rev. Msgr. Charles D. BALVO, Apostolic Nunciature, Amman (JORDAN)

Rev. Msgr. Mark L. BARTCHAK, Judicial Vicar, Diocese of Erie, PA (USA)

Sr. Mary Ann BARTOLAC, SCL, Marriage Case Advocate, Archdiocese of Kansas City, KS (USA)

Sr. Virginia L. BARTOLAC, SCL, Director, Diocese of Kansas City-St. Joseph, MO (USA)

Rev. Msgr. Ricardo E. BASS, Pastor St. Joan of Arc Church, St.Clair Shores, Archdiocese of Detroit, MI (USA)

Rev. Yethi Raju-John BATTHULA, Advocate, Coventry (UNITED KINGDOM)

Very Rev. Anthony E. BAWYN, Judicial Vicar, Archdiocese of Seattle, WA (USA)

Rev. Msgr. Raymond F. BEGIN, Judicial Vicar Emeritus, Diocese of Portland, ME (USA)

Rev. Msgr. John P. BELL, Judicial Vicar, Diocese of Dallas, TX (USA)

Rev. Msgr. Austin P. BENNETT, Special Consultant to the Bishop, Diocese of Brooklyn, NY (USA)

Mrs. Sherie BERG, Advocate, Archdiocese of Indianapolis, IN (USA)

Rev. Joseph BINZER, Judge, Archdiocese of Cincinnati, OH (USA)

Rev. Gregory T. BITTNER, Judicial Vicar, Diocese of Birmingham, AL (USA)

Rev. Michael A. BOCCACCIO, Pastor of St. Philip Church, Diocese of Bridgeport, Norwalk (USA)

Rev. Msgr. Kenneth E. BOCCAFOLA, Judge, Roman Rota, Rome (ITALY)

Rev. James BONKE, Defender of the Bond, Archdiocese of Indianapolis, IN (USA)

Rev. Msgr. Anthony BORRELLI, Associate Judge, Diocese of Columbus, OH (USA)

Very Rev. James BRACKIN, SCJ, President - Rector of Sacred Heart School of Theology, Hales Corner, WI (USA)

Sr. Marie A. BREITENBECK, OP, Canonical Consultant, Dominican Sisters, Adrian, MI (USA)

Rev. Thomas BRUNDAGE, Judicial Vicar, Archdiocese of Milwaukee, WI (USA)

Rev. Brian BURNS, OFM, Defender of the Bond, Diocese of Calgary, Alberta (CANADA)

Rev. Dennis J. BURNS, Pastor, Star of the Sea Parish, Archdiocese of Boston, MA (USA)

Rev. Randolph R. CALVO, Pastor of Our Lady of Mount Carmel Church, Archdiocese of San Francisco, CA (USA)

Rev. John F. CANARY, Rector/President Mundelein Seminary, Archdiocese of Chicago, IL (USA)

Rev. Msgr. Michael J. CARIGLIO JR., Adjutant Vicar General, Diocese of Youngstown, OH (USA)

Rev. Msgr. Denis E. CARLIN, Rector Royal Scots College, Salamanca (SPAIN)

Rev. John CARONAN, O. Praem., St. Michael's Abbey, Silverado, CA (USA)

Rev. Gregory V. CARROLL, Archdiocese of Perth, (AUSTRALIA)

Rev. John T. CATOIR, Judicial Vicar Emeritus, Diocese of Paterson, NJ (USA)

Rev. Msgr. James F. CHECCHIO, Moderator of the Curia, Diocese of Camden, NJ (USA)

Rev. J. Michael CLARK, Student, Diocese of Owensboro, KY (USA)

Rev. Msgr. John K. CODY, Judge, Diocese of Columbus, OH (USA)

Rev. Patrick COGAN, SA, Faculty of Canon Law, St. Paul University, Ottawa (CANADA)

Rev. William A. COLLINS, Adjutant Judicial Vicar, Archdiocese of Baltimore, MD (USA)

Rev. Patrick A. CONDRON, Pastor, St. Alphonsus Church, Diocese of Wheeling-Charleston, WV (USA)

Rev. Msgr. William J. CONNELL, Judicial Vicar, Diocese of Youngstown, OH (USA)

Rev Michael C. CONNOLLY, OSFS, Pastor, St. Brendan the Navigator, Ocean Isle Beach, NC (USA)

Very Rev. Paul D. COUNCE, Judicial Vicar, Diocese of Baton Rouge, LA (USA)

Dr. Frank W. COUNTRYMAN, Psychiatrist/Consultant, Archdiocese of Indianapolis, IN (USA)

Rev. Msgr. Craig A. COX, Vicar for Clergy, Archdiocese of Los Angeles, CA (USA)

Rev. Msgr. J. James CUNEO, Judge, Diocese of Bridgeport, CT (USA)

Dr. Barbara Anne CUSACK, Chancellor, Archdiocese of Milwaukee, WI (USA)

Sr. Catherine C. DARCY, RSM, Tribunal Judge, Diocese of Las Cruces, NM (USA)

Rev. James W. DE ADDER, Judge Auditor, Archdiocese of Boston, MA (USA)

Rev. Louis L. DE NINNO, Defender of the Bond, Diocese of Pittsburgh, PA (USA)

Rev. Msgr. Dacian DEE, Judicial Vicar, Diocese of St. Petersburg, FL (USA)

Rev. Msgr. Robert P. DEELEY, Pastor of St. Anne's, Wollaston, Archdiocese of Boston, MA (USA)

Rev. Jonathan DEFELICE, OSB, President of Saint Anselm College, Manchester, NH (USA)

Very Rev. Lawrence A. DI NARDO, Office of Canonical Affairs, Diocese of Pittsburgh, PA (USA)

Rev. Paul DIGIROLAMO, Tribunal Judge, Archdiocese of Philadelphia, PA (USA

Rev. Msgr. George E. DOBES, Judicial Vicar, Archdiocese for the Military Services, Washington, DC (USA)

Rev. John V. DOLCIAMORE, Associate Professor Canon Law Mundelein Seminary, Archdiocese of Chicago, IL (USA)

Rev. James I. DONLON, Judicial Vicar, Diocese of Albany, NY (USA)

Rev. John P. DONOVAN, Tribunal Judge, Diocese of Syracuse, NY (USA)

Rev. Joseph DOOGAN, Adjutant Judicial Vicar, Archdiocese of Seattle, WA (USA)

Ms. Judith A. DOUGLAS, Advocate, Diocese of Richmond, VA (USA)

Rev. Msgr. Jerald A. DOYLE, Judicial Vicar, Diocese of Bridgeport, CT (USA)

Rev. William R. DU BUISSON, OMI, Adjutant Judicial Vicar, Archdiocese of San Antonio, TX (USA)

Ms. Patricia M. DUGAN, Dugan and Kosinski, Philadelphia. PA (USA)

Rev. Msgr. Frederick C. EASTON, Judicial Vicar, Archdiocese of Indianapolis, IN (USA)

Rev. John F. EDWARDS, Pastor, Archdiocese of Hartford, CT (USA)

Rev. Arthur J. ESPELAGE, OFM, Executive Coordinator, Canon Law Society of America, Washington, DC (USA)

Chor-bishop John D. FARIS, Assistant Secretary General, CNEWA, New York, NY (USA)

Very Rev. Dr. Adrian G. FARRELLY, Judicial Vicar, Archdiocese of Brisbane, (AUSTRALIA)

Rev. Msgr. Francis J. FAZZALARO, Pastor, St. Gabriel Church, Pompano Beach, Archdiocese of Miami, FL (USA)

Rev. Rick FILARY, Assumption of the Blessed Virgin Mary Parish, Diocese of Saginaw, MI (USA)

Rev. Michael Smith FOSTER, Judicial Vicar, Archdiocese of Boston, MA (USA)

Rev. Msgr. Donald J. FRUGE, Moderator of the Curia, Diocese of Austin, TX (USA)

Rev. Msgr. Lawrence E. GAUTHREAUX, Archdiocese of New Orleans, LA (USA)

Rev. Msgr. William A. GENUARIO, Judge, Diocese of Bridgeport, CT (USA)

Rev. Robert J. GILDAY, Adjunct Vicar Judicial, Archdiocese of Indianapolis, IN (USA)

Mrs. Margaret GILLETT, Director of the Tribunal, Diocese of Dallas, TX (USA)

Ms. Catherine A. GILLIGAN, Director of the Tribunal, Diocese of Savannah, GA (USA)

Rev. James M. GILLIGAN, MM, Korean Foreign Mission Society, Seoul (SOUTH KOREA)

Rev. Msgr. George P. GRAHAM, Appeals Court Judge, Diocese of Rockville Centre, NY (USA)

Rev. Ed GRIMES, CSSp, Director PMS Holy Ghost College, Dublin (IRELAND)

Rev. Robert D. GROSCH, Judicial Vicar, Diocese of Great Falls-Billings, MT (USA)

Rev. Ralph C. GROSS, Pastor St. Margaret Mary Church, Archdiocese of Milwaukee, WI (USA)

Rev. Msgr. James C. GURZYNSKI, Retired Judicial Vicar and Vicar General, Diocese of Amarillo, TX (USA)

Rev. Michael HACK, Judge, Archdiocese of Chicago, IL (USA)

Rev. Mr. Joseph HANNAWACKER, Deacon, Archdiocese of Trenton, NJ (USA)

Rev. Ken HARDER, Tribunal Judge, Diocese of Tulsa, OK (USA)

Rev. Msgr. J. Wayne HAYES, St. Joseph Church, Las Bravos, Diocese of Fresno, CA (USA)

Rev. Msgr. John J. HEDDERMAN, Judicial Vicar, Diocese of Salt Lake City, UT (USA)

Rev. John C. HERGENROTHER, Judge, Archdiocese of Chicago, IL (USA)

Dr. Michael HIGGINS, Executive Director, Justice for Priests and Deacons, San Diego, CA (USA)

Rev. Msgr. Philip W. HILL, Archdiocese of New York, NY (USA)

Rev. James A. HOLTZ, Adjutant Judicial Vicar, Diocese of Gaylord, MI (USA)

Rev. Joseph A. HOWARTH, Judge, Archdiocese for the Military Services, Washington, DC (USA)

Very Rev. Michael J. IBACH, Judicial Vicar, Diocese of Yakima, WA (USA)

Sr. Lynn JARRELL, OSU, Teacher, San Bruno, CA (USA)

Rev. Msgr. John G. JOHNSON, Adjutant Judicial Vicar, Diocese of Columbus, OH (USA)

Rev. Gareth Adrian JONES, Student of Canon Law, Archdiocese of Cardiff, Wales (UNITED KINGDOM)

Mrs. Rita F. JOYCE, Judge, Diocese of Pittsburgh, PA (USA)

Rev. Donald J. JOYCE, OMI, Director of Libraries, Oblate School of Theology Library, San Antonio, TX (USA)

Rev. Lawrence JURCAK, Adjutant Judicial Vicar, Diocese of Cleveland, OH (USA)

Rev. Robert J. KABAT, Judicial Vicar, Diocese of Green Bay, WI (USA)

Rev. Lee J. KAHRS, Defender of the Bond, Diocese of Green Bay, WI (USA)

Rev. Robert L. KEALY, Judicial Vicar, Archdiocese of Chicago, IL (USA)

Rev. Msgr. Kurt H. KEMO, Judicial Vicar, Diocese of Steubenville, OH (USA)

Rev. Laurence W. KENNEDY, Pastor of St. Brigid and St. Joseph Church, Diocese of Syracuse, NY (USA)

Rev. Msgr. Walter F. KENNY, Judicial Vicar, Archdiocese of New York, NY (USA)

Rev. B. D. KILLEEN, Orange, CT (USA)

Ms. Charlotte M. KINCH, Tribunal Assessor, Diocese of Las Cruces, NM (USA)

Rev. David J. KLEIN, Sacred Heart Catholic Church, Diocese of Camden, NJ (USA)

Rev. Dennis C. KLEMME, Tribunal, Retired, Archdiocese of Milwaukee, WI (USA)

Rev. Msgr. Thomas J. KLINZING, Judicial Vicar, Diocese of West Palm Beach, FL (USA)

Rev. Msgr. Edward J. KURTYKA, Judicial Vicar, Diocese of Paterson, NJ (USA)

Rev. Michael A. KURZ, Adjutant Judicial Vicar, Diocese of Rockford, IL (USA)

Rev. Patrick R. LAGGES, Judicial Vicar, Archdiocese of Chicago, IL (USA)

Rev. William F. LAIRD, Pastor, Diocese of Rochester, NY (USA)

Rev. Msgr. Kenneth E. LASCH, Diocese of Patterson, NJ (USA)

Very Rev. Joel A. LECUIVRE, Judicial Vicar, Diocese of Providence, RI (USA)

Rev. Msgr. Michael LENIHAN, Pastor, St. Lawrence Martyr Church, Archdiocese of Los Angeles, CA (USA)

Chor-Bishop William J. LESER, Judicial Vicar, Eparchy of Our Lady of Lebanon Of Los Angeles, CA (USA)

Sr. Grace Dorothy LIM, MM, Bishop's Delegate for Ethnic Ministries, Diocese of Honolulu, HI (USA)

Mrs. Katharine LOZANO, Judge Instructor, Archdiocese of Indianapolis, IN (USA)

Rev. Edward J. LUCA, Associate Judicial Vicar, Diocese of Cleveland, OH (USA)

Rev. John P. LUCAS, Adjutant Judicial Vicar, Court of Appeals, Province of Chicago, IL (USA)

Rev. Gregory T. LUYET, Adjutant Judicial Vicar, Diocese of Little Rock, AR (USA)

Rev. Richard C. MACEY, Our Lady of the Woods Church, Woodhaven, Archdiocese of Detroit, MI (USA)

Rev. Thomas C. MACHALSKI, Associate Judicial Vicar, Diocese of Brooklyn, NY (USA)

Sr. Ishbel M. MACPHERSON, SND, Judge, Scottish National Tribunal (SCOTLAND)

Rev. John J. MAHONEY, JR., Judicial Vicar, Diocese of Manchester, NH (USA)

Rev. Msgr. Michael MANZELLI, Judicial Vicar Emeritus, Diocese of Rockville Centre, NY (USA)

Ms. Ariel MARTIN, Lay Eucharistic. Minister/Advocate, Diocese of Springfield, IL (USA)

Rev. Justin D. MARTIN, Associate Pastor, St. Luke Catholic Church, Archdiocese of Indianapolis, IN (USA)

Rev. Lucian C. MARTINEZ, SJ, Judge, Diocese of Charlotte, NC (USA

Rev. Jeremiah J. MCCARTHY, Judicial Vicar, Diocese of Savannah, GA (USA)

Rev. Msgr. John J. MCCARTHY, Archdiocese of Hartford, CT (USA)

Rev. Albert MCGOLDRICK, Tribunal Judge, Diocese of Bridgeport, CT (USA)

Rev. Aidan MCGRATH, OFM, Vice-Officialis, Dublin Regional Marriage Tribunal, (IRELAND)

Rev. Martin MCGUILL, St. Luke Catholic Church, Diocese of Arlington, VA (USA)

Rev. Kevin E. MCKENNA, President of the CLSA, Diocese of Rochester, NY (USA)

Rev. Edward J. MCLEAN, Church of St. Brigid, Archdiocese of Hartford, CT (USA)

Rev. Msgr. Charles W. McNamee, Retired Chancellor, Diocese of Rockford, IL (USA)

Rev. Brian E. McWeeney, St. Martin de Porres, Archdiocese of New York, NY (USA)

Very Rev. George P. Miller, Judicial Vicar, Archdiocese of Detroit, MI (USA)

Rev. Walter D. Miller, Judicial Vicar, Diocese of Burlington, VT (USA)

Rev. Joseph M. Mills, Diocese of Owensboro, KY (USA)

Rev. Carl T. Morrison, Defender of Bond, Archdiocese of Miami, FL (USA)

Very Rev. Lawrence O'Keefe, Judicial Vicar, Diocese of Gallup, NM (USA)

Rev. Mark O'Connell, Assistant for Canonical Affairs, Archdiocese of Boston, MA (USA)

Rev. Robert M. O'Grady, Archdiocese of Boston, MA (USA)

Rev. Nilo S. Peig, Vicar General, Diocese of Bangued (PHILIPPINES)

Rev. Msgr. Mark A. Plewka, Judicial Vicar, Diocese of Pueblo, CO (USA)

Rev. Robert D. Ponticello, Church of the Nativity, Diocese of Memphis, TN (USA)

Rev. John F. Porter, Judicial Vicar Retired, Diocese of Grand Rapids, MI (USA)

Rev. Paul Quirk, Board Member, Canon Law Society of Australia and New Zealand, Renmark (AUSTRALIA)

Very Rev. Norbert Raszeja, CR, Procurator General, Congregation of the Resurrection, Rome (ITALY)

Rev. John W. Robertson, Judicial Vicar, Diocese of Helena, MT (USA)

Rev. Ed Roden-Lucero, Diocese of El Paso, TX (USA)

Sr. Carolyn A. Roeber, OP, Leadership Team, Dominican Sisters of Edmonds, WA (USA)

Rev. Msgr. Joseph R. ROTH, DD, Vicar General, Diocese of Charleston, SC (USA)

Rev. Msgr. Charles H. ROWLAND, Judicial Vicar, Diocese of Charleston, SC (USA)

Rev. Caesar RUSSO, Diocese of St. Augustine, FL (USA)

Rev. Fred SACKETT, OMI, Judicial Vicar, Appellate Court of Texas, San Antonio, TX (USA)

Rev. Joseph A. SALERNO, Tribunal Judge, Diocese of Camden, NJ (USA)

Rev. Robert J. SANSON, Pastor, Saint Joseph Church, Diocese of Cleveland, OH (USA)

Rev. John M. SANTONE, CSC, Holy Cross Church, South Easton, MA (USA)

Rev. Mr. Gerald SCHERKENBACH, Assessor-Auditor, Archdiocese St. Paul and Minneapolis, MN (USA)

Rev. Charles H. SCHETTLER, Judicial Vicar, Archdiocese of Oklahoma City, OK (USA)

Rev. Arthur C. SCHRENGER, Defender of the Bond, Archdiocese of Mobile, AL (USA)

Ms. Carol L. SCOTT, Tribunal Assessor, Diocese of Sacramento, CA (USA)

Rev. Msgr. Leonard G. SCOTT, Judicial Vicar, Diocese of Camden, NJ (USA)

Rev. Gilbert J. SEITZ, Cathedral of Mary Our Queen, Archdiocese of Baltimore, MD (USA)

Rev. Msgr. John T. SEKELLICK, Judicial Vicar, Byzantine Catholic Eparchy of Passaic, NJ (USA)

Rev. John SHAMLEFFER, Judicial Vicar, Archdiocese of St. Louis, MO (USA)

Bro. Patrick SHEA, OFM, Legal Counsel, Diocese of Springfield, IL (USA)

Rt. Rev. Msgr. Gerard SHEEHY, Officialis, Dublin Regional Marriage Tribunal (IRELAND)

Rev. Jerry M. SHERBA, Judicial Vicar, Diocese of Raleigh, NC (USA)

Rev. James J. SHIFFER, Columban Fathers, Los Angeles, CA (USA)

Rev. Paul SHIKANY, Adjunct Vicar Judicial, Archdiocese of Indianapolis, IN (USA)

Rev. Kevin SLATTERY, Judicial Vicar, Diocese of Jackson, MI (USA)

Rev. Daniel A. SMILANIC, Adjutant Judicial Vicar, Archdiocese of Chicago, IL (USA)

Rev. Myles SMITH, Defender of the Bond, Archdiocese of Indianapolis, IN (USA)

Rev. Michael SMYTH, Judicial Vicar, Galway Marriage Tribunal (IRELAND)

Very Rev. J. Mark SPALDING, Judicial Vicar, Archdiocese of Louisville, KY (USA)

Rev. John J. STACK, Professor of Religious Studies, St. Joseph College, West Hartford, CT (USA)

Rev. Msgr. Paul F. STEFANKO, Judicial Vicar, Diocese of Portland, ME (USA)

Ms. Amy Jill STRICKLAND, Judge, Archdiocese of Boston, MA (USA)

Rev. Marek SUCHOCKI, Judge, Archdiocese of New York, NY (USA)

Rev. Msgr. William V. SULLIVAN, Judicial Vicar, Diocese of Richmond, VA (USA)

Sr. Margaret L. SULLIVAN, CSJ, General Councilor, Congregation of the Sisters of St. Joseph of Boston, MA (USA)

Rev. Alfred A. TACHIAS, Adjutant Judicial Vicar, Diocese of Gallup, NM (USA)

Rev. Charles F. TAYLOR, Defender of the Bond, Diocese of Cheyenne, WY (USA)

Rev. Charles L. TORPEY, Judge, Diocese of Grand Island, NE (USA)

Rev. Patrick J. TRAVERS, Judicial Vicar, Diocese of Juneau, AK (USA)

Mrs. Ann TULLY, Advocate, Archdiocese of Indianapolis, IN (USA)

Rev. Michael J. TULLY, Judicial Vicar, Diocese of Lancaster (UNITED KINGDOM)

Sr. Susan L. VANNICE, Diocesan Canonist, Diocese of Richmond, VA (USA)

Rev. John C. VARGAS, CSsR, Development Director, Academia Alfonsiana, Rome (ITALY)

Sr. Lucy VAZQUEZ, OP, Chancellor, Diocese of Orlando, FL (USA)

Rev. Albert E. VERBRUGGHE, Judicial Vicar, Diocese of Tucson, AZ (USA)

Rev. Michael VIGIL, Tribunal Office, Diocese of Gallup, NM (USA)

Rev. Wilbur J. VOTRAW, Associate Judge, Appeals Court, Diocese of Syracuse, NY (USA)

Rev. Dennis A. WAGNER, Judicial Vicar, Diocese of Grand Rapids, MI (USA)

Sr. Waldia A. WARDEN, OP, Defender of the Bond, Archdiocese of New Orleans, LA (USA)

Rev. John S. WEBER, Judicial Vicar, Diocese of Las Cruces, NM (USA)

Ms. Linda A. WEIGEL, Director of the Tribunal, Archdiocese of Portland, OR (USA)

Rev. S. C. WELLENS, Judicial Vicar, Retired, Heythusysen (NETHERLANDS)

Rev. Ray WILHELM, OMI, Defender of the Bond, Appellate Court of Texas, San Antonio, TX (USA)

Rev. Robert H. WILLIAMS, Metropolitan Tribunal, Archdiocese of Detroit, MI (USA)

Rev. Thomas WISNIEWSKI, Advocate, Archdiocese of Philadelphia, PA (USA)

Rev. Joseph M. WOLF, Judicial Vicar, Diocese of Davenport, IA (USA)

Rev. Gary D. YANUS, Adjutant Judicial Vicar, Diocese of Cleveland, OH (USA)

FAMILY AND FRIENDS

Rev. Lucius ANNESE, OFM, Director of Religion in Society Institute, Somerville, MA (USA)

Mrs. Lorraine M. BRENNAN, Friend, West Hartford, CT (USA)

Ms. Peggy COOK, University of Alabama Bounds Law Library, Tuscaloosa, AL (USA)

Dr. Rosalie J. FORD, Ph.D., West Springfield, MA (USA)

Abbot Gabriel GIBBS, OSB, Friend from St. Bernard's in Rochester, Abbot, Still River, MA (USA)

Dr. Marie T. HILLIARD, Ph.D., Executive Director, Connecticut Catholic Conference, Archdiocese of Hartford, CT (USA)

Very Rev. Terence KRISTOFAK, CP, Provincial, Passionists Community, South River, NJ (USA)

Rev. William MULLEN, Co-Pastor, St. Mark Catholic Church, Archdiocese of Hartford, CT (USA)

ORATORIAN COMMUNITY, Monterey, CA (USA)

Rev. Msgr. John D. REGAN, Classmate and Friend, Archdiocese of Hartford, Middlebury, CT (USA)

Mr. & Mrs. Kenneth and Marilyn RUZICK, Loving Friends, Cincinnati, OH (USA)

Mr. Norman A. VERNATI, NAV CO/LLC, Upper Darby, PA (USA)

Mr. Brent J. WILLIAMS, St. Louis, MO (USA)

Anne Marie WRENN-BESSMER, Nicholas, Lucian, Ella and Charlotte, Grateful and Adoring Family, Needham, MA (USA)

Mrs. Joan WRENN JASKI, Sacramento, CA (USA)